TOUGH ON CRIMINAL WEALTH

Tough on Criminal Wealth

Exploring the Practice of Proceeds from Crime Confiscation in the EU

by

BARBARA VETTORI

TRANSCRIME, Joint Research Centre on Transnational Crime, Università di Trento - Università Cattolica di Milano, Italy

Springer

A C.I.P. Catalogue record for this book is available from the Library of Congress.

ISBN-10 1-4020-4128-4 (HB)
ISBN-13 978-1-4020-4128-0 (HB)
ISBN-10 1-4020-4129-2 (e-book)
ISBN-13 978-1-4020-4129-7 (e-book)

Published by Springer,
P.O. Box 17, 3300 AA Dordrecht, The Netherlands.

www.springer.com

Printed on acid-free paper

Printed in the Netherlands.

CONTENTS

ACKNOWLEDGEMENTS

I would like to express my gratitude to the following experts who contributed, in their various roles, to the development of this book. Without their very kind and generous help this work would have never been possible.

For Austria

- W. Pilgermair, President of the Court of Appeal, Innsbruck;
- F. Zeder, Deputy Head of Unit, Austrian Ministry of Justice, Vienna.

For Belgium

- V. De Wolf, Head of the Proceeds of Crime Unit, Belgian Federal Police, Brussels;
- E. Francis, Public Prosecutor, Director of the Central Office for Seizure and Confiscation, Brussels.

For Denmark

- S. Ponikowski, Deputy Public Prosecutor, The Public Prosecutor for Serious Economic Crime, Danish Ministry of Justice, Copenhagen.

For Finland

- L. Kuitunen, National Bureau of Investigation—Money Laundering Clearing House, Vantaa;
- M. Sunell, District Prosecutor, Prosecutor's Office of the Helsinki Local District, Helsinki.

For France

- A. Kostomaroff, Magistrat, *Bureau de la lutte contre la criminalité organisée, le trafic de stupéfiants et le blanchiment*, French Ministry of Justice, Paris;
- J.-F. Pascal, *Avocat General*, Court of Appeal Aix en Provence, Aix en Provence.

For Germany

- J. Klaas, *Referatsleiter Organisierte Kriminalität*, North Rhein-Westphalian Ministry of Justice, Düsseldorf;

– H. H. Plump, Leader of the Joint Financial Task Force *Bundeskriminalamt/ Zollkriminalamt*, *Bundeskriminalamt*, Wiesbaden.

For Greece

– P. Nikoloudis, Public Prosecutor, Greek Ministry of Justice, Athens;
– A. Vgontzas, Adviser, Greek Ministry of Justice, Athens.

For Ireland

– B. Galvin, Solicitor in Cork and former Bureau Legal Officer of the Criminal Assets Bureau, Dublin;
– W. Ryan, Detective Superintendent, Criminal Assets Bureau, Dublin.

For Italy

– P. L. Dell'Osso, *Sostituto Procuratore Nazionale Antimafia, Direzione Nazionale Antimafia*, Rome;
– G. Fidelbo, *Direzione Generale Affari Penali*—Office I, Italian Ministry of Justice, Rome.

For Luxembourg

– J.-P. Frising, *Procureur d'Etat adjoint*, *Parquet du Tribunal d'Arrondissement*, Luxembourg;
– C. Konsbruck, *Conseiller de direction*, Luxembourg Ministry of Justice, Luxembourg.

For the Netherlands

– E. van der Steeg, Legal Advisor on International Affairs, Criminal Assets Deprivation Bureau (BOOM), Dutch Public Prosecution Service, Leeuwarden;
– T. Brandsma, Financial Detective, Office of Financial Support, Police of the Netherlands, Heeuwarden.

For Portugal

– J. Davin, Public Prosecutor, *Procuradoria Geral Republica DIAP*, Portuguese Ministry of Justice, Lisbon;
– M. Romão, Legal Adviser, Legal Policy and Planning Office, Portuguese Ministry of Justice, Lisbon.

For Spain

- J. M. Alvarez Luna, Head of Group I of the Laundering Section—Economic and Financial Crime Squad, National Police, Madrid;
- I. Navia Osorio, Public Prosecutor, *Audiencia Nacional—Fiscalia Antidroga*, Madrid.

For Sweden

- N. Wågnert, Legal Advisor, Swedish Ministry of Justice, Stockholm;
- A. von Sydow, Chief Prosecutor, Prosecutor General's Office, Stockholm.

For the United Kingdom

- D. Evans, Judicial Cooperation Unit, Home Office, London;
- C. Hugill, Head of Asset Forfeiture Unit, HM Customs and Excise, London.

INTRODUCTION[1]

Over the past twenty years, awareness of the importance of destabilising the financial basis of criminal organisations has grown significantly. In the 1980s, as the illicit production of drugs and their trafficking grew apace, organised crime's financial power increased substantially, and so did its ability to penetrate and corrupt the legitimate sphere by introducing dirty money into the legal system. The so called 'War on Drugs', launched at that time in the United States and which then spread elsewhere, inaugurated a new era in the fight against criminal organisations which Gallant (1999, 323) has aptly labelled 'the age of proceeds'. Given the awareness that the traditional device used to combat crime, that is, imprisonment, is entirely inadequate to counteract what is essentially an entrepreneurial criminal phenomenon whose strength lies more in its financial basis (the proceeds from crime) than in its personal one (criminal members), international policymakers rethought the strategies adopted to tackle criminal groups. The slogan 'tough on criminal wealth' quickly spread, and as a consequence of the emphasis now placed on criminal revenues, a tool familiar to most of the European Union countries—albeit one used intermittently and with narrow scope in national legislation at that time—was rediscovered: namely the confiscation of the proceeds from crime.

Various documents issued at both the international and European Union levels in the past two decades have stressed the importance of a well-developed proceeds-oriented strategy in disrupting criminal organisations and invited nations to strengthen their confiscation provisions. In response to these recommendations, the European Union Member States have gradually enhanced their existing confiscation regulations or introduced such provisions *ex novo*.

The problem, however, is that although a considerable amount of legislation—inspired by the idea that it is necessary to be 'tough on criminal wealth' to combat criminal organisations effectively—has been passed on the confiscation of crime proceeds, there is very little quantitative and qualitative information on how confiscation provisions are enforced within the European Union. No statistics—or at most very limited, partial and unreliable data—are collected on the implementation of such provisions, and the lack of such a significant platform for analysis has affected the studies produced on the topic. Such literature as does exist refers to just under half of the

[1] This book is based on the author's Ph.D. thesis. Also worth mentioning is that the author of this book started developing knowledge of the topic dealt with here when she acted as the Project Manager for the study *The Seizure and Confiscation of the Proceeds from Crime in the European Union Member States: What Works, What Does Not and What is Promising*, awarded by the European Commission to Transcrime under the Falcone 2000 Annual Programme, and as co-author of the final report on the study.

original fifteen EU Member States, and it is generally limited and partial in that it does not provide a complete picture of the enforcement of confiscation provisions from the very beginning of proceedings (when proceeds from crime are located) to their conclusion (when confiscation orders are enforced).

As a result, more that twenty years after the War on Drugs was launched, our knowledge of how confiscation provisions are concretely applied is scant in the extreme. To use the terminology coined by Roscoe Pound at the beginning of the last century (Pound, 1910), when he distinguished between 'law in the books', that is, the mere legal text, and 'law in action', that is, "the life of law in its enforcement" (Ibidem), our knowledge of proceeds from crime confiscation is still at the level of 'law in the books', while almost completely lacking is thorough understanding of how the legal provisions on the matter are enforced.

This situation entails that shedding light on the enforcement of the legal provisions of each EU Member State—as regards the entire process undertaken to confiscate and dispose of criminal proceeds (from investigation to trial and hence to the disposal of the assets)—requires knowledge to be built from scratch. This is what this work seeks to do, its aim being *to explore the practice ('law in action') of proceeds from crime confiscation so as to understand how legal provisions on proceeds from crime confiscation are enforced in the original fifteen European Union Member States. This will be in order to identify the main obstacles against the implementation of confiscation provisions, and to highlight the related best practices that could be emulated by other jurisdictions.*

The questions that this book will address are therefore the following:

- How are legal provisions on proceeds from crime confiscation enforced in the original fifteen European Union Member States?
- In particular, what are the main obstacles against their implementation and the related best practices?

To this end, the book is organised as follows.

Chapter 1 introduces the subject of proceeds from crime confiscation by examining the rationale for revival of the measure in the last two decades, its translation into documents enacted at the international and European Union levels, and the main evolutionary path—inspired by the idea that it is necessary to be 'tough on criminal wealth'—followed by European Union national systems in this area.

Chapter 2 seeks to answer the following question: what do we know about the implementation of tough legal provisions? For this purpose, the chapter reviews the information, both quantitative and qualitative, currently available on the practice of proceeds from crime confiscation. The review of the state of the art reveals that such information is extremely meagre and clarifies why there is a need for an exploratory study in this area.

Chapter 3 elucidates the methodology used in the book to explore the practice of crime proceeds confiscation across the original fifteen European Union Member States. After clarifying the relevant concepts, the chapter describes all the methodological steps followed to achieve the aim of this work.

Chapter 4 presents the findings obtained from implementation of the methodology described in the previous chapter. It contains, for each of the original fifteen Member States, a country profile that describes the law in action and juxtaposes it with the law in the books. In particular, for each country, the law in the books is first presented. A description of the law in action is then provided for each of the three phases of confiscation proceedings—the investigative phase, the judicial phase and the disposal phase—the purpose being to identify the main difficulties that arise in enforcing the legal provisions relevant in each phase, and the related best practices. This descriptive analysis of the law in action is followed by quantification of the law in action itself. Thus, the description of each phase is accompanied by a Figure representing the extent to which the law in the books is enforced in that phase, so as to provide graphic illustration of the magnitude of the problems that arise when the legal provisions relevant to each phase of confiscation proceedings are implemented.

Chapter 5 provides an overview of the enforcement of crime proceeds confiscation in the European Union. On the basis of the country-by-country analysis set out in the previous chapter, this chapter carries out horizontal analysis of the fifteen EU Member States in order to sum up, for each phase of the confiscation proceedings, the most recurrent problems and the related best practices. Some concluding remarks complete the book.

Finally, two annexes are appended to the end of this work. Annex 1 reproduces the questionnaires prepared for the development of this study. Annex 2 is its methodological appendix.

CHAPTER 1

THE REVIVAL OF CONFISCATION IN THE FIGHT AGAINST CRIMINAL ORGANISATIONS: THE INTERNATIONAL/EU AGENDA AND THE EVOLUTION OF THE MEASURE IN THE ORIGINAL FIFTEEN EU MEMBER STATES

This chapter introduces the subject of proceeds from crime confiscation by examining the rationale for the revival of the measure in the last two decades (section 1), and its translation into documents enacted at the international and European Union levels (section 2). The main evolutionary path followed by EU national systems in this area, also as a consequence of international and regional pressure, is then presented (section 3).

1.1 THE REVIVAL OF CONFISCATION IN THE FIGHT AGAINST CRIMINAL ORGANISATIONS

The term proceeds of crime confiscation can be defined as the permanent deprivation, by order of a court or some other competent authority, of any property (i.e. assets of every kind, whether corporeal or incorporeal, movable or immovable, tangible or intangible, and legal documents or instruments evidencing title to, or interest in, such assets) derived or obtained, directly or indirectly, through the commission of an offence. Seizure powers are normally available in order to secure the proceeds from crime and to prevent them from being dissipated before confiscation. Seizure can be defined as temporarily prohibiting the transfer, conversion, disposition or movement of property, or temporarily assuming custody or control of property, on the basis of an order issued by a court or a competent authority.[1]

To prevent confusion, it is necessary immediately to differentiate between what is technically defined as confiscation, as above defined, and what is generally referred to as 'forfeiture'. Forfeiture is an age-old term that denotes the removal of items whose possession is an offence (e.g. prohibited drugs, firearms, etc.), and of property used in

[1] These definitions are largely based on pertinent international conventions, whose provisions will be considered in detail in the following section.

the commission of the crime itself (Cabinet Office, Performance and Innovation Unit 2000, 26; Thomson 2000, 1).[2]

While traditional forfeiture powers continue to be provided for by law worldwide—and their application has been enhanced in recent times—the past few decades have also seen a revival of confiscation as a crime control strategy, in Europe as elsewhere.[3] The sanction, familiar to most countries, but used intermittently or almost completely abandoned for two hundreds years, was rediscovered in the last quarter of the twentieth century (Pieth 2002, 118) as a consequence of the new emphasis placed upon criminal revenues.

In the 1980s, in fact, as the illicit production and trafficking in drugs grew apace, the financial power of criminals, especially criminal organisations, increased significantly, and so did their ability to penetrate and corrupt the legitimate sphere by introducing dirty money into the legal system.[4] In response to widespread concern about the flow of illegal drugs and the spread of organised crime, there began what Gallant (1999, 323) has incisively called 'the age of proceeds'. This was initiated by the War on Drugs, which was launched in the United States in the 1980s to enhance Federal and State powers in fighting the illegal drug trade and whose message of the new folk-devils—that is organised crime and drugs problems—to be combated rapidly spread throughout the world (Levi 1997, 1; Pieth 2002, 119). This 'age of proceeds' was characterised by the awareness that monetary gain is one of the most important incentives for engaging in serious crimes, and that it provides criminals with the capital necessary to commit further offences and to infiltrate and corrupt the legitimate economy. Accordingly, the traditional approach to crime control—based on the arrest and imprisonment of criminal offenders—was deemed inadequate to combat criminal behaviours intended to produce and accumulate exorbitant wealth (Gallant 1999, 323; Thornton 1990, 72).

As a consequence, confiscation of ill-gotten gains was seen as a key element in any modern strategy to fight organised crime. Not only, in fact, did the measure satisfy the retributive principles that 'crime should not pay' and that 'no-one should profit from an illegal act', by removing unjust enrichment and restoring the legitimate distribution of wealth in society, but it also fulfilled further valuable objectives for crime prevention

[2] Given the EU focus of this work, the term 'forfeiture' is here used in its British English meaning (which is typically the EU significance), and not in that of American English, where it has a much wider coverage. It should be noted, however, that still today the two terms—forfeiture and confiscation—are used interchangeably, so that the potential for confusion is high (Broadbridge & Blair 2001, 9).

[3] As a matter of fact, the renaissance of confiscation did not occur solely in the original fifteen EU Member States—these being the focus of this work—but came about worldwide as well. Confiscation was rediscovered, for example, in the USA, where the War on Drugs had been launched and the regulations on the removal of criminal wealth were first enhanced (for an analysis of the US system see Salsich 1995; Levy 1996; Jensen & Gerber 1996; US Department of Justice, Criminal Division, Asset Forfeiture and Money Laundering Section 1998; Ehlers 1999; Baldwin 2000; Worrall 2001; Cassella 2001; Williams 2002); in Australia (see Clarke 2001; Fisse 1992; Lusty 2002; Thornton 1990; The Australian Law Reform Commission 1999); in Canada (see Maddocks 2000; Naylor 2000; Scott 1993); in South Africa (Gupta 2002; Redpath 2000; Schönteich 2000) and in Eastern Europe countries (Council of Europe 2001).

[4] On the infiltration of the licit economy by criminal organisations see, for example, Albanese (1985, 9); Savona (1996, 8–10); Adamoli, Di Nicola, Savona & Zoffi (1998, 21–22).

(Albrecht 1998, 169). By removing the rewards associated with crime, which constitute the main motive for illegal activity, confiscation would reduce the attractiveness of crime by decreasing its expected monetary benefits, and thereby act as a deterrent. In the end, indeed, it would dismantle criminal organisations by removing their working capital for investment in further criminal activities and infiltration of the legitimate economy (Bell 1999, 371; Hawkins 1999, 25–26; Levi 1997, 12).[5]

On the basis of these underlying principles, therefore, traditional criminal confiscation laws—which had been in place in most countries for many years—were revised and reinforced for use in the fight against Mafia-type organisations. Far from being mere imitations of those that they replaced, the confiscation provisions enacted worldwide in the aftermath of the War on Drugs were substantially more stringent than their predecessors. Those provisions, in fact, were now perceived to be too limited in scope, and only effective in straightforward cases (e.g. when a drug trafficker was caught in possession of the proceeds from his/her last sale), but not in more complex—and by now usual—ones involving the use of money laundering techniques to conceal the criminal origin of the proceeds (Financial Action Task Force on Money Laundering 1997, 12). Moreover, whereas tough confiscation provisions were initially restricted to the context from which they originated, namely drug trafficking activities, they were shortly therafter extended to the profits earned from most serious crimes, those typically committed by criminal organisations, and most recently to terrorism (Albrecht 1998, 167; Pieth 2002).

The policy development described in this section is now elaborated in greater detail by examining the international and EU documents that, in the past two decades, have emphasised the importance of proceeds from crime confiscation, and also the evolutionary paths followed by the EU Member States in this area.

1.2 THE INTERNATIONAL AND THE EU AGENDA

At the international level, over the last twenty years the significance of seizure and confiscation measures has been commented on in the following Conventions: the United

[5] Doubts about the effective capacity of confiscation to fulfil the various aims assigned to it have been expressed by some commentators. Levi and Osofsky (1995, 12–14) have noted that the risk of confiscation, rather than deterring people from crime, may simply induce criminals to refine their concealment techniques, and that the deterrence factor is modest when the ill-gotten gains are spent before prosecution. Furthermore, Levi and Osofsky maintain, confiscation does not typically target either criminal organisations or their heads. Naylor (1999, 11–14), in an extensive critique of the 'follow-the-money' approach in crime control policies, has pointed out that a) criminals are motivated by factors other than profit; b) most criminals are 'profligate spenders', so that, rather than deterring them from crime, confiscation risk simply intensifies their inherent propensity to spend; and c) it is not clear how the measure could put criminal organisations out of business, since as long as the underworld offers them credit, they can easily get back into business. It is finally worth noting that, especially in those countries where the law foresees the disposal of the proceeds from crime in favour of the law enforcement agencies that initiated the proceedings (as in the US), a large part of the literature claims that the true rationale of confiscation is not the noble goal of controlling crime, but rather its profitable nature for law enforcement agencies. On this point see, for example, Hyde (1995); Blumenson & Nilsen (1998 and 1999); Payne (1999); Walsh (2000); Worrall (2001).

Nations Convention against Illicit Traffic in Narcotic Drugs and Psychotropic Substances, signed in Vienna on 20 December 1988; the Convention on Laundering, Search, Seizure and Confiscation of the Proceeds from Crime, signed in Strasbourg on 8 November 1990; the United Nations Convention against Transnational Organised Crime, signed in Palermo from 12 to 15 December 2000.

The 1988 United Nations Convention against Illicit Traffic in Narcotic Drugs and Psychotropic Substances (henceforth 'Vienna Convention') was the first international response to the major threat to global financial stability raised by the laundering of the huge profits reaped by criminals from drug trafficking. The Vienna Convention came into force on 11 November 1990 and has been signed and ratified by all the original fifteen European Union Member States. Article 3 of this Convention requires that each Party adopts measures to criminalise: (1) any activity related to the production, possession, purchase, transport and distribution of narcotic drugs and psychotropic substances; (2) the laundering of the profits from drug trafficking activities. Since one of the aims of the Vienna Convention is, as stated in the Preamble, "to deprive persons engaged in illicit traffic of the proceeds of their criminal activities and thereby eliminate their main incentive for so doing", criminalising the above activities should be accompanied by measures permitting the removal of the proceeds from such offences. Article 5 of the Vienna Convention requires each Party to introduce into their domestic legislation measures enabling the competent authorities to seize and confiscate the proceeds from drug related offences, or the value thereof. Furthermore, any economic benefit arising from such proceeds is to be seized and confiscated. In order to facilitate the deprivation of criminal assets, each Party is invited to consider introducing a reversal of burden of proof in confiscation cases.

The Vienna Convention was followed, in 1990, by the Convention on Laundering, Search, Seizure and Confiscation of the Proceeds from Crime promoted by the Council of Europe (henceforth 'Strasbourg Convention'), which came into force on 1 September 1993 and was signed and ratified by all the original fifteen European Union Member States. This Convention, whose Preamble considers confiscation to be one of the 'modern and effective methods' for use on an international scale to combat serious crime, differs from the Vienna Convention as regards the predicate offences, which are no longer restricted to drug-related offences but include any type of crime. Chapter 2 of the Strasbourg Convention sets out measures to be taken at the national level. According to the provisions in this chapter, each Party must adopt the measures necessary to enable the tracing, seizure (article 3) and confiscation of the proceeds from crime, also in the form of value confiscation (article 2). Particular emphasis is placed on the adoption of those measures necessary to empower the competent authorities to order that bank, financial or commercial records be made available in confiscation proceedings, as well as to enable the use of special investigative techniques (such as interception of telecommunications, access to computer systems, etc.) facilitating the identification of the ill-gotten gains (article 4).

The issue of seizure and confiscation of the proceeds from crime has more recently been addressed at the international level by the United Nations Convention against Transnational Organised Crime signed in Palermo from 12 to

15 December 2000 (henceforth 'Palermo Convention'), the purpose of which was "to promote cooperation to prevent and combat transnational organised crime more effectively".[6] The Convention, which covers all the serious offences committed by transnational criminal groups, considers deprivation of the financial basis of organised crime as a significant means towards this end. Article 12 of the Convention obliges each Party to introduce measures providing for the seizure and confiscation of the proceeds directly or indirectly derived from criminal activity, or the value thereof, as well as the income and other economic benefits generated by the said proceeds. Furthermore, the same article invites each Party to consider the possibility of introducing reversal of the burden of proof in confiscation proceedings.

Again at the international level, also to be mentioned are the Forty Recommendations drawn up by the Financial Action Task Force on Money Laundering (henceforth FATF) in 1990 and revised since that date on various occasions, the most recent being in June 2003 (Financial Action Task Force on Money Laundering 2003). Recommendation 3 of the latest version of the Forty Recommendations requires the parties to adopt, on the basis of the principles established by the Vienna and Palermo Conventions, measures that enable their authorities to conduct appropriate investigations of property which is subject to confiscation and to seize and confiscate it, also in value form. The same Recommendation suggests that countries adopt measures making confiscation possible without the need for a criminal conviction, or ones that would shift onto the offender the onus of demonstrating the lawful origin of the property liable to confiscation in order to prevent adoption of the measure.

Turning from the international to the European level, the importance of proceeds confiscation in order to combat organised crime effectively has frequently been emphasised by the European Union. The following documents are a selection of those recently issued by the European Union to stress the importance of a well-developed confiscation system in action against criminal groups.

The Council Action Plan to Combat Organised Crime of 28 April 1997 stated that "the major driving force behind organised crime is the pursuit of financial gain". For this reason, in Political Guideline no. 11, "the European Council stresses the importance for each Member State of having well-developed and wide ranging legislation in the field of confiscation of the proceeds from crime [. . .]".[7] On the basis of this Political Guideline, Recommendation 26(c) suggests, among other things, the admissibility of confiscation regardless of the presence of the offender, such as when the offender has died or absconded.

In 1998, the Joint Action of 3 December 1998 adopted by the Council on the Basis of Article K.3 of the Treaty on European Union, on Money Laundering, the Identification, Tracing, Freezing, Seizing and Confiscation of the Instruments of and the Proceeds from Crime, emphasised the need to improve "the potential for disrupting criminal activity in the field of organised crime, by more effective cooperation between

[6] See article 1 of the Palermo Convention.

[7] Council Action Plan to Combat Organised Crime of 28 April 1997, in *Official Journal L 251*, 15 August 1997.

Member States in identifying, tracing, freezing or seizing, and confiscating the assets deriving from crime".[8] This Act calls on each Member State not to make or uphold reservations in respect of some articles of the Strasbourg Convention and to introduce value confiscation.

In 2000, the Council Action Plan of 27 March 2000 'The Prevention and Control of Organised Crime: A European Union Strategy for the Beginning of the New Millennium' asserted that "political attention should be devoted to depriving organised crime of its major motivation, the proceeds from crime".[9] Recommendations 17, 19 and 20 of the Action Plan are specifically focused on confiscation issues: Recommendation 17 invites Member States to establish units specifically dedicated to the tracing of ill-gotten gains; Recommendation 19 suggests exploring the feasibility of mitigating, either under criminal or civil law, the onus of proof regarding the source of the assets held by a person convicted of a Mafia-related offence; and Recommendation 20 proposes investigating the possibility that confiscation might apply regardless of the presence of the offender in order to cover cases where the latter has died or absconded.

The subject of seizure and confiscation was addressed in 2001 by the Council Framework Decision of 26 June 2001 on Money Laundering, the Identification, Tracing, Freezing, Seizing and Confiscation of the Instruments of and the Proceeds from Crime.[10] This Act calls on each Member State not to make or uphold reservations in respect of some articles of the Strasbourg Convention and to introduce value confiscation.

The topic of financial investigations aimed at identifying the proceeds from crime was addressed by the Council Recommendation of 25 April 2002 on Improving Investigation Methods in the Fight Against Organised Crime Linked to Organised Drug Trafficking: Simultaneous Investigations into Drug Trafficking by Criminal Organisations and Their Finances/Assets.[11] This recommends that such investigations should be conducted from the very beginning of proceedings in order to identify criminal organisation's finances. Also encouraged is the setting up of groups specialised in such investigations.

Finally to be mentioned is a document issued in 2005, namely the Council Framework Decision of 24 February 2005 on Confiscation of Crime-Related Proceeds, Instrumentalities and Property.[12] Article 3 of this Act provides for the adoption by MSs of an extended confiscation regime in the case of conviction for offences committed

[8] Joint Action of 3 December 1998 adopted by the Council on the basis of Article K.3 of the Treaty on European Union, on Money Laundering, the Identification, Tracing, Freezing, Seizing and Confiscation of the Instruments of and the Proceeds from Crime, in *Official Journal L 333*, 9 December 1998.

[9] Council Action Plan of 27 March 2000 'The Prevention and Control of Organised Crime: A European Union Strategy for the Beginning of the New Millennium', in *Official Journal C 124*, 3 May 2000.

[10] Council Framework Decision of 26 June 2001 on Money Laundering, the Identification, Tracing, Freezing, Seizing and Confiscation of the Instruments of and the Proceeds from Crime, in *Official Journal L 182*, 5 July 2001.

[11] Council Recommendation of 25 April 2002 on Improving Investigation Methods in the Fight Against Organised Crime Linked to Organised Drug Trafficking: Simultaneous Investigations into Drug Trafficking by Criminal Organisations and Their Finances/Assets, in *Official Journal C 114*, 15 May 2002.

[12] Council Framework Decision of 24 February 2005 on Confiscation of Crime-Related Proceeds, Instrumentalities and Property, in *Official Journal L 68*, 15 March 2005.

within the framework of a criminal organisation or for the purposes of terrorism if the court is convinced that the property has derived from other criminal activities (similar or otherwise to the one for which conviction has been passed) in a period prior to the conviction, and if the value of the property is disproportionate to the lawful income of the convicted person. The property of the closest relations of the person and of his/her business partners should also be liable to confiscation.

1.3 THE EVOLUTION OF NATIONAL CONFISCATION REGIMES IN THE EU FRAMEWORK[13]

International and EU pressure has played a significant role in persuading countries to enhance proceeds from crime confiscation provisions, or to introduce them *ex novo*. Of course, the evolution of national confiscation regimes has been due to a variety of factors, including the publication of reports stressing the need for changes to existing legislation, the activity of national authorities, failure in high-profile cases,[14] and recognition of the magnitude of the 'organised crime' problem (Bell 2000, 24–27), as well as a wave of sensational murders which have put the fight against organised crime high on the political agenda.[15] However, one can plausibly maintain that supranational pressure is probably "the major driver of change in respect of proceeds of crime legislation in many nations" (Ibidem, 24).[16]

Although the evolution of national confiscation regimes in the original fifteen EU Member States differs among them in many respects—and, as always when talking about policies, should be seen as an on ongoing process—in all countries it has nevertheless followed a clearly recognisable evolutionary pattern that can be described, given the severity of its constitutive elements, as being based on the motto 'tough on criminal wealth'. This signifies that, in recent decades, all the EU Member States considered here have revised their confiscation systems by introducing, to a greater or lesser extent, draconian provisions designed to increase the effectiveness of the measure

[13] This section reviews the main components of the common evolutionary pattern followed by the original fifteen EU Member States in the field of confiscation in the past two decades. For a more detailed account of the specific features of national legislation, see chapter 4.

[14] This happened, for example, in the United Kingdom following a notorious drug trafficking case, that is, that of *R v. Cuthbertson*. In this case, about £750,000 of drug trafficking proceeds were traced into the hands of the offenders and forfeited by Bristol Crown Court. However, the money had to be released 'with considerable regret' by the House of Lords, which recognised that forfeiture powers were not intended to be used to strip drug traffickers of the total proceeds of their criminal enterprises, but merely the instruments of crime. This case played a significant role in the development of confiscation in the country, since it clearly showed the inadequacy of the limited forfeiture powers. For a more detailed analysis of this case, see Howard League for Penal Reform (1984).

[15] This happened, for example, both in Italy and in Ireland. In Italy, Parliament member La Torre was killed by the Mafia in April 1982. In 1980 he presented a bill aimed at depriving criminal organisations of their ill-gotten gains. In September 1982, General Dalla Chiesa, who had been sent to Sicily to combat the Mafia, was murdered. In Ireland, on 6 June 1996 Gerry McCabe, detective of the *Garda Síochána* (the Irish police) was murdered. Some weeks later, on 26 June, Veronica Guerin, an investigative reporter for the *Sunday Independent* in Dublin, was killed.

[16] This view is also supported by Keyser-Ringnalda (1992, 512–513).

and especially in the fight against the serious crimes typically committed by criminal organisations.

Before examining the new philosophy referred to as 'tough on criminal wealth' in detail, it should first be noted that, in Europe, confiscation has largely evolved within the measure's natural setting, that is, criminal proceedings. This is because confiscation has traditionally been, and to a large extent still is today, *in personam,* that is, enacted as a sanction that follows a person's criminal conviction for the commission of a profit-generating crime (criminal confiscation). Only a very small number of EU Member States, in fact, have decided not only to strengthen their criminal confiscation laws but also to make the overall discipline even harsher by providing for confiscation in civil proceedings as well (civil confiscation). These are *in rem* proceedings, i.e. instituted against the proceeds rather than the alleged criminal, so that the focus is on the ill-gotten gains themselves.

The evolutionary pattern of criminal confiscation in the EU framework can be summed up as follows.

First, in consideration of the wide spectrum of potentially profitable activities, the coverage of confiscation provisions, which were restricted to drug trafficking offences when the War on Drugs was launched in the 1980s, has been extended in subsequent decades to all serious crimes, and often to all offences (Albrecht 1998, 167).

Also, given that the gains from a crime may no longer be in the convicted person's possession when the measure is enacted (it may have already been spent or converted into other assets/proceeds), value confiscation (i.e. the confiscation of a sum of money equal to the value of the proceeds from crime) has been introduced in addition to, or as the regular surrogate for, property confiscation (i.e. the confiscation of property found to be the proceeds of a crime) (Financial Action Task Force on Money Laundering 1997, 2).

Another important feature of the vast majority of EU national confiscation systems is that the measure no longer exclusively targets the alleged criminal, as it did in the past, but third parties as well. While Member States respect the rights acquired on assets representing the proceeds of a crime by *bona fide* third parties, they foresee the application of the measure to *mala fide* third parties, i.e. the straw men to whom the defendant has formally transferred his/her criminal wealth in order to avoid confiscation while continuing substantially to enjoy it. It is consequently now possible to confiscate assets owned by persons other than the defendant, and using dissimilar criteria (e.g. the property is a gift from the defendant; the third party knew of its criminal origin; the assets are under the defendant's effective control) (Ibidem, 5). Also, so that potential straw men can be subjected to the measure, legislation has been introduced whereby wide investigative powers can be exercised in their regard (Nanula 1999, 50).

Again, in some EU countries, conviction of the defendant is not always a prerequisite for confiscation of his/her assets in criminal proceedings—although this generally applies in a very limited number of circumstances (e.g. the defendant has died before confiscation, the defendant has absconded). Furthermore, some Member States have introduced, especially with reference to criminal typologies like drug trafficking, extended confiscation measures enabling the confiscation not only of the proceeds from the crime for which conviction has been adjudged but also other proceeds presumed to derive from previous crimes for which the defendant has not been convicted. The idea behind this development is that organised criminals are unlikely to be engaged in criminal activities on a one-off basis, so that it is presumed that gains acquired in a given period (normally five or six years) before conviction derive from crime and are confiscated unless the defendant can prove their licit origin (Fornari 1997, 209).

This consideration links with another feature of most national confiscation systems. The normal probatory rules which require public prosecutors fully to justify the measures requested have in fact been altered in most of the EU Member States, where, especially with reference to most serious offences, the onus is now on the defendant to show the legitimate origin of his/her assets in order to prevent their confiscation. This reversal of the burden of proof is probably the best known and most controversial element of modern confiscation laws. Its introduction, considered to be particularly important so that the purpose of the measure is not frustrated, was justified on the basis of the following considerations. While it may be extremely difficult for public prosecutors to show that proceeds stem from crime, because of the increasing ease with which the illicit origin of criminal proceeds can be concealed through money laundering, the defendant is the person in the best position to know how his/her property has been acquired and to furnish proof of its legal origin (Lusty 2002, 349).

Turning to civil confiscation, only four out of the original fifteen EU Member States, namely Greece, Ireland, Italy and the United Kingdom, have supplemented their confiscation systems with new civil confiscation powers. Although the civil confiscation regimes of these countries differ in many respects,[17] the guarantees for those involved are by definition lower than in criminal cases: for example, the threshold of proof (i.e. on the balance of probabilities) is lower than the criminal one (i.e. beyond reasonable double); and no conviction is required because the procedure is *in rem*, that is, only against the proceeds from the crime (Gallant 1999, 326).

To be finally noted is that this evolution of confiscation has been accompanied by a strengthening of investigators' powers to collect information on a suspect's financial situation. This has come about because financial investigations are the gateway to confiscation. Therefore, financial investigation units with particular responsibility for the financial aspects of crime have been set up in most of the EU Member States, and powers to obtain information and to use special investigative means have been boosted,

[17] Among the four civil confiscation regimes mentioned, that of Italy seems the most distinctive. Persons suspected of participating in a criminal organisation can be subject, as individuals deemed 'socially dangerous', not only to *misure di prevenzione personale* (literally, preventive personal measures) but also to confiscation as a preventive measure (*confisca di prevenzione*). Preventive measures (*ante* or *praeter delictum*) are intended to prevent certain individuals considered 'socially dangerous' from committing offences. The commission of previous offences is not a consideration when a decision is rendered and a preventive measure is issued. These measures are both personal, that is, directed against the person (e.g. special surveillance, prohibition and obligation to stay in a particular place), and financial, that is, directed against his/her wealth (e.g. confiscation). To be noted, however, is that confiscation normally follows the issue of a preventive personal measure. This makes Italian civil confiscation a hybrid between criminal and civil confiscation. For further details, see section 4.9.

also through enactment of anti money laundering regulations (Financial Action Task Force on Money Laundering 1997, 6).[18]

The above-described evolutionary process from traditional to modern confiscation has everywhere been accompanied by debate on the admissibility of such stringent criminal and civil confiscation measures, which, to some extent (greater or lesser according to the EU Member State concerned) undoubtedly conflict with fundamental rights enshrined by all European Constitutions and by the European Convention on Human Rights: to wit, the right to the enjoyment of property, the proportionality of the punishment to the gravity of the offence and to the personal culpability of the offender, as well as the presumption of innocence and the right to a fair trial.[19] Although these debates have generally been influential in shaping the evolution of the measure, the very fact that national legislators have passed the said provisions indicates that they have taken a clear stance on the matter, namely the position—fully upheld by national constitutional courts, as well as by the European Court on Human Rights[20]—that the public interest accruing from the protection of society against particularly aggressive forms of criminality well justifies some restrictions on due process protections. So, for example, the Irish Supreme Court, in the judgement *Murphy v. Mitchell; Gilligan v. Criminal Assets Bureau* of 18 October 2001, stated that "People engage in this activity (drug trafficking) to make money and it is notorious that they hide what they are doing. Direct proof of the proceeds is often difficult, if not impossible. The nature of the activity and the harm it does to the community provide a sufficient basis for the making of these assumptions (i.e. assumptions that property held by the accused could in certain circumstances be assumed to have been received in connection with drug trafficking). They serve a legitimate aim in the public interest of combating that activity. They do so in a way that is proportionate. They relate to matters that ought to be within the accused's knowledge, and they are rebuttable by him at a hearing before a judge on the balance of probabilities. In my opinion a fair balance is struck between the legitimate aim and the rights of the accused". The basic idea of a general public interest—that is ensuring that the use of ill-gotten gains does not procure for the applicant, or for the criminal organisation to which s/he was suspected of belonging, advantages to the detriment of the community—as the rationale for tough confiscation provisions had previously been affirmed by the European Court of Human Rights in the judgement

[18] For wider analysis on this point, see Council of Europe, European Committee of Crime Problems, Group of Specialists on Criminal Law and Criminological Aspects of Organised Crime (1997).

[19] The constitutionality of the measure has been discussed in a large number of documents produced in every part of Europe. See, for example, Alexander (1998); Murphy (1999); Bell (2000a); Wadham (2000); Maugeri (2001); Liberty (2001, 2001a, 2001b); Friedman (2001); Joint Committee on Human Rights (2001, 2002); Criminal Assets Bureau (2002, 2003).

[20] On this point see, for example, the following decisions by the European Court of Human Rights: European Court of Human Rights, *Phillips v. United Kingdom*, Judgment of 5 July 2001; European Court of Human Rights, *Raimondo v. Italy*, Judgment of 22 February 1994. The following are instead decisions by national courts: Scottish Privy Council, *Her Majesty's Advocate v. McIntosh*, Judgment of 5 February 2001; Italian Constitutional Court, Ordinance n. 18 of 22–29 January 1996; Irish High Court, *Gilligan v. Criminal Assets Bureau*, Judgment of 26 June 1997; Irish Supreme Court, *Murphy v. Mitchell; Gilligan v. Criminal Assets Bureau*, Judgment of 18 October 2001.

Raimondo v. Italy of 22 February 1994. On that occasion the court—well aware of the difficulties encountered by the Italian State in fighting Mafia-type organisations, as well as of the enormous profits earned by those organisations from their illegal activities and which are often invested, *inter alia*, in the real property sector—recognised that confiscation is an effective and necessary weapon with which to combat such a dangerous criminal phenomenon.

CHAPTER 2

WHY AN EXPLORATORY STUDY INTO THE PRACTICE OF PROCEEDS OF CRIME CONFISCATION ACROSS THE ORIGINAL FIFTEEN EU MEMBER STATES?

Having reviewed the evolutionary pattern of proceeds from crime confiscation in the last two decades in the original fifteen EU Member States—with modern and especially tough confiscation measures replacing traditional ones in order to bolster the fight against organised crime—it is now of interest to ask: what do we actually know about the implementation of these stringent legal provisions?

This chapter accordingly reviews what we know, in terms of both quantitative (section 1) and qualitative (section 2) information, about the practice of proceeds from crime confiscation—or in other words, about the enforcement of legal provisions which discipline the removal of ill-gotten gains. The survey which follows reveals that knowledge is extremely meagre, in fact, and clarifies why there is a need for an exploratory study in this area (section 3).

2.1 THE LACK OF STATISTICS ON THE IMPLEMENTATION OF CONFISCATION PROVISIONS IN THE EU FRAMEWORK

No statistics, or only very scarce, partial and unreliable ones, are collected on the implementation of confiscation provisions (for instance, data on the number, value, typology of seized, confiscated and disposed of assets; the ratio between the number of confiscation orders and the number of convictions for a given offence).

The FATF is especially interested in evaluating the effectiveness of confiscation as a necessary component of an anti-money laundering strategy. This interest is because "the criminals' concern that their proceeds of crime may be confiscated is a major factor in motivating them to launder the proceeds of crime" (Financial Action Task Force on Money Laundering 1997, 1). In 1997, the FATF carried out a survey of confiscations in its members, which include the original fifteen EU Member States. The study's main conclusion, which it reached by analysing the members' replies to a questionnaire, was that "[. . .] only twelve members kept statistics, and of these only nine had statistics on a year by year basis [. . .]", so that "[. . .] it is difficult to discern any clear trends" (Ibidem, 7). The FATF also warns that the existing statistics must be treated with caution, since countries may collect data in different ways, and account should also be taken of the time lag between the commencement of a case and its conclusion (Ibidem, 7). Because the replies to the questionnaires furnished 'a considerable amount of qualitative information and a limited amount of quantitative information' (Ibidem, 1), what was initially intended to be an evaluation of confiscation policies was perforce transformed into a description of the evolution and main features of the FATF members' confiscation systems.

A year later, in 1998, similar conclusions were drawn by the the Council of the European Union, which reported that "Member States had hardly any information available at national level about the seizure and confiscation of criminal proceeds. [...] In most of the EU Member States there seems to be no mechanism in place to report this type of information at national level" (Council of the European Union 1998, 36).

The lack of quantitative information on proceeds from crime confiscation was again remarked upon by the FATF in a report produced in 2001. On that occasion, the FATF stressed that the statistics available in this area are "limited, and are also rather out of date" (Financial Action Task Force on Money Laundering 2001, 13). As a consequence, the report was only able to present, in its Annex 1, some partial statistics collected in mutual evaluation reports. As the report admits, this situation makes it difficult to assess whether confiscation provisions and the institutional system set up to enforce them are effective (Ibidem, 11).

These findings were replicated in 2001 by a research project financed by the European Commission under the Falcone 2000 Annual Programme and carried out by Transcrime in cooperation with the University of Palermo and the Italian Ministry of Justice, in which the author of this book took part (Transcrime 2001a). The research covered the fifteen EU Member States and employed the following methodology to obtain quantitative data on the functioning of confiscation systems. In order to retrieve existing data on the number, value, typology of seized, confiscated and disposed of assets, a questionnaire was sent to one expert for each EU Member State who had previously been selected by the Ministry of Justice of each country. The findings of the Project furnish a detailed panorama of existing quantitative data on confiscation in the European Union which is worth briefly reviewing here. *Austria* has no reliable data on confiscations. Since the national confiscation system was reformed in 1996, public prosecutors must complete a form used to collect information on the quantity of assets seized and then confiscated. This data collection system fails to work, however, because the information provided by the public prosecutors at the Ministry of Justice is incomplete. In *Belgium* some data are collected autonomously and without coordination among the different institutions concerned: the police, the *Gendarmerie* and the Financial Intelligence Units (henceforth FIU). The data collected are sometimes partial because they concern either the initial phase of confiscation proceedings, when seizure takes place, or the final phase. There are no reliable data on seizures and confiscations in *Denmark*: this situation is due to both a lack of interest in the matter and the absence of the resources necessary for collection of these statistics. There is a shortage of data on seizure and confiscation in *Finland*. This is because statistics are collected separately by the agencies involved in the various phases of confiscation proceedings (the police and the executive authorities) and the different initiatives are inefficiently coordinated. Reliable statistics on the implementation of seizure and confiscation provisions are not available in *France*. Data on the implementation of confiscation in *Germany* are not included in official statistics; statistics on the value of seized and confiscated assets are provided by the *Bundeskriminalamt* only since the year 2000. No reliable data exist on the implementation of confiscation provisions in *Greece*. Reliable data on the implementation of criminal confiscation are not available in *Ireland*, although the country has a complete and computerised data collection system with regard to civil confiscation. There are no reliable data on the implementation of criminal confiscation in *Italy*, but civil confiscation (the so called *confisca di prevenzione*) is monitored by the Ministry of Justice, which collects statistics in a computerised database set up in 1997.[21] The system, however, does not function properly: the Ministry of Justice only supplies partial figures, and the database should gather data sent by all the courts, but a large number of them do not cooperate (Ministero della Giustizia, Dipartimento per gli affari di giustizia, Direzione generale della giustizia penale, Ufficio I 2002, 9). The quality of the information recorded is poor, moreover, and in most cases the value of confiscated assets is not stated (Ibidem, 11). A further shortcoming is that not only the Ministry of Justice but also other institutions, like the Ministry of Finance and the *Direzione Investigativa Antimafia*, collect statistics in this field, and do so in uncoordinated manner. In *Luxembourg*, the Ministry of Justice publishes annual statistics on the performance of the judicial system. These are general data, however; specific figures on seizure and confiscation are not systematically collected. In the *Netherlands* some statistics are provided by a centralised office, the BOOM (i.e. the Criminal Assets Deprivation Bureau set up within the Public Prosecution Service), which started collecting data in 1997. Since then it has provided estimates of the amounts confiscated, although discrepancies have been signalled between those estimates and courts' activity (Daams 2002, 314). Reliable statistics on the implementation of seizure and confiscation measures are not available for *Portugal*, where various institutions—the police, the customs offices, the *Guarda Nacional Republicana* and the Ministry of Justice—collect general data. However, because these different initiatives are not coordinated, contradictory and non-comparable statistics are produced. In *Spain*, partial and non-comparable data are collected by various bureaux (police, customs authorities, etc.) but with no coordination among them. In *Sweden*, the Crime Prevention Bureau, a specialised authority, gathers statistics on the activity of the police and the judicial system. However, figures relating to the implementation of confiscation are not collected at present, one of the main reasons being the competent agencies' scant awareness of the importance of dispossessing criminals of their wealth. Finally, in the *United Kingdom*, data on the implementation of the confiscation provisions are "[...] not collected in any systematic way. What little data exists shows that the UK's confiscation track record is poor" (Cabinet Office, Performance and Innovation Unit 2000, 29). With reference to criminal confiscation, only statistics on the value of property confiscated and then recovered are available for the UK. They evidence a wide gap between the amount collected and the amount confiscated. There are no reliable figures on the value of property frozen and seized in the UK, owing to the fact that public prosecutors do not have to declare the value of

[21] This database should provide figures on confiscation *ex* article 12-*sexies* as well, although in practice these data are not collated.

goods involved in the confiscation procedure until the final confiscation hearing. With regard to civil forfeiture, neither in this case is it possible to compare the value of cash forfeited with the value of that seized.

To sum up, a complete lack of reliable statistics on seizure and confiscation is commonplace in the original fifteen European Union Member States. In some countries, data are not collected at all, owing to a lack of both culture and resources. In others, such as Finland, Italy, Spain and Portugal, various offices collate statistics but their operations are not coordinated. As a result, contradictory and non-comparable data are produced, with a consequent great waste of time and resources. The only exception is Irish civil confiscation, the implementation of which is monitored by means of a complete and computerised data collection system.

This lack of trustworthy statistics on the implementation of confiscation provisions prompts a number of considerations.

Firstly, because the existence and accuracy of such information is indicative of the importance given by national institutions (political, judicial and law enforcement agencies) to confiscation, *it seems that only low priority is given to the matter at present.* At the political level—perhaps also because of the constant budgetary constraints with which they must contend—politicians seem satisfied with having developed a tough and well publicised policy merely by enacting some legislation. With reference to judicial and law enforcement agencies, for understandable reasons they tend to see the collection of related statistics as a burden (Council of the European Union 1999, 2).

Secondly, and more importantly, because such statistics are a significant source of information for the evaluation of confiscation policies, *the lack of them hampers review of the effectiveness and efficiency of such policies*, so that it is difficult to determine whether the measure has achieved its expected outputs/outcomes[22] (i.e. whether it is *effective* in depriving criminals of their ill-gotten gains—this being its output—or in reducing organised crime activities, deterring from the commission of crime by reducing/removing its expected benefits, and strengthening public confidence in the criminal justice system by showing that crime does not pay—these being its possible outcomes), and whether it achieves these expected outputs/outcomes at the lowest cost[23] (i.e. whether it is *efficient*).

Evaluation of public policies, while commonplace in areas such as economics and financial affairs—where it is supported by statistics—is less common in the area of the judiciary and law enforcement, also owing to the low priority given to the collection of statistical information by national institutions, as well as to the logistical and functional problems of such collection, which normally involves a variety of institutions (Ibidem). The case of confiscation policy is emblematic in this respect.

[22] "*Outputs* are defined narrowly as the direct products of the process of implementation. [. . .] *Outcomes* are defined as the consequences of the intervention. These can arise both during and after the implementation period. [. . .] Key outcomes will relate to the stated objectives of the intervention. But there are likely to be wider outcomes such as a change in the fear of crime or the reduction in other types of crime" (Dhiri & Brand 1999, 12).

[23] "*Costs* are defined as the monetary value of *inputs*, [which are] defined as any additional human, physical and financial resources that are used to undertake a project" (Dhiri & Brand 1999, 12).

It is therefore impossible to evaluate the *effectiveness* of the measure in producing its output, which is to deprive criminals of their ill-gotten gains. Answering the question of whether or not the measure is effective requires a complete set of data on the value, number and typology of seized, confiscated and disposed of assets. It can be reasonably assumed that (a) the *higher* the percentage of criminal wealth seized, (b) the *higher* the percentage of seized assets confiscated and (c) the *higher* the percentage of confiscated assets disposed of, the *greater* the effectiveness of the process from (a) the investigative phase, to (b) the judicial phase, and finally to (c) the disposal phase. However, this process of reasoning is at present impracticable. Nobody knows how much money criminals have; and, as seen, no or very few data are collected in the European Union Member States on the value of seized, confiscated and disposed of assets. Measuring the effectiveness of confiscation in achieving its possible outcomes would require a wider set of data, and the exercise is at the moment simply not feasible.

An even wider set of data would be needed to evaluate the *efficiency* of confiscation policies, whether one wants to carry out a cost effectiveness analysis or a cost-benefit analysis.[24]

2.2 THE SCANT LITERATURE PRODUCED ON THE IMPLEMENTATION OF CONFISCATION PROVISIONS IN THE EU FRAMEWORK

As seen, the EU framework is marked by the scarcity and, when it exists, the unreliability of quantitative information on the way confiscation provisions are applied. The lack of such a significant platform for analysis has affected the literature produced on the topic, as clearly emerges when reviewing it.[25]

Regarding Austria, a study was carried out by Löschnig-Gspandl and Kilchling (2002). Since criminal statistics still have no specific section devoted to confiscation, Löschnig-Gspandl and Kilchling's work is based on the analysis of case studies and on limited quantitative information (Löschnig-Gspandl & Kilchling 2002, 119), which at least enables them to draw the general conclusion that the use of confiscation is infrequent in the country.

With reference to Germany, an analysis by Benseler in 1997 focused—owing to the paucity of quantitative data—on the law in the books rather than on the law in action. Consequently, the author emphasised "the great importance to investigate a more detailed and comparable data basis regarding the effect of national forfeiture laws" (Benseler 1997, 209). The lack of reliable information on the practice of proceeds from

[24] Cost-effectiveness analysis "is articulated in terms of the *input cost per unit of output or outcome* achieved. [. . .]. In order to derive a measure of cost-effectiveness, therefore, we need to know the level of inputs used to implement an intervention, the cost of these inputs and the nature and level of outputs and outcomes. [. . .] Cost-benefit analysis (CBA) takes cost-effectiveness analysis a stage further by attaching monetary values to the outcomes of an intervention. Once both the costs of inputs and the value of outcomes (benefits) are expressed in monetary terms a direct comparison can be made" (Dhiri & Brand 1999, 13–14).

[25] This section conducts a rapid survey of studies on the implementation of confiscation provisions in the EU Member States covered by this work. A more detailed account of the findings of these studies is given in chapter 4, when the country profiles are presented.

crime confiscation, as well as on the practical problems that hamper the application of specific confiscation provisions, has been expressly stated by Kilchling (2002, 36–37), who, on the basis of the incomplete statistics available, of concluded cases and of some previous studies, offers some preliminary reflections on police and judicial practice in this area.

For Italy, in 1997 Paoli cross-checked various sources, both quantitative and qualitative, to question the effectiveness of confiscation. Although Paoli was aware of the scant scientific reliability of existing statistics, and therefore of the need to interpret them with caution (Paoli 1997, 263–264), her conclusions highlighted the ineffectiveness of the existing legal framework (Ibidem, 270). More recently, the same conclusions were reached in a research project conducted by Transcrime and in which the author of this book took part (Transcrime 2001), as well as in an article by the present author (Vettori 2003). Both studies highlighted the limitations of the existing data and their negative consequences for the evaluation of confiscation policies, and they both reviewed the existing literature on the subject (legal theory, case law, the 'grey' literature, and reports by an *ad hoc* Committee, namely the *Commissione Parlamentare Antimafia*) in order to identify the main problems that arise in implementing the legal provisions of relevance from the very beginning of confiscation procedures, when financial investigations are conducted, to its conclusion, when confiscation orders are enforced. A different methodology, whereby the literature review was supplemented by interviews with ten law enforcement officers, was employed by Paoli to shed light on the subject (Paoli 2002).

With reference to France, in 1997 an article by Godefroy and Kletzlen reviewed the evolution of the measure in the country and concluded by stressing "the little interest [. . .] in regard of the confiscation issue" shown by politicians and the media (1997, 280). In 2000, the same authors compiled a report (Godefroy & Kletzlen 2000), which was later published in a collected volume (Godefroy & Kletzlen 2002), which offered a tentative evaluation, based on existing quantitative information and analysis of court cases, of confiscation measures adopted with regard to money laundering and drug related offences. The statistical analysis, for all its limitations, showed that the measure is infrequently applied, while the qualitative analysis highlighted some practical problems.

In the Netherlands, detailed analysis of the impact of the new confiscation provisions introduced in 1993 was conducted in 1998 in a report requested by the Ministry of Justice and prepared by its Research and Documentation Centre (WODC) (Nelen & Sabee 1998). The report employed various research methods (so that existing statistics were integrated with case studies, interviews with officials involved in the application of the legislation, and surveys of police forces) to analyse the application of the newly-introduced draconian provisions. The conclusion of the study was that confiscation has not yet taken firm root in the country. Although the findings should be interpreted with caution, as the authors themselves stress, owing to the short evaluation period (insufficient since most confiscation cases last more than five years), the report gives useful insights into the obstacles—grouped under the heading "lack of expertise, of resources and of willingness"—that hamper the implementation of confiscation provisions from the very beginning of the case to its conclusion. Indications on how confiscation provisions are applied (in terms of the offences most frequently subject to them, the amounts confiscated, the nationalities of the defendants) were also provided by Daams (2002), who analysed sixty-four cases from eight courts. The author comes to the conclusion that the results achieved by the legislation are still not as good as was expected when it was introduced, owing to practical problems and unrealistic expectations (Daams 2002, 315).

The United Kingdom is probably the EU country in which closest attention has been paid to confiscation issues, from both the theoretical and practical points of view, with the two levels closely intertwined, given that identification of the practical problems hampering the implementation of the legal provisions has been the driver of legislative change. There follows a selection of the main items of research on the subject. In 1995, a study commissioned by the Home Office Police Research Group (Levi & Osofsky 1995) identified a series of factors explaining why confiscation orders cover only a tiny fraction of the estimated ill-gotten gains, and why the amount recovered when enforcing confiscation orders is generally low, putting forward some recommendations to improve the situation. In 1998, the Home Office Working Group on Confiscation also reported on the enforcement of confiscation provisions (Home Office Working Group on Confiscation 1998).[26] Drawing on existing statistics and on the replies to a questionnaire sent to Justices' Clerks, the report proposed a number of amendments to the criminal confiscation system so as to improve the confiscation order recovery rate; the extension of limited powers for confiscation without a criminal conviction in emulation of the Irish model; and the creation of a central confiscation agency. These proposals were reprised and developed further in a report produced in 2000 by the Performance and Innovation Unit of the Cabinet Office (Cabinet Office, Performance and Innovation Unit 2000), whose conclusions provided the basis for the 2002 Proceeds of Crime Act. The last study to be mentioned was produced in Scotland in 2000 (Her Majesty's Inspectorate of Constabulary for Scotland 2000). This was a thematic inspection of the effectiveness of Scottish police services in identifying assets in order to make them available for subsequent confiscation by Her Majesty's Inspectorate of Constabulary (HMIC). The study was conducted by means of questionnaires administered individually to officers conducting financial investigations, and interviews with line managers, heads of department and support staff. The findings identified some weaknesses in assets tracing practice.

The following considerations sum up the literature produced on the enforcement of confiscation provisions.

First, at least some information on the practice of confiscation is available for just less than a half of the original fifteen EU Member States, while for the remaining States the enforcement of confiscation provisions is still unexplored.

Second, even when one or more items of research are available, in the vast majority of cases they provide only limited information.

[26] This is only the latest of a series of reports produced by the Working Group, all of which have been very influential in shaping legislative changes. For example, the first report of 1991 led to significant amendment of the Drug Trafficking Offences Act 1986, the Criminal Justice Act 1993 and the consolidating Drug Trafficking Act of 1994. Its second report of 1992 influenced first the contents of the Criminal Justice Act 1993 and then those of the Proceeds of Crime Act 1995.

Third, such knowledge as is available generally concerns, depending on the methodology employed and on the statistics available, the practice in a particular phase of confiscation proceedings. *A complete picture of the enforcement of confiscation provisions from the very beginning of proceedings (when proceeds from crime are located) to their conclusion (when confiscation orders are enforced) is almost completely lacking.* To be noted on this point is that the existing literature deals mainly with (a) the very beginning of confiscation proceedings, that is the investigative phase, when proceeds from crime are located by investigators, or (b) the immediately subsequent phase, that is, the judicial phase, when proceeds suspected of originating from criminal activities are seized and eventually confiscated. Almost totally neglected is the disposal phase, despite its extreme importance for the effectiveness of the overall confiscation system. The disposal phase, in fact, is when the fruits of confiscation must be concretely harvested, so that problems occurring at this stage may nullify the efforts made in the previous phases.[27]

2.3 THE NEED FOR AN EXPLORATORY STUDY OF THE PRACTICE OF PROCEEDS FROM CRIME CONFISCATION

More than twenty years after the War on Drugs was launched and confiscation provisions were significantly 'reinforced', one might reasonably expect mechanisms to be now in place to furnish information on how these provisions are applied in practice in the EU Member States. However, as the previous two sections have shown, this is not the case.

Current knowledge of the way in which confiscation provisions are implemented is scant from both:

- *a quantitative point of view*, given that a complete lack of reliable statistics on seizure and confiscation is commonplace in the original fifteen European Union Member States, and
- *a qualitative point of view*, given that knowledge, relative to just less than half of the EU Member States analysed here, is generally limited and partial because it does not constitute a complete picture of the enforcement of confiscation provisions from the very beginning of proceedings (when proceeds from crime are located) to their conclusion (when confiscation orders are enforced).

To use the terminology coined by Roscoe Pound at the beginning of the last century (Pound 1910), when he distinguished between 'law in the books' (i.e. the mere legal text), and 'law in action', that is "the life of law in its enforcement" (Ibidem), our knowledge of proceeds from crime confiscation is still at the level of 'law in the books', while almost completely lacking is sound comprehension of the 'law in action', that is of the enforcement of legal provisions on confiscation.

This situation entails that shedding light on the enforcement of the legal provisions relevant, in each EU Member State, on the entire process of confiscating and disposing of the proceeds from crime (from investigation to trial, and then to disposal of the

[27] Regarding the scant attention generally paid to the disposal phase see, for example, Shelley (2000, 47).

assets), requires that knowledge must be built from scratch. To this end, and because evaluation research is at present precluded by a lack of the data with which to assess the effectiveness and efficiency of confiscation policies, exploratory research seems particularly appropriate. Research of this kind, in fact, can be especially useful when investigating "[. . .] criminal justice policies about which little is known" (Maxfield & Babbie 2000, 18), because such inquiry is "[. . .] usually undertaken, when there is not enough information available about the research subject. In certain cases it is undertaken in order to provide a basis for further research, for example to define some concepts, [. . .] or to operationalise variables; in other cases it is undertaken to gain information on the issue *per se* [. . .]" (Sarantakos 1998, 7).

The aim of this book is to explore the practice ('law in action') of proceeds from crime confiscation, the purpose being to understand how legal provisions disciplining proceeds from crime confiscation are enforced in the original fifteen EU Member States. This will lead to identification of the main obstacles against the implementation of confiscation provisions, and of the related best practices that could be emulated by other jurisdictions.

The questions that this work will address are therefore the following:

– How are legal provisions disciplining proceeds from crime confiscation enforced in the original fifteen EU Member States?
– In particular, what are the main obstacles against their implementation and the related best practices?

Hence, as the above makes clear, this work intends to start building knowledge on how legal provisions disciplining proceeds from crime confiscation work in practice. Besides producing new and systematised knowledge on this neglected topic, the study seeks to provide a first definition and operationalisation of concepts so as to stimulate further research.

CHAPTER 3

HOW TO EXPLORE THE PRACTICE OF PROCEEDS OF CRIME CONFISCATION ACROSS THE ORIGINAL FIFTEEN EU MEMBER STATES?

The aim of this study, as said, is to explore how legal provisions on the tracing, confiscation and disposal of the proceeds from crime are enforced in the original fifteen EU Member States, the purpose being to identify the main obstacles against their implementation and the related best practices. It is necessary, therefore, to elucidate the methodology used in pursuit of this aim.

This chapter first clarifies the meanings with which this study uses terms such as 'proceeds of crime confiscation', 'national confiscation system and its phases' and 'law in action' (or practice) of each phase of the national confiscation system (section 1). It then explains the methodology used by describing all the methodological steps followed (section 2).

3.1 DEFINING CONCEPTS

The following terms require definition in regard to the meaning with which they are used in this work.

A) Proceeds of crime confiscation

In what follows, the term 'proceeds of crime confiscation' refers to the permanent deprivation, by order of a court or some other competent authority, of any property (i.e. assets of every kind, whether corporeal or incorporeal, movable or immovable, tangible or intangible and legal documents or instruments evidencing title to, or interest in, such assets) derived or obtained, directly or indirectly, through the commission of an offence. The term, therefore, does not refer to the permanent deprivation of those items which it is an offence to possess or use, those that were used in the commission of a crime, or those with regard to which a crime was committed (a form of deprivation often referred to as 'forfeiture').

B) National confiscation system and its three phases (investigative, judicial and disposal phases)

A broad notion of 'national confiscation system' is adopted here in order to yield a complete picture of the enforcement of confiscation provisions in the original fifteen European Union Member States.

First, the concept 'national confiscation system' is used to refer to all national provisions on the confiscation of criminal proceeds, i.e. not only criminal provisions but also civil ones, where they exist. The legislation of some EU countries, in fact, provides for confiscation not only in criminal proceedings but in civil ones as well. Civil confiscation is envisaged by the legal systems of four Member States: Greece, Ireland, Italy and the United Kingdom.

Second, the term 'national confiscation system' is used to refer to national provisions regarding the entire body of proceedings intended to deprive criminals of their illicit gains. Consequently, the entire process of confiscating illicit wealth from criminal organisations is considered. Owing to the complexity and dissimilarity of the actors/procedures/rules involved in confiscation proceedings, the latter have been divided into three phases:

1. investigative phase, when proceeds from crime are located and evidence on their owners is collected;
2. judicial phase, when the ill-gotten gains may be seized and eventually confiscated once their criminal origin has been judicially ascertained;
3. disposal phase, when a decision is taken on the destination of the confiscated proceeds.

C) Law in action (or practice) of each of the three phases of the national confiscation system

In order to clarify the concept 'law in action' in each of the three mentioned phases of the national confiscation system—here used as a synonym for 'practice' (the two terms, in fact, are employed interchangeably in the context of this book)—the necessary starting point is the difference between 'law in the books' and 'law in action'. The great divide between these two concepts was first described by Roscoe Pound at the beginning of the twentieth century. Pound explained that "if we look closely, distinctions between law in the books and law in action, between the rules that purport to govern the relations of man and man and those that in fact govern them, will appear [...]" (Pound 1910). Therefore, whilst 'law in the books' is the mere legal text, 'law in action' is "the life of law in its enforcement" (Ibidem), and thus represents the real world of the present-day criminal justice system.

Transferring this definition to the topic dealt with here, the term 'law in action' (or practice) with regard to each of the three phases of a national confiscation system denotes the *enforcement of the legal provisions of relevance to each of the three phases by the institutions responsible for doing so.* The legal provisions themselves are instead the 'law in the books'.

The above definition can be translated, for each phase, into the following equation:

$$LA_P = ELB_P$$

where:

LA_P = the "law in action" of the phase.

ELB_P = the enforcement of the law in the books, i.e. of the legal provisions of relevance in the phase.

3.2 METHODOLOGICAL STEPS

Now that the concepts employed in this study have been clarified, there follows a description of the methodological steps followed to explore the practice of proceeds from crime confiscation. They are as follows:

Step 1. Operationalisation of the concept 'law in action'.
Step 2. Preparation of a questionnaire, and its administration to one high profile expert per Member State by means of a telephone interview.
Step 3. Building a country profile that describes the law in action and juxtaposes it with the law in the books.
Step 4. Quantifying the law in action.

STEP 1. Operationalisation of the Concept 'Law in Action'

In order to explore the law in action during each phase of the confiscation proceedings, it was first necessary to operationalise the concept 'law in action' so that it was empirically observable and measurable.

The starting point of this operationalisation was the assumption that the law in action, that is, the enforcement of the legal provisions of relevance in each of the three phases of the confiscation proceedings, depends on two elements.

First, it depends on how specific legal provisions relative to the phase are implemented. Hence it was assumed that the greater the extent to which such provisions are implemented, the better the law in action. To be noted is that a limited number of legal provisions were selected, and essentially those distinctive of the recent evolution of national confiscation systems brought about by the War on Drugs.[28]

Second, it depends on a series of factors in which shape practice during the overall phase. The basic idea was that the enforcement of legal provisions is influenced by such factors as: the training and competence of institutional actors; the amount of human resources and material resources available for the purpose; information exchange and cooperation both among institutional actors and between those institutional actors and the external ones that may play a role in confiscation cases, like financial and non financial institutions and informants. It was assumed that the better these factors (i.e. the higher the level of training and competence of institutional actors, the greater the amount of material and human resources devoted to the phase, the closer the information exchange and cooperation both among institutional actors and between those institutional actors and the external ones that may play a role in confiscation cases), the better the law in action. Although these factors may also impact on the implementation of one or more of the specific legal provisions considered,[29] they nevertheless

[28] Therefore, most of the legal provisions considered are those that incorporated the principles of the 'tough on criminal wealth' philosophy presented in section 1.3 into the EU national confiscation systems.
[29] By way of an example, the amount of human resources devoted to the investigative phase is a factor that impacts on implementation of the specific provision on the investigation of the financial situations of persons suspected of acting as straw men for the defendant, given that without adequate manpower the provision may not be applied at all, or may have limited coverage (so that potential straw men are not investigated). It is

shape practice during the phase as a whole—including the implementation of the myriad legal provisions not specifically considered but anyhow applied in confiscation cases.

This assumption can be translated, for each phase, into the following mathematical expression:

$$LA_P = (ESP_P \; U_P)$$

where:

LA_P = The law in action of the phase.
ESP_P = The enforcement of specific legal provisions of relevance in the phase.
U_P = Factors relevant to the overall enforcement of the law in the books during the phase.

Therefore, (a) the greater the extent to which specific legal provisions of relevance in the phase are implemented, and b) the better a series of factors relevant to the overall enforcement of the law in the books during the phase, the better the law in action is assumed to be.

On the basis of this assumption, a set of variables were identified for ESP_P and for U_P in order to measure the law in action of each phase.

These variables and the related modalities are listed in the tables below for each of the three phases. The tables also indicate why the variable was assumed to contribute to the law in action of the phase. The contribution to the law in action by the variables identified with reference to ESP_P is self evident. Less clear, however, is that of the variables identified with reference to U_P. Consequently, the reason why each variable was assumed to be relevant to measurement of the law in action during the phase is explained, also by referring to the literature that highlights this significance.

For the investigative phase, considering that the law in action of the phase can be expressed with the following mathematical expression,

$$LA_{IP} = (ESP_{IP} \; U_{IP})$$

where:

LA_{IP} = The law in action of the investigative phase.
ESP_{IP} = The enforcement of specific legal provisions of relevance in the investigative phase.
U_{IP} = Factors relevant to the overall enforcement of the law in the books during the investigative phase.

the following variables were selected for ESP_{IP} and U_{IP} in order to measure the law in action of the phase:

also clear, however, that the effect of this factor is not limited to this aspect alone, but is much wider and shapes practice during the entire phase.

Variables for ESP_{IP}	*Modalities of the variable*
1. Frequency of the use of special investigative means, if their use is envisaged. *The more frequent the use of special investigative means, the better the law in action is assumed to be.*	a range from 1 to 5, where 1 = never used; 5 = always used
2. Frequency of financial investigations on third parties believed to be acting as the defendant's straw men, if such investigations of third parties are envisaged. *The more frequently financial investigations are conducted on third parties believed to be acting as a defendant's straw men, the better the law in action is assumed to be.*	a range from 1 to 5, where 1 = never made; 5 = always made

Variables for U_{IP}	*Modalities of the variable*	*Reason why the variable is assumed to be relevant to measurement of the law in action*
3. Level of cooperation by banks in the investigative phase. *The higher the level of cooperation by banks, the better the law in action is assumed to be.*	a range from 1 to 5, where 1 = no cooperation at all; 5 = high level of cooperation	Since banks are among the places in which criminal proceeds are placed and/or invested in order to conceal their dirty origin, they may significantly contribute to the identification of illicit wealth, and therefore to fuller enforcement of confiscation provisions. *Mentioned by:* Council of the European Union Directive 2001/97/EC of 4 December 2001 amending Council Directive 91/308/EEC of 10 June 1991 on prevention of the use of the financial system for the purpose of money laundering; Masciandaro (1994); Donato & Masciandaro (1997).
4. Level of cooperation by non banking financial institutions in the investigative phase. *The higher the level of cooperation by non banking financial institutions, the better the law in action is assumed to be.*	a range from 1 to 5, where 1 = no cooperation at all; 5 = high level of cooperation	Since non banking financial institutions are among the places in which criminal proceeds are placed and/or invested in order to conceal their dirty origin, they may significantly contribute to the identification of illicit wealth, and therefore to fuller enforcement of confiscation provisions. *Mentioned by:* Council of the European Union Directive 2001/97/EC of 4 December 2001 amending Council Directive 91/308/EEC of 10 June 1991 on prevention of the use of the financial system for the purpose of money laundering.

(*continued*)

(Continued)

Variables for U_{IP}	*Modalities of the variable*	*Reason why the variable is assumed to be relevant to measurement of the law in action*
5. Level of cooperation by non financial institutions in the investigative phase. *The higher the level of cooperation by non financial institutions, the better the law in action is assumed to be.*	a range from 1 to 5, where 1 = no cooperation at all; 5 = high level of cooperation	Since non financial institutions are among the places in which criminal proceeds are placed and/or invested in order to conceal their dirty origin, they may significantly contribute to the identification of illicit wealth, and therefore to fuller enforcement of confiscation provisions. *Mentioned by:* Council of the European Union Directive 2001/97/EC of 4 December 2001 amending Council Directive 91/308/EEC of 10 June 1991 on prevention of the use of the financial system for the purpose of money laundering.
6. Level of financial investigation training. *The higher the level of financial investigation training, the better the law in action is assumed to be.*	a range from 1 to 5, where 1 = no training; 5 = high level of training	Financial investigations are highly complex and require investigators to have special forms of expertise (in civil law, financial law, commercial law, etc.). Full enforcement of the law in the books therefore requires adequate training to be provided to investigators. *Mentioned by*: Council of the European Union Joint Action of 3 December 1998; Council of the European Union (2000); Council Action Plan of 27 March 2000; Europol (2000); Cabinet Office, Performance and Innovation Unit (2000); Council of Europe (2001).
7. Level of multidisciplinary composition of the office/s conducting financial investigations. *The greater the multidisciplinary composition of the office/s conducting financial investigations, the better the law in action is assumed to be.*	a range from 1 to 5, where 1 = no multidisciplinary composition; 5 = marked multidisciplinary composition	Financial investigations are highly complex. Full enforcement of the law in the books is therefore assisted by the input of the skills, powers and knowledge (accounting, civil law, financial law, commercial law, etc.) possessed by different agencies within the investigative phase. *Mentioned by:* Financial Action Task Force on Money Laundering (2001); Bell (2003).

(continued)

(Continued)

Variables for U_{IP}	*Modalities of the variable*	*Reason why the variable is assumed to be relevant to measurement of the law in action*
8. Level of inter-agency cooperation, i.e. cooperation among different national law enforcement agencies (police forces, revenue agencies, prosecution services, etc.) in the development of financial investigations. *The higher the level of inter-agency cooperation in the development of financial investigations, the better the law in action is assumed to be.*	a range from 1 to 5, where 1 = no cooperation; 5 = high level of cooperation	Different agencies are able to collect, for different purposes (prosecution, taxation, etc.), information relevant to building a person's financial profile. The exchange and crosschecking of all relevant information on an individual's assets can support the enforcement of legal provisions and enhance their potential. *Mentioned by:* Council of the European Union (2000); Council of Europe (2001); Financial Action Task Force on Money Laundering (2001).
9. Degree of cooperation by informants/witnesses with financial investigations. *The higher the degree of cooperation by informants/witnesses with financial investigations, the better the law in action is assumed to be.*	a range from 1 to 5, where 1 = no cooperation at all; 5 = high level of cooperation	Because they have been involved in the activities of criminal organisations or otherwise have insight into them, informants/witnesses can reveal useful details on the location of unlawful profits, thereby assisting the law enforcement agencies in the enforcement of confiscation provisions. *Mentioned by:* The Law Reform Commission of Ireland (1991); Commissione Parlamentare Antimafia (1998).
10. Frequency of financial investigations in organised crime cases, also taking account of the stage at which they are conducted. *The more frequent and the earlier the conduct of financial investigations in organised crime cases, the better the law in action is assumed to be.*	six modalities, i.e.: 1. never OR rarely made, and generally at an early stage (i.e. before charges are brought) 2. never OR rarely made, and generally late (i.e. after charges) 3. sometimes made, and generally at an early stage (i.e. before charges)	Given that organised crimes typically generate large revenues, enforcement of the law in the books is supported by the systematic use of financial investigations, especially if conducted from the outset, i.e. before charges, so as to prevent criminals from concealing their assets in order to avoid confiscation. *Mentioned by:* Council Recommendation of 25 April 2002; Europol (2000); Cabinet Office, Performance and Innovation Unit (2000).

(continued)

(Continued)

Variables for U_{IP}	*Modalities of the variable*	*Reason why the variable is assumed to be relevant to measurement of the law in action*
	4. sometimes made, and generally late (i.e. after charges) 5. often OR always made, and generally at an early stage (i.e. before charges) 6. often OR always made, and generally late (i.e. after charges)	
11. Adequacy of the human resources devoted to identification of the proceeds from crime, with reference to their overall number. *The more adequate the human resources devoted to identification of the proceeds from crime, the better the law in action is assumed to be.*	a range from 1 to 5, where 1 = inadequate; 5 = fully adequate	Without human resources there can be no enforcement of the law in the books. Therefore, full application of the law in the books requires an adequate number of human resources to be devoted to financial investigations. *Mentioned by:* Council Action Plan of 27 March 2000; Council of Europe (2001).
12. Adequacy of the material resources devoted to identification of the proceeds from crime, with reference to their overall consistency. *The more adequate the material resources devoted to the identification of the proceeds from crime, the better the law in action is assumed to be.*	a range from 1 to 5, where 1 = inadequate; 5 = fully adequate	Without material resources there can be no enforcement of the law in the books. Therefore, full application of the law in the books requires an adequate number of material resources to be devoted to financial investigations. *Mentioned by:* Council Action Plan of 27 March 2000; Council of Europe (2001).

For the judicial phase, considering that the law in action of the phase can be expressed with the following mathematical expression,

$$LA_{JP} = (ESP_{JP}\ U_{JP})$$

where:

LA_{JP} = The law in action of the judicial phase.
ESP_{JP} = The enforcement of specific legal provisions of relevance in the judicial phase.
U_{JP} = Factors relevant to the overall enforcement of the law in the books during the judicial phase.

the following variables were selected for ESP_{JP} and U_{JP} in order to measure the law in action of the phase:

Variables for ESP_{JP}	*Modalities of the variable*
13. Level of impediment against the issue of a confiscation order raised by the need for a conviction, if a conviction is (always or sometimes) a prerequisite for confiscation. *The lower the level of impediment against the issue of a confiscation order raised by the said prerequisite (conviction), the better the law in action is assumed to be.*	a range from 1 to 5, where 1 = no impediment; 5 = significant impediment
14. Level of implementation of extended confiscation, if such a legal provision exists. *The higher the level of implementation of extended confiscation, the better the law in action is assumed to be.*	a range from 1 to 5, where 1 = not applied to a satisfactory extent; 5 = applied to a satisfactory extent
15. Frequency of confiscation, if application of the measure is sometimes or always discretionary. *The more frequently confiscation is ordered, if the application the measure is sometimes or always discretionary, the better the law in action is assumed to be.*	a range from 1 to 5, where 1 = never applied; 5 = always applied
16. Level of implementation of the legal provision allowing for the reversal of the burden of proof, if such a legal provision exists. *The higher the level of implementation of the legal provision allowing for the reversal of the burden of proof, the better the law in action is assumed to be.*	a range from 1 to 5, where 1 = not applied to a satisfactory extent; 5 = applied to a satisfactory extent

(*continued*)

(*Continued*)

Variables for ESP_{JP}	*Modalities of the variable*
17. Level of implementation of property confiscation, if provided for by the legal system. *The higher the level of implementation of property confiscation, the better the law in action is assumed to be.*	a range from 1 to 5, where 1 = not applied to a satisfactory extent; 5 = applied to a satisfactory extent
18. Level of implementation of value confiscation, if provided for by the legal system. *The higher the level of implementation of value confiscation, the better the law in action is assumed to be.*	a range from 1 to 5, where 1 = not applied to a satisfactory extent; 5 = applied to a satisfactory extent
19. Level of implementation of a legal provision which requires the seizure and confiscation of proceeds presumed to have derived from crime if owned or held by a third person, if such a legal provision exists. *The higher the level of implementation of the legal provision which requires the seizure and confiscation of proceeds presumed to have derived from crime if owned or held by a third person, the better the law in action is assumed to be.*	a range from 1 to 5, where 1 = not applied to a satisfactory extent; 5 = applied to a satisfactory extent

Variables for U_{JP}	*Modalities of the variable*	*Reason why the variable is assumed to be relevant to measurement of the law in action*
20. Adequacy of the human resources devoted to the judicial phase, with reference to their overall number.	a range from 1 to 5, where 1 = inadequate; 5 = fully adequate	Without human resources there can be no enforcement of the law in the books. Therefore, full application of the law in the books requires an adequate number of human resources to be devoted to the judicial phase. *Mentioned by:* Council Action Plan of 27 March 2000; Council of the European Union (2000); Council of Europe (2001).
21. Adequacy of the material resources devoted to the judicial phase, with reference to their overall consistency.	a range from 1 to 5, where 1 = inadequate; 5 = fully adequate	Without material resources there can be no enforcement of the law in the books. Therefore, full application of the law in the books requires an adequate number of material resources to be devoted to the judicial phase.

(*continued*)

(*Continued*)

Variables for U_{JP}	*Modalities of the variable*	*Reason why the variable is assumed to be relevant to measurement of the law in action*
The more adequate the material resources devoted to the judicial phase, the better the law in action is assumed to be.		*Mentioned by:* Council Action Plan of 27 March 2000; Council of the European Union (2000); Council of Europe (2001).
22. Level of training of the officials (such as public prosecutors) who take legal action against defendants in criminal/civil proceedings in the field of seizure and confiscation of the proceeds from crime. *The higher the level of training of officials (such as public prosecutors) who take legal action against defendants in criminal/civil proceedings in the field of seizure and confiscation of the proceeds from crime, the better the law in action is assumed to be.*	a range from 1 to 5, where 1 = no training; 5 = high level of training	In order to ensure full enforcement of the law in the books, officials (such as public prosecutors) who take legal action against defendants must have a sound knowledge of financial matters, accounting, civil law, etc. Adequate training must therefore be provided for them, so that they can correctly interpret and apply the relevant legal provisions and fully exploit their potential. *Mentioned by:* Council of the European Union Joint Action of 3 December 1998; Council of the European Union (2000); Europol (2000); Council of Europe (2001).
23. Level of training of judges in the field of seizure and confiscation of the proceeds from crime. *The higher the level of training of judges in the field of seizure and confiscation of the proceeds from crime, the better the law in action is assumed to be.*	a range from 1 to 5, where 1 = no training; 5 = high level of training	In order to ensure full enforcement of the law in the books, judges must have a sound knowledge of financial matters, accounting, civil law, etc. An adequate training must therefore be provided for them, so that they can correctly interpret and apply the relevant legal provisions. *Mentioned by:* Council of the European Union Joint Action of 3 December 1998; Council of the European Union (2000); Europol (2000); Council of Europe (2001).

(*continued*)

(*Continued*)

Variables for U_{JP}	*Modalities of the variable*	*Reason why the variable is assumed to be relevant to measurement of the law in action*
24. Level of competence of the authority/ies managing seized assets. *The higher the level of competence of the authority/ies managing seized assets, the better the law in action is assumed to be.*	a range from 1 to 5, where 1 = incompetent; 5 = highly competent	Management of seized assets is a highly complex task which is crucial for the enforcement of confiscation provisions. Poor management, in fact, may partially or entirely frustrate all the efforts made by law enforcement agencies and prosecutors to secure assets value before confiscation. Therefore, the specialist expertise of those managing seized assets is a factor to be taken into account. *Mentioned by:* Council of the European Union (1998); Council of the European Union Joint Action of 3 December 1998.
25. Level of the current management of seized assets. *The better the current management of seized assets, the better the law in action is assumed to be.*	a range from 1 to 5, where 1 = not satisfactory, i.e. not able to maximise the value/ minimise the deterioration of seized assets; 5 = satisfactory, i.e. able to maximise the value/minimise the deterioration of seized assets	The management of seized assets is crucial for the enforcement of confiscation provisions. Bad management, in fact, may partially or entirely frustrate all the efforts made by law enforcement agencies and prosecutors to secure assets value before confiscation. *Mentioned by:* Council of the European Union Joint Action of 3 December 1998; The Australian Law Reform Commission (1999); Council of the European Union (2000).
26. Period of time usually necessary to conclude the judicial procedure leading to the confiscation of the proceeds from crime. *The shortest the period of time usually necessary to conclude the judicial procedure leading to the confiscation of the proceeds from crime, the better the law in action is assumed to be.*	a range from 1 to 5, where 1 = long; 5 = short	Given the costs in terms of human and material resources sustained by the State during the judicial procedure, as well as the perishable nature of some categories of assets subject to confiscation, it is important to take account of the time factor when evaluating the enforcement of legal provisions, since a lengthy procedure hampers full enforcement of the law in the books. *Mentioned by:* Commissione Parlamentare Antimafia (1997b); The Australian Law Reform Commission (1999).

For the disposal phase, considering that the law in action of the phase can be expressed with the following mathematical expression,

$$LA_{DP} = (ESP_{DP}\ U_{DP})$$

where:

LA_{DP} = The law in action of the disposal phase.
ESP_{DP} = The enforcement of specific legal provisions of relevance in the disposal phase.
U_{DP} = Factors relevant to the overall enforcement of the law in the books during the disposal phase.

the following variables were selected for ESP_{DP} and U_{DP} in order to measure the law in action of the phase:

Variables for ESP_{DP}	*Modalities of the variable*
27. Level of implementation of legal provisions disciplining each disposal option (i.e. sale, destruction, use for social purposes, rent, liquidation, other). *The higher the level of implementation of the legal provisions disciplining each disposal option, the better the law in action is assumed to be.*	for each disposal option, a range from 1 to 5, where 1 = not applied to a satisfactory extent; 5 = applied to a satisfactory extent

Variables for U_{DP}	*Modalities of the variable*	*Reason why the variable is assumed to be relevant to measurement of the law in action*
28. Level of inter-agency cooperation, i.e. cooperation among the various offices involved in the disposal phase. *The higher the level of inter-agency cooperation during the disposal phase, the better the law in action is assumed to be.*	a range from 1 to 5, where 1 = no cooperation; 5 = high level of cooperation	The disposal of confiscated assets usually requires the cooperation of more than one agency (court, police, execution offices, etc.). This implies that the prompt communication and exchange of information among the agencies involved supports the enforcement of legal provisions in the disposal phase. *Mentioned by:* Financial Action Task Force on Money Laundering (2001).
29. Adequacy of the human resources devoted to the enforcement of confiscation orders/ disposal of confiscated	a range from 1 to 5, where 1 = inadequate; 5 = fully adequate	Without human resources there can be no enforcement of the law in the books. Therefore, full application of the law in the books requires an adequate number of human resources to be devoted to the disposal phase.

(*continued*)

(*Continued*)

Variables for U_{DP}	*Modalities of the variable*	*Reason why the variable is assumed to be relevant to measurement of the law in action*
assets, with reference to their overall number. *The better the adequacy of the human resources devoted to the enforcement of confiscation orders/disposal of confiscated assets, the better the law in action is assumed to be.*		*Mentioned by:* Council Action Plan of 27 March 2000; Council of the European Union (2000); Council of Europe (2001).
30. Adequacy of the material resources devoted to the enforcement of confiscation orders/ disposal of confiscated assets, with reference to their overall consistency. *The better the adequacy of the material resources devoted to the enforcement of confiscation orders/ disposal of confiscated assets, the better the law in action is assumed to be.*	a range from 1 to 5, where 1 = inadequate; 5 = fully adequate	Without material resources there can be no enforcement of the law in the books. Therefore, full application of the law in the books requires an adequate number of material resources to be devoted to the disposal phase. *Mentioned by:* Council Action Plan of 27 March 2000; Council of the European Union (2000); Council of Europe (2001).
31. Level of competence of the authority/ies managing confiscated assets. *The higher the level of competence of the authority/ies managing confiscated assets, the better the law in action is assumed to be.*	a range from 1 to 5, where 1 = incompetent; 5 = highly competent	The management of confiscated assets is crucial for the enforcement of confiscation provisions. Bad management, in fact, may partially or entirely frustrate all the efforts made by law enforcement agencies, prosecutors and judges to secure assets value during disposal. Specialist expertise is therefore necessary for the execution of confiscation orders. *Mentioned by:* The Australian Law Reform Commission (1999); Council of the European Union (2000).

(*continued*)

(Continued)

Variables for U_{DP}	*Modalities of the variable*	*Reason why the variable is assumed to be relevant to measurement of the law in action*
32. Period of time usually necessary to dispose of confiscated assets/enforce confiscation orders. *The shorter the period of time usually necessary to dispose of confiscated assets/enforce confiscation orders, the better the law in action is assumed to be.*	a range from 1 to 5, where 1 = long; 5 = short	Given the perishable nature of some categories of assets subject to confiscation, as well as the costs in terms of human and material resources sustained by the State during the disposal phase, it is important to take account of the time factor when evaluating the enforcement of legal provisions. *Mentioned by:* Financial Action Task Force on Money Laundering (1997a).

STEP 2. Preparation of a Questionnaire and Administration to One High Profile Expert per Member State by Means of a Telephone Interview

The variables for the law in action of each phase of confiscation proceedings were incorporated into two questionnaires respectively designed to explore the practice of proceeds from crime confiscation (a) within *criminal proceedings* and (b) within *civil proceedings*, for the limited number of countries where civil confiscation is possible (namely Greece, Ireland, Italy and the United Kingdom). The two questionnaires were identical, with two exceptions, viz. *Variable 13. Level of impediment against the issue of a confiscation order raised by the need for a conviction, if a conviction is (always or sometimes) a prerequisite for confiscation,* and *Variable 14. Level of implementation of extended confiscation, if such a legal provision exists.* These were not included in questionnaire (b) because of the non applicability of the legal requirement of conviction in civil proceedings, given that they are *in rem*. Both questionnaires are contained in Annex 1.

The questionnaires consisted entirely of closed-ended questions. The order of the questions followed that of the activities in a confiscation proceedings, from the very beginning (investigative phase—section 1 of the questionnaire) to its intermediate passage (judicial phase—section 2 of the questionnaire) to its conclusion (disposal phase—section 3 of the questionnaire). Each variable was translated into a question, with five possibile answers for each question. As shown above while presenting the modalities of each variable of the law in action, these replies were always on a scale from 1 to 5. The only exception was the question translating *Variable 10. Frequency of financial investigations in organised crime cases, also taking account of the stage at which they are conducted.* Since there were six modalities for this variable, in this case the national expert could choose 1 out of 6 possible answers.

Each question was followed by the prompt "Give brief reasons for your choice". The purpose of this prompt was to invite the national expert to give a explanation for the score just given in reply to the question and to obtain further comments on the point.

The questionnaire was given this format in order to achieve two main objectives.

First, the use of closed-ended questions enabled *immediate quantification of the law in action* (on this point, see step 4). It also potentially raised the response rate, because the possibility of replying rapidly encouraged respondents to answer the questionnaire.

Second, the inclusion of the prompt "Give brief reasons for your choice" after each question allowed the researcher not only to control in some way for the subjectivity of the expert's opinion (this point will be further developed below), but also to obtain from the expert comments crucial for better understanding of current obstacles/best practices, and to collect qualitative information with which to build *a country profile describing the law in action* (on this point, see step 3).

The questionnaire was sent by e-mail to one high profile expert for each Member State and was administered some time after its dispatch by means of a telephone interview. This manner of administering the questionnaire gave the researcher closer control over data collection (in terms of immediate clarification of wording/terminology, identification and resolution of misunderstandings, etc.), while also fostering interactive dialogue between the researcher and the interviewee.

The foregoing implies that, in order to explore the practice of confiscation, it was decided to rely on the opinions of high profile experts in the field of proceeds from crime confiscation. The data collection technique selected, which is in fact a specific type of survey, was therefore the so-called 'expert opinion' method. This is a data collection technique that relies on the necessarily subjective views of experts—selected on the basis of their knowledge and experience in a given area—in order to shed light on the object of the study (Corbetta 1999, 420). The basic idea behind the method is that persons with direct and deep knowledge of the phenomenon under investigation are able to provide the researcher with useful insights into it.

This data collection technique was chosen on the basis of the following considerations. First, its employment is particularly recommended and useful in areas, like the one dealt with here,[30] where objective data are poor (Nagarajan & Vanheukelen 1997, 54). Thus, in the absence of reliable quantitative and qualitative information on the implementation of proceeds of crime confiscation provisions, individuals concerned with the application of confiscation provisions as a part of their routine work are assumed to have remarkable insight into the practice of confiscation. They are thus in the best position to identify what problems arise in implementing these provisions and what aspects, on the contrary, make the identification, confiscation and disposal of ill-gotten gains easier. They were consequently regarded as prime sources of information with which to start building knowledge on this neglected topic. It should also be borne in mind that this technique makes it possible to collect information in a fairly inexpensive and rapid way (Ibidem).

[30] On this point, see chapter 2.

Of course, the weaknesses of the method cannot be glossed over. Like any subjective judgment, an expert opinion raises a credibility problem, besides that of the not necessarily representative nature of the expert's point of view. Furthermore, it has been noted that experts are unlikely to be uniformly and completely informed about a particular area (Ibidem).

Some basic rules were followed in order to remedy these weaknesses as far as possible.

First, in order to ensure that the informants selected were high profile experts, they were identified by the Ministries of Justice of the EU Member States considered here. Each Ministry, in fact, was requested to choose, preferably from among public prosecutors, a person with particular expertise in the area of proceeds from crime confiscation, with special reference to cases involving criminal organisations.[31]

Second, the inclusion of the prompt "Give brief reasons for your choice" after each question, as briefly mentioned above, enabled some sort of control to be exerted on the subjectivity of the expert's opinion, because it required him/her to explain the score just given in reply to the question. S/he was thus called upon in some way to 'justify' the reply and to comment on it further. Another potential problem when relying on the opinion of experts is that they may not be uniformly and completely informed about a particular area. The choice of public prosecutors is the best way to minimise the effect of this possible difficulty, because they are the practitioners most closely involved in confiscation proceedings (and in criminal investigations in general). They have an overview on investigations (although it is wider in civil law countries than in common law countries) and are the main actors in the judicial phase. Their involvement in the disposal phase is generally less frequent: indeed, when the replies of the experts to the questionnaire were collected, some of them admitted that their replies were based on discussions with colleagues and/or officials involved in the disposal phase.

STEP 3. Building a Country Profile that Describes the Law in Action and Juxtaposes it to the Law in the Books

The third step involved the building of a country profile which described the law in action and juxtaposed it with the law in the books. This was done on the basis of the experts' replies to the questionnaire, and in particular on the basis of the comments stimulated by the prompt "Give brief reasons for your choice" after each question. Such comments, in fact, made it possible to obtain comments crucial for better understanding of current obstacles/best practices from the expert.

The description of the law in action based on the expert's opinion was integrated, where possible, with secondary sources, such as reports produced on the theme by international institutions (for example, the Financial Action Task Force, the Council of

[31] The experts were first selected in 2001 to cooperate in the study *The Seizure and Confiscation of the Proceeds from Crime in the European Union Member States: What Works, What Does Not and What is Promising*, financed by the European Commission under the Falcone 2000 Annual Programme. They were then contacted again for this work.

Europe) or by national ones, and the literature on the subject, these being essentially the few sources of information, already mentioned in chapter 2, currently available on the practice of confiscation.

STEP 4. Quantifying the Law in Action

The fourth step was to quantify the law in action, that is, the level of enforcement of the legal provisions (law in the books) of relevance in each of the three phases of confiscation proceedings.

On the basis of the replies by the experts to the questions, a numerical value on a scale from 0 to 100 was assigned to each modality of each variable selected for the phase. The closer the value to 100, the better the law in action (the numerical values assigned to the modalities of each variable are set out in Annex 2).

These values were subsequently aggregated, for each phase, into a Law in Action Index, so that calculation could be made of an Investigative Phase Law in Action Index, a Judicial Phase Law in Action Index and a Disposal Phase Law in Action Index. These Indexes express, on a scale from 0 to 100, the extent to which the law in the books is enforced in each phase. They were obtained by calculating the average of the values assigned to the modalities of each variable for the phase. *The higher the index, the better the law in action of the phase in the country.*

The two extreme situations depicted by this quantification are the following. When one of these Indexes scores 100, it denotes the ideal situation in which the enforcement of the law in the books is the best possible. When, on the contrary, one of these Indexes scores 0, it denotes the worst possible situation in which the enforcement of the law in the books is nil.

CHAPTER 4

LAW IN THE BOOKS, LAW IN ACTION

This chapter presents the findings obtained by employing the methodology described in the previous chapter. The chapter first provides, for each of the original fifteen Member States, a country profile which describes the law in action and juxtaposes it with the law in the books.

In particular, first presented for each country is the law in the books (letter A). This description is necessary because, obviously, it makes no sense to talk about the implementation of the legal provisions on a given matter unless one already has an idea of the content of those legal provisions. It also shows the extent to which the 'tough on wealth' philosophy has been absorbed by the country in question. Finally, and incidentally, the combining the main legal provisions on proceeds from crime confiscation into a single text, although it is not the aim of this work, is a worthwhile undertaking if one considers that no comprehensive collection of such legislation exists at present.

The law in action is then described for each of the three phases of confiscation proceedings—the investigative phase, the judicial phase and the disposal phase (letter B)—so as to identify the main difficulties that arise in enforcing the legal provisions relevant to each phase, and the related best practices. This descriptive analysis of the law in action is followed by quantification of the law in action itself. At this point, a figure graphically represents the country's Investigative Phase Law in Action Index, the Judicial Phase Law in Action Index, and the Disposal Phase Law in Action Index, all of which express, on a scale from 0 to 100, the level of enforcement of the law in the books in each phase.

4.1 AUSTRIA

A) Law in the Books

Investigations of the proceeds from crime are undertaken by the *Einsatzgruppe der Gruppe D zur Bekämpfung der Organisierten Kriminalität* (EDOK), the Austrian FIU, set up within the Federal Ministry of Interior. Investigators may make use of such special investigative techniques as wire-tapping, electronic surveillance and undercover operations.

The Austrian Parliament entirely revised sanctions pertaining to confiscation of the proceeds from crime in 1996, when Federal Law no. 762 introduced new regulations for the removal of the financial basis of organised crime into the Criminal Code, that is section 20 (*Abschöpfung der Bereicherung*) and section 20b (*Verfall*).

According to section 20, paragraph 1, the economic benefit obtained by a person from or for the commission of an offence must be confiscated by sentencing the offender to payment of a sum of money equal to the value of the illicit benefit. To be noted is that section 20 refers to the commission of an offence. This implies that imposition of the sanction does not require, as its prerequisite, conviction of the offender. Consequently, confiscation may occur both following the conviction of the offender and as an independent sanction without conviction (Löschnig-Gspandl 1997, 216).

Execution of the measure is excluded, *ex* section 20a, (1) if the offender has satisfied civil claims lodged as a consequence of the criminal act (paragraph 1); (2) if the sum of money to be confiscated or the likelihood that the order is enforceable are disproportionate to the expenditure that would be required to proceed with the order or to enforce it (paragraph 2, no. 2); (3) if the payment of the confiscation order would unreasonably jeopardise the continued existence of the offender or would constitute inappropriate hardship for him/her (paragraph 2, no. 3). Furthermore, in the case of profits obtained from commission of an offence, confiscation is waived if the proceeds from crime do not exceed ATS 300,000 (around 22,000 euro) and if confiscation is not necessary to prevent the commission of further crimes (paragraph 2, no. 1).

Reversal of the burden of proof is envisaged by section 20, paragraph 2. In the case of the repeated commission of crimes, confiscation covers not only the relative profits but also the further economic benefits obtained by the defendant in the same period. These further profits are presumed to derive from criminal activities, and consequently the onus of proving their legitimate origin is placed on the defendant. A similar presumption of illicit origin applies in the case of membership of a criminal organisation. According to section 20, paragraph 3, the profits acquired by a person during membership of a criminal group are presumed to be illicit and are consequently subject to confiscation unless their licit source is proved by the defendant.

As stated by section 20, paragraph 4, confiscation also applies to third parties—both natural and legal persons—which have illegally profited from the commission of a crime. Should the offender die, or if the legal person ceases to exist, before the confiscation order has been completed, the measure can be applied to the legal heir.

In the case of non applicability of section 20,[32] section 20b applies in order to deprive criminal organisations of their illicit wealth. The section provides for the confiscation of property under the control of a criminal organisation. Control of assets by an organisation is interpreted with reference to "[. . .] the notion of custody, which means that not the legal right but the factual disposal of the proceeds is important" (Kathrein 1999, 369). The measure does not apply (1) if the property belongs to *bona fide* third parties; (2) if assets are removed from the criminal group by means of other legal measures; (3) if the measure would be disproportionate to the gravity of the offence.

To secure confiscation, a provisional measure can be applied in accordance with section 144a of the Austrian Code of Criminal Procedure. Conditions for its issue are

[32] This happens in the case of: (1) property belonging to the criminal group which cannot be related to a specific crime committed by a specific offender; (2) proceedings against unknown persons; (3) property located in the territory of a State but obtained by means of offences committed outside it. See Kathrein (1999, 368).

the expectation that profits will be confiscated and the risk that the confiscation order may not be enforceable.

With reference to the disposal phase, if the confiscation order concerns (as normally happens) payment of a sum of money, it is executed by the State. If the order relates to objects (e.g. cars), these are usually sold at public auction.

B) Law in Action

With regard to the law in action, and starting with the investigative phase, to be noted in general is that the philosophy of financial investigation—although fully affirmed at the legislative level with the setting up of a dedicated agency and the availability of special investigative means—still seems to be shallowly rooted.

Financial investigations are not conducted in any systematic way in organised crime cases, and they usually take place once the trial has begun, with the consequence that the defendants have all the time they need to conceal their ill-gotten gains. Moreover, the use of financial investigative means seems to be rather rare. The multidisciplinary composition of the offices conducting financial investigations (i.e. EDOK and, in general, the police), is quite marked. The ability of these offices to trace the proceeds from crime has until very recently been compromised by the modest level of financial investigation training received by their officials, as well as by understaffing and underresourcing. This situation has only now been improved by an increase in the financial and human resources available and by improved training provision. Investigators are trained through attendance at interdisciplinary meetings, and they also receive training from the Ministry of Finance, the Ministry of Justice and university representatives. The training does not consist in mere theory but is closely focused on practice (e.g. by means of analysis of case studies). There is a good level of information exchange between the police and prosecution agencies. Other agencies, like the financial surveillance authority, cooperate to a satisfactory extent as well.

With reference to the level of cooperation by banks, other financial and non financial institutions with financial investigations, banks cooperate closely because they are fully aware of their vulnerability to money laundering operations and consequently assist with investigations. A problem is the scant cooperation forthcoming from other financial and non financial institutions. A further drawback is the information provided by informants, which in most cases is not particularly precise and therefore of limited use in identifying the proceeds from crime.

Turning to the judicial phase, and in particular to implementation of reversal of the burden of proof foreseen by section 20, paragraph 2, this measure is only limited in its impact. This is because firstly it can be used solely in specific and restricted circumstances, and secondly because, at least in certain cases, the provisions relative to such reversal are substantially purposeless, being not correctly understood and interpreted—especially by judges. Linked to the probatory issue is the question of the general level of implementation of value confiscation, which is particularly interesting because the system is value based. Value confiscation does not seem entirely satisfactory for two main reasons: the enormous difficulties faced by public prosecutors in linking defendants with the ill-gotten gains whose value is to be confiscated, and the court practice whereby public prosecutors are required to fulfil a very high standard of proof. Hence, in many cases, value confiscation proves to be impotent. The same applies, according to the existing literature, to section 20b, which to date has been implemented in an extremely limited number of cases (Löschnig-Gspandl & Kilchling 2002, 123).

Although the human and material resources devoted to the judicial phase are adequate, to be stressed is that public prosecutors and judges are often loath to apply the legislation designed to deprive criminals of their illicit profits. Furthermore, although the training they receive has improved in the past few years, it still falls short of what is required. Although it is of good quality—seminars are held by a very wide range of experts (university lecturers, experts from the Ministries and private industry, lawyers) and theoretical as well as practical points are dealt with—the time devoted to it is insufficient.

The disposal phase works well when the confiscation order relates (as usually happens, given that the system is value based) to money, that is to an asset that by its nature allows rapid definition of the procedure at very low costs. The advantages of a value based system in the enforcement of the order is particularly evident in those rare cases where the measure affects specific objects. In this case, problems arise in the disposal of the goods, because the offices involved in the procedure lack the necessary human and financial resources and because the procedure is excessively complex.

By way of summary, Figure 1 shows the Investigative Phase Law in Action Index, the Judicial Phase Law in Action Index, and the Disposal Phase Law in Action Index for Austria. These Indexes quantify the law in action of that country by expressing, on a scale from 0 to 100, the extent to which the law in the books is enforced in each phase. *The higher the index, the better the law in action of the phase.*

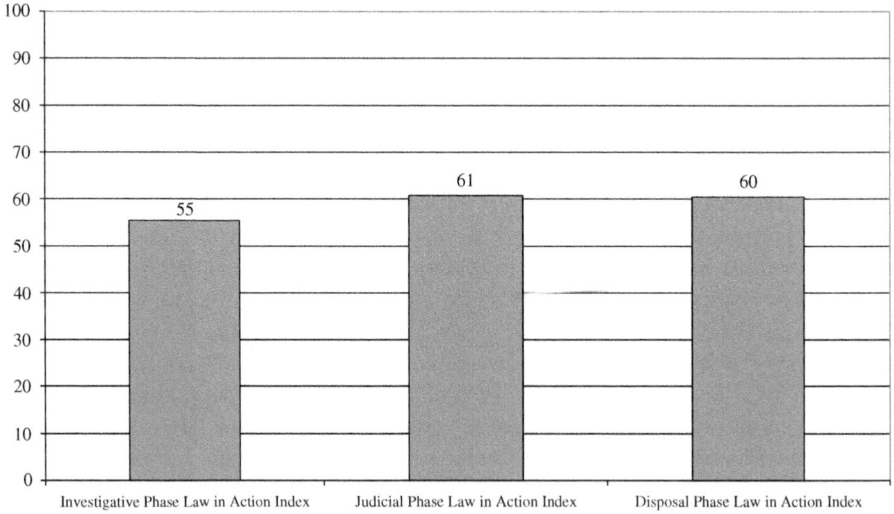

Figure 1. Law in Action Indexes of the Investigative, Judicial and Disposal Phases in Austria. Source: Author's elaboration of the national expert's replies to the questionnaire.

4.2 BELGIUM

A) Law in the Books

Until 1990, Belgium had a traditional confiscation system consisting of the provisions contained in article 42, 1° and 2°, of the Criminal Code. This article provides for the compulsory removal of the objects of the crime (i.e. the assets subject to the criminal act), the means used or intended for use in its commission and the products of the crime (i.e. the objects created by the offence). These provisions, still in existence, were strengthened by a law enacted on 17 July 1990 which introduced proceeds of crime confiscation,[33] and, more recently, by laws adopted in 2002 and 2003.

Article 42, 3°, added in 1990, provides for the optional confiscation of proceeds directly acquired from a criminal act by the offender. The income deriving from criminal proceeds is also subject to confiscation. If the offender has in the meantime converted the illicit gains into assets, the measure covers these substitute assets as well. Another provision introduced in 1990 is article 43-*bis*, which introduces value confiscation. This article states that if criminal proceeds are no longer part of the defendant's assets, the judge shall sentence the defendant to payment of a sum of money equal to their estimated value. With reference to the position of *bona fide* third parties, these may in principle not be deprived of their assets if they themselves have not been convicted of an offence.[34] If their assets have previously derived from crime, they can only be affected by a confiscation penalty inflicted on another person if they are unable to prove that their possession of those assets is legitimate. A specific application of this rule is envisaged by article 505 of the Criminal Code, paragraph 3, with reference to money laundering, in which case the proceeds are to be confiscated from third parties. The confiscation of the proceeds from crime, which is optional for offenders under article 42, 3°, becomes compulsory for them and for *mala fide* third parties in money laundering cases. In the latter, in fact, the illicit profits are deemed to be objects of the crime and compulsorily subject to confiscation *ex* article 42, 1°.

Law of 19 December 2002[35] introduced article 43-*quarter* of the Criminal Code, which envisages an especially severe confiscation regime for a list of serious offences, such as those committed by a criminal organisation, drug trafficking related offences, trafficking in human beings, international fiscal fraud, etc. In case of conviction for one of these offences, the proceeds directly acquired therefrom, as well as the income deriving from the criminal proceeds and the substitute assets into which the illicit gains have been converted, can be confiscated, also in value form, on request by the public prosecutor. If there are serious and concrete grounds for suspecting that the convicted person has acquired, in the five-year period before the conviction, further proceeds, either from the offence to which the conviction refers or from similar ones,

[33] For analysis of the Belgian confiscation system before and after the entry into force of the law of 17 July 1990, see Jakhian (1991).

[34] "The *nulla poena sine crimen* principle and the guilt principle implied that confiscation could only be imposed on the frontman if he too was convicted of a criminal offence". See Verbruggen (1997, 318).

[35] Law of 19 December 2002 was published in the *Moniteur belge* of 14 February 2003.

these proceeds too are confiscated, unless the defendant or interested third parties are able to give plausible grounds for believing that, on the balance of probabilities, the assets did not originate from the type of crime for which the conviction has been passed, or from similar crimes. Proceeds under the control of a criminal organisation must also be confiscated, unless they belong to *bona fide* third parties. The law also introduced article 35-*ter* of the Code of Criminal Procedure, which allows the seizure of assets of a value equal to the amount of the suspected criminal assets, if these are no longer available. The said law also augments the Code of Criminal Procedure with articles 524-*bis* and -*ter*, which deal with special inquiry into the proceeds from crime (*enquête particulière sur les avantages patrimoniaux*). Under article 524-*bis*, the public prosecutor may request the court to order a separate property inquiry in order to assess the value of the criminal proceeds foreseen under articles 42, 3°, 43-*bis* and 43-*quater* when convicting the defendant. For this inquiry to be admissible, the public prosecutor must provide the court with concrete evidence that the defendant has profited from the crime. Seizure may be made during this inquiry. On termination of the investigation, the public prosecutor resubmits the case to the court, which decrees confiscation by separate verdict. In this way, preliminary investigations are not overly delayed as a result of a criminal assets inquiry. Mention should also be made of a law enacted on 6 January 2003[36] and providing for a wide range of special investigative techniques, which can also be used to locate ill-gotten gains in all investigations into serious crime (i.e. generally carrying more than one year of imprisonment).

The management of seized assets is now regulated by a law of 26 March 2003.[37] Before enactment of this law, the entire body of Belgian legislation had only one relevant article, which specified that the court clerk was responsible merely for conservation of the assets deposited in his office (article 1 of the Royal Decree of 24 March 1936). The new law has innovated with what it calls "management of seized assets at constant value". Under this provision, the magistrate leading the case is responsible for administration of the seized assets, which either can be managed in such a way as to prevent any decrease in their value or they can be sold. The assistance of the newly established *Organ Central pour la Saisie et la Confiscation* (Central Office for Seizure and Confiscation—COSC) is foreseen in performing this task.

The Central Office just mentioned has been established within the public prosecutor's structure by the same law, with the participation of liaison officers from the Federal police and the Ministry of Finance. Its mission is to assist the judicial authorities in the entire procedure to be followed in the investigation, seizure, confiscation and disposal of assets removed from the offender under articles 42, 3°, 43-*bis*, 43-*quarter* and 505 of the Criminal Code. In order to accomplish this mission, the office is called upon, in particular, (a) to provide the Ministry of Justice and the Prosecutors General Organisation with its opinions on amendments to the current legislation and its implementation; (b) to ensure the centralised and computerised collection of data on seized, confiscated

[36] Law of 6 January 2003 was published in the *Moniteur belge* of 12 May 2003.

[37] Law of 26 March 2003 was published in the *Moniteur belge* of 2 May 2003. This law should be read together with the law of 19 March 2003, published in the same *Moniteur belge*.

and disposed of assets; (c) to handle, on behalf of the court or the public prosecutor, the sale of seized assets, when this is possible, or otherwise to attend to their management at constant value (above-mentioned); (d) to coordinate the execution of confiscation orders; (e) to assist the courts in specific cases, if requested; (f) to give general information on the matter to the police and the judicial authorities.

Seizure is provided for by article 35 of the Code of Criminal Procedure. If the proceeds of crime consist of real property, article 35-*bis* of the same Code applies.[38]

With reference to the disposal phase, the Ministry of Finance is responsible for execution of the measure. Under article 197 of the Code of Criminal Procedure, confiscation orders are executed by the Director of Registration, that is a tax officer. Assets may be destroyed, if so ordered by the court, or sold at a public auction, with the money thus realised being paid into the Treasury. Confiscated and previously seized money is deposited in the Treasury, whilst confiscated but not previously seized money is recovered from the convicted person in order to be deposited in the Treasury. There are also protocols whereby certain confiscated goods (e.g. vehicles) can be used by the police forces.

B) Law in Action

The recent legislative amendments have made the police and magistrates aware of the new—and thus the already existing—possibilities in the realm of seizure and confiscation. Interest in the topic is increasing, and the COSC receives a large number of requests for help from practitioners in field—currently more than the office can handle. However, since the system has only just been put in place, it is too early to comment on its results. There consequently follows a description of the confiscation practice under the less recent—and to a large extent still in force—legislation.

In the past, financial investigations were not a priority in organised crime cases. Today, there is greater awareness of the importance of depriving organised criminals of their ill-gotten gains. However, such investigations—which normally also concern persons suspected of acting as straw men if the existing information justifies this preliminary conclusion—are still infrequently employed. Moreover, investigators feel obliged to investigate every financial detail, instead of focusing on the most relevant portions of the criminal proceeds and thereby accelerating the investigation.

Regarding the way in which information on criminal wealth circulates among law enforcement agencies either through the multidisciplinary composition of the investigative units, or through inter-agency cooperation, with reference to the former aspect over the past few years the branch of the Federal police specialised in financial investigations (ECOFIN) has been assisted by a number of seconded tax officers, who have been given the rank of 'officer of judicial police' and support the police in their investigations into fiscal matters (VAT, revenue tax and customs). With reference to public prosecutors offices, these comprise civil servants from the Ministry of Finance

[38] For detailed commentary on seizure in the Belgian system see Vermeulen, De Ruyver & Vander Beken (1997). For specific commentary on article 35-*bis* see Vandermeersch (1997, 700–703).

who assist specialist prosecutors on technical matters. Thus, the public prosecutors offices are able to draw on the technical skills of detached tax officers when dealing with financial matters—a possibility that has existed for several years and is meant to compensate for the fact that legislation in the 1980s and 1990s made the close exchange of information between the judicial and the special tax services no longer possible. Cooperation between public prosecutors and tax officers in the public prosecutors offices is now adequate, but by no means perfect—owing, amongst other things, to an overload of work on the prosecutors engaged in criminal investigations (who lack time to confer) and the different working habits of some detached tax officers. Furthermore, the latter can only give technical assistance; they are not allowed to disclose any tax-related information to the prosecutors. There are also police liaisons at the FIU, and currently working at the COSC are liaison officers detached from the Federal police force and the Ministry of Finance, who perform their duties within the office and in close cooperation with the latter. However, it should be pointed out that the administrations of origin were initially rather reluctant to release personnel on secondment to work elsewhere. This resulted from the more general problem affecting most administrations: a shortage of human resources. Nevertheless, cooperation within the COSC is good and looks set to improve even further, largely because of the present liaison's motivation and skills. With reference to inter-agency cooperation, public prosecutors and police forces always work together in criminal investigations. This is also the case when financial crimes are investigated. However, the prosecutors' needs and police priorities do not always coincide. Problems may also arise owing to the fact that different forces are working together with, for example, differing capabilities, and owing to disputes among them. With this exception, and apart from the occasional freely given collaboration or on specific request by a prosecutor, there is no specific inter-agency cooperation (e.g. between police and customs). Consequently, too much expertise goes unexploited because most administrations do not work together, with each of them instead sticking to its own field. Recently, however, a new kind of inter-agency cooperation has been established in the form of two cells set up to combat VAT fraud and petroleum fraud. Each cell is composed of specialised police officers and tax officers, and they give support to both administrations of origin.

Because the legislation enhancing financial investigations is very recent and to a large extent not yet implemented, the human and material resources devoted to such investigations are still inadequate. Consequently, although the situation is improving, much remains to be done. The same applies to the training of financial investigators, where seminars are mostly designed for senior officers. On the other hand, a police school has now been created in which some classes on financial investigation are being organised. Visits to foreign institutions—which sometimes take place—are not considered to be a form of education but serve more the purpose of international cooperation in certain cases.

The level of cooperation received by investigators from financial and non financial institutions is strongly influenced by the legal framework, which does not envisage bank secrecy and requires both financial and non financial institutions to provide the investigating magistrates with all information that they request and to inform the FIU if they suspect money laundering is taking place. Financial institutions are more co-operative than non financial ones. Although the legal obligation is the same in both cases, the closer cooperation of banks and some other financial institutions is probably due to the close disciplinary supervision—with the related sanctions—exercised by the supervising authorities (e.g. the Bank Commission). The use, and consequently the level of cooperation by informants with financial inquiries is still very limited, mainly because of the suspicion with which they are viewed.

Moving to the judicial phase, the extent of property confiscation differs from court to court. Also because confiscation is an accessory punishment which ensues from a conviction, courts evaluate the relative severity of the sanctions that they can apply. Since confiscation is mostly not compulsory, in practice it is often not ordered even though the criminal standard of proof has been met. As for value confiscation, until the law of 19 December 2002 this was subsidiary to property confiscation. Only when the real criminal profits were not to be found among the convicted person's assets could the court estimate their amount and order the confiscation of that amount. However, this procedure, which is regularly applied, encounters the same problems as property confiscation—and indeed even more so, because the court must make the additional effort of calculating the profit. Moreover, judges skilled in criminal matters are not always financial experts as well, and they sometimes have—for reasons of their own—little interest in confiscation. Assets owned by the convicted person but held by third persons are normally seized and confiscated, although obstacles may be created by third party claims on the confiscated assets. In money laundering cases, specific problems arise from the fact that, according to recent rulings by the Supreme Court (*Cour de cassation*), although laundered money is compulsorily subject to confiscation, it can be recovered only in the execution phase, if identified as such, no matter who may be in possession of it,[39] except for *bona fide* persons. It cannot be substituted by other money found in the patrimony of the convicted. While apparently excessively severe towards third parties, these rulings make it harder to confiscate laundered money, which, if not seized in advance will seldom be found afterwards, no matter where it is located.

The situation of seized assets was very poor until recently. This was closely connected with the legal framework, which did not provide until very recently for their 'active' management. As said, the only relevant legal provision, that of 1936, merely stated that the court clerk was responsible for the conservation (not management) of the assets deposited in his/her office. Since enactment of that decree, there had been a increase in the number and variety of seized goods, a large number of which could not be deposited in a clerk's office. An example was provided by vehicles, which were often left for several years on unguarded parking lots, where they were vandalised and deteriorated enormously. They were sometimes left in commercial garages, which charged fees of up to fifteen euro a day, which gave the magistrate no alternative than to return the car to the offender. No person with specific responsibility for the goods was defined, and the situation was exacerbated by the long duration of judicial proceedings,

[39] *Cour de cassation*, 14 January 2004, contradicted by *Cour de cassation*, 21 October 2003 and partially by *Cour de cassation*, 11 January 2005. See at www.cass.be.

including the procedures leading to confiscation. Since the creation of COSC in 2003, matters have improved, but the situation is certainly not yet ideal. Since September 2003, it has been permitted to sell seized assets and replace them with the revenue obtained, in order to ensure the value constant management of those assets. As of today, COSC has sold assets for a total value of more than one million euro, and the more public prosecutors and investigative judges become familiar with the new legislation—presently being revised for the purpose of simplification—the more seized assets will be replaced by their value, further managed by the COSC.

Scant human and material resources are allocated to confiscation in the judicial phase. Also unsatisfactory is the level of training, although it is interesting to note that public prosecutors and police officers are better trained than judges. Since the Ministry of Justice now has its own department for the training of magistrates, and since interest in asset recovery has been stimulated by the enactment of the above-mentioned legislation, there is now adequate training in seizure and confiscation. Experience has shown, however, that training sessions are generally attended more by public prosecutors than by judges.

The disposal phase is theoretically under the supervision of the public prosecutor's office, but in fact it is not, because no real control is exerted over the process. The court clerks must deliver the confiscated goods to the competent services of the Ministry of Finance, which arrange for their disposal. The provisions on the sale of confiscated assets work better than those on their use for social purposes (police forces may sometimes receive specific goods like cars), which are rarely applied. Numerous difficulties and misunderstandings occur in the phase. For example, the clerk's offices only occasionally provide general lists of confiscated assets which have been previously seized and which are sold by the Ministry of Finance, so that the real amount obtained from the sale of those assets is never known. This implies that, except for some specific valuable assets, statistics can only be drawn up on money not previously seized and recovered by the Ministry of Finance. Moreover, in a number of cases the police have had to transfer all confiscated goods to the Ministry of Finance, because the latter is not equipped to undertake the effort or cost of collecting them. On the other hand, they assign the proceeds of the sale directly to the Treasury without furnishing feedback to the Department of Justice. In fact, the Ministry of Finance has scant human and material means with which to enforce confiscation orders. In order to develop closer cooperation with the Ministry of Finance so that results obtained in the execution phase are reported to the Ministry of Justice, the COSC has tasked with coordinating the execution of confiscation orders jointly with the Ministry of Finance. As a result of this collaboration, a number of assets previously considered irretrievable have already been recovered.

The situation in Belgium, and in particular the many problems highlighted by the national expert who completed the questionnaire, are summarised by Figure 2, which shows the Investigative Phase Law in Action Index, the Judicial Phase Law in Action Index, and the Disposal Phase Law in Action Index for Belgium. These Indexes quantify the law in action of the country by expressing, on a scale from 0 to 100, the extent to which the law in the books is enforced in each phase. *The higher the index, the better the law in action of the phase.*

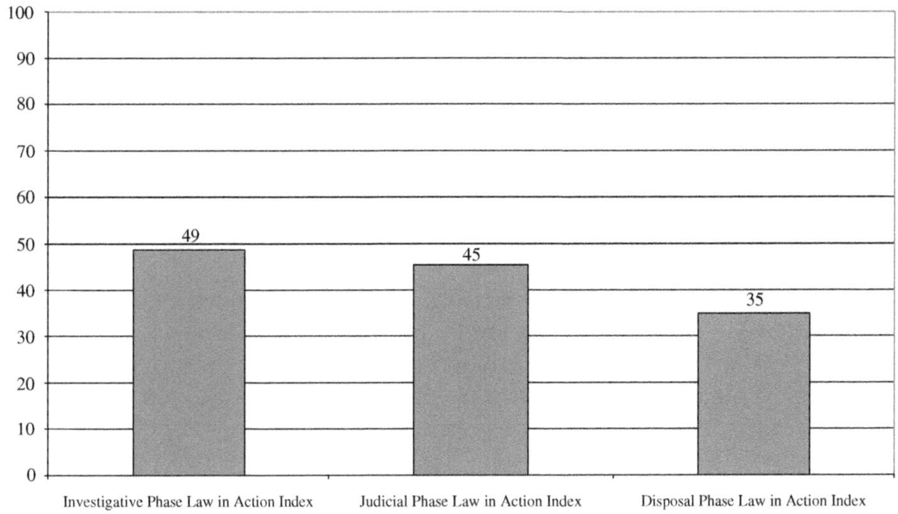

Figure 2. Law in Action Indexes of the Investigative, Judicial and Disposal Phases in Belgium. Source: Author's elaboration of the national expert's replies to the questionnaire.

4.3 DENMARK

A) Law in the Books

In Denmark, investigation to locate the proceeds from crime is not separate from the criminal investigation; rather it is an integral part of it, and there are no special financial units which undertake such investigations. Consequently, the same investigators who handle the criminal case also investigate the economic benefits obtained from the offence. They are able to deploy a wide range of investigative instruments, such as electronic surveillance, undercover operations, interceptions, etc. Subject to investigation is any person suspected of detaining assets in the defendant's name; such persons, depending on their role, are regarded as abetting execution of the crime (article 23 of the Criminal Code) or as receiving stolen goods (article 290 of the Criminal Code).

Confiscation regulations are contained in the Criminal Code, from section 75 to section 77a. The optional confiscation of the proceeds from crime is provided under section 75, subsection 1, which stipulates that the profits gained from any criminal act, or an amount of money equal to their value, shall be confiscated. Confiscation of illicit proceeds applies to the offender and to those persons to whom the proceeds have been directly transferred (section 76, subsection 1). Should the former or the latter die, their heirs are subject to the measure (section 76, subsection 5).

If the criminal assets have been transferred to a third party, confiscation applies both if the third person knew of the illicit origin of the assets and if the transfer was at no cost to him/her (section 76, subsection 4).

To be noted is that, in order to obtain issue of a confiscation order, the public prosecutor must fully prove that the assets derive from criminal activities.

Section 76a was introduced by law no. 411 of 10 June 1997 in order to facilitate the work of the public prosecutor. This new section, at subsection 4, in certain circumstances shifts to the defendant the onus of proving the legal origin of assets in order to prevent their confiscation. This reversal of the burden of proof is applicable to the property of a person found guilty of a crime punishable by imprisonment for six years or more and of such nature as to create sizeable proceeds (section 76a, subsection 1). Value confiscation is allowed in this case as well.

Some specific third-party categories to whom illicit gains may have been transferred are considered by subsections 2 and 3 of the provision, viz.:

1) *the spouse or cohabitant of the offender*: property from these persons is confiscated, unless cohabitation did not exist at the time of the acquisition, or if the property was acquired more than five years before commission of the crime;
2) *the corporation in which the offender participates*: property transferred to such a corporation can usually be removed, unless the transfer occurred more than five years before commission of the crime.

Under section 77, in the case of victims of a crime who claim damages, the goods and proceeds confiscated shall be used for their compensation. Otherwise, confiscated assets are sold and, together with money already confiscated, transferred to the State.

Seizure provisions are contained in the Danish Administration of Justice Act, from section 801 to section 807d. Under section 801, the provisional measure is applied "to secure the claim of the State [. . .] to confiscation".

B) Law in Action

In major cases (e.g. mainly those involving motorbike gangs, since traditional organised crime is not a significant problem in the country) financial investigations are conducted systematically, and at a very early stage (i.e. before charges are made). The opportunity to use special investigative means is normally exploited, when needed. Investigations of third parties suspected of acting as straw men for the suspected criminal are also conducted on a regular basis. Although the law does not require a multidisciplinary composition of the offices conducting financial investigations this composition is created when warranted by the nature and circumstances of the case. Thus, for example, in large-scale financial investigations accountants are employed to follow the cash flow. In addition, there is a tradition of close inter-agency cooperation in Denmark. Police and public prosecutors collaborate to a very satisfactory extent with the tax and financial authorities.[40] To be noted is that financial inquiries are quite frequently conducted jointly with private experts, whose knowledge proves very useful in the search for criminal proceeds.

The resources—both human and material—devoted to the investigative phase are adequate. Also good is the training given to law enforcement officers, who are trained

[40] On this point, see also Financial Action Task Force on Money Laundering (1997a, 15).

in the conduct of financial investigations as part of their basic education. Moreover, officers may apply to attend more specialised courses on financial crimes.

Cooperation with banks, other financial and non financial institutions—which are required by anti-money laundering legislation[41] to report suspicious transactions—works very well.[42] In order to gain such cooperation, however, the investigators must obtain a court order which overrides the legal provisions on professional secrecy. When this order has been obtained, banks, other financial and non financial institutions are highly cooperative. The level of cooperation with financial investigations by witnesses depends on the individual case, on the personal interests involved, and on whether the witness is afraid of the suspect, as is frequently the case. Consequently, in the case of financial fraud, for example, where substantial personal interests are usually involved, the level of cooperation increases.

The material and human resources allocated to the judicial phase are adequate. As regards training issues, public prosecutors are trained as part of their basic education. Specialised books and manuals are distributed to them as support when they deal with concrete cases. These handbooks provide very useful guidance, illustrating the most recurrent problems and ways to handle them. Less satisfactory, it seems, is the level of training given to judges—at least as far as one gathers from the literature.[43] A document issued by the European Committee of Crime Problems of the Council of Europe, in fact, states that the more recent confiscation provisions introduced in 1997 are "[...] reluctantly applied by judges [...]" (Council of Europe, European Committee of Crime Problems, Group of Specialists on Criminal Law and Criminological Aspects of Organised Crime 2000, 19) and that there is "[...] little experience and no special training for judges on s. 76a" (Ibidem). In general, no particular problems arise in applying confiscation provisions: prosecutors are generally able to prove a criminal case, and although in theory confiscation is never compulsory, in practice it is always applied. Depending on the case, property or value confiscation is chosen. A practice that works particularly well allows the defendant to suggest the arrangements necessary to manage the seized assets in order to maximise their value/minimise their deterioration. Such suggestions are met if reasonable (as they generally are). In this way the system strikes a good balance between public and private interest. The administrators responsible for the management of assets before confiscation—typically law enforcement officials—are competent. Nevertheless, mistakes are sometimes made, also because the conservation of perishable goods like cars is difficult, owing to the nature of those assets themselves, which often decrease in value before confiscation is enacted.

Particular problems do not arise on conclusion of the confiscation proceedings, during the disposal phase, when confiscated assets are sold rapidly and the revenue goes directly to the State. The offices dealing with the disposal of confiscated

[41] The various pieces of the anti money laundering legislation (i.e. law no. 348 of 1993, law no. 1058 of 1998, law no. 295 of 2000 and law no. 422 of 2002) have been recently consolidated by law no. 734 of 2002.

[42] This has also been pointed out by the Financial Action Task Force on Money Laundering (1997a, 15), which noted that the financial sector is "[...] facilitating investigations, prosecutions and confiscation [...]".

[43] The Danish expert, in fact, did not assign a score to this.

assets—special agencies handling the assets (one agency deals with their sale, the other with the administration of cash money) located within the police and the prosecutor service—cooperate to a great extent. For this reason there is usually no difference between the amount of assets confiscated and the amount of those disposed of.

By way of summary, and in particular of the very good level of enforcement of confiscation provisions remarked on by the national expert who completed the questionnaire, Figure 3 shows the Investigative Phase Law in Action Index, the Judicial Phase Law in Action Index, and the Disposal Phase Law in Action Index for Denmark. These Indexes quantify the law in action of the country by expressing, on a scale from 0 to 100, the extent to which the law in the books is enforced in each phase. *The higher the index, the better the law in action of the phase.*

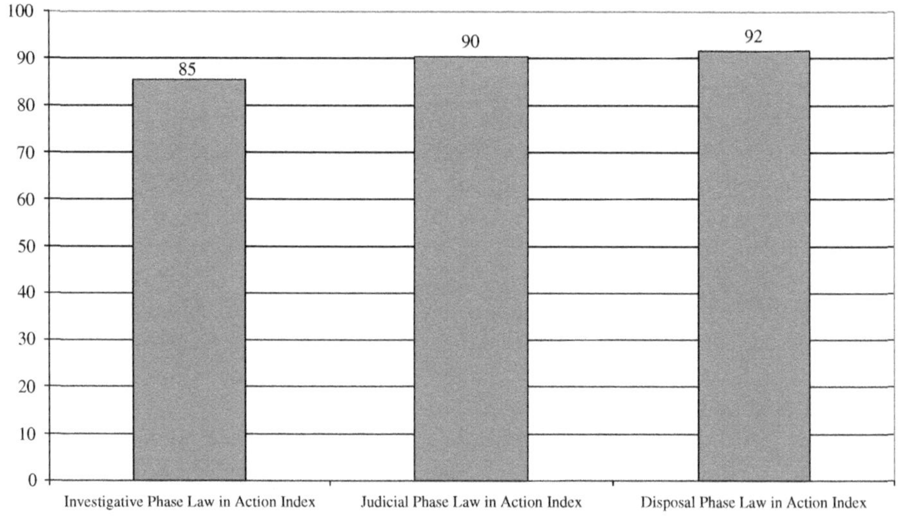

Figure 3. Law in Action Indexes of the Investigative, Judicial and Disposal Phases in Denmark. Source: Author's elaboration of the national expert's replies to the questionnaire.

4.4 FINLAND

A) Law in the Books

Various specialised units address the problem of locating criminal proceeds in Finland: the Money Laundering Clearing House (the Finnish FIU, set up in 1998), which is a division of the National Bureau of Investigation, and other special units established both within the same Bureau and in local police forces. Their officers can make use of special investigative means such as electronic surveillance, phone tapping and undercover operations.

Regarding confiscation provisions, law no. 875 of 2001 entirely revised the confiscation regime, which is now contained in chapter 10 of the Penal Code.

The chapter in question, at section 1, states that a conviction is a necessary prerequisite for confiscation.

Section 2 specifically disciplines proceeds from crime confiscation, which must be ordered against the offender, a participant or a person on whose behalf or to whose advantage the offence has been committed, where these have benefited from the offence. If there is no evidence as to the amount of the proceeds of crime, or if such evidence is difficult to present, the proceeds are estimated taking into account the nature of the offence, the extent of the criminal activity and the other circumstances. Confiscation may not be ordered if the ill-gotten gains have been or will be returned to the injured party.

Particularly severe measures are envisaged by section 3, which sets out an extended confiscation regime applicable to serious offences, that is (a) offences punishable with imprisonment for at least four years and (b) a list of specific crime typologies including money laundering, smuggling and narcotics offences. In the case of conviction for one of the mentioned offences, if there is reason to believe that the convicted person's property derived from criminal activity considered not insignificant, confiscation may cover some or all of the property acquired by the person in the five-year period prior to commission of the offence. The measure also applies to accomplices and to people on whose behalf or to whose advantage the offence has been committed. Extended confiscation can also be ordered for proceeds held by third parties—whether these are close to the defendant or have a business relationship with him/her, if there is reason to believe that property has been conveyed to them in order to avoid confiscation.

Full proof of the criminal origin of the assets must be provided by the public prosecutor.

Once the assets have been confiscated, they pass to the State. Goods subject to confiscation do not, partially or entirely, devolve to the State if they are used to compensate damages arising from the offence. This happens in cases where it is impossible to collect these damages from the offender. Furthermore, confiscated assets may be used to pay *bona fide* third parties.

Seizure is provided for under the Coercive Measures Act, chapter 4, section 1, according to which the provisional measure can be adopted for objects "likely to be confiscated by a court order". The Coercive Measures Act also provides for restraint and freezing orders under chapter 3.

B) Law in Action

Moving from the law in the books to the law in action, and starting with the investigative phase, although in past years the importance of tracing the proceeds of crime has been widely emphasised in Finland, financial investigations are still not systematically conducted in organised crime cases. Neither, with the exception of the freezing of money in laundering cases, are special investigative means used to any frequent extent, one reason being their limited range.

The amount of human resources devoted to financial investigations is generally sufficient, although they are normally redeployed (depending on the priority at any given time) to fight particular types of crime. In the past, financial investigators dealt mainly with economic crimes; drug cases are now the priority and attract more resources. The material resources available to investigators are adequate. Investigators receive a good level of training, with seminars and courses being run on a regular basis. The topics covered are, for instance, money laundering techniques, the investigation of crime proceeds in offshore jurisdictions and new confiscation provisions. With regard to the processing and exchange of information on a person's financial situation, to be noted is that the Money Laundering Clearing House has a very good multidisciplinary composition. The office is highly active and co-operates with various authorities, such as special units in the local police forces of the biggest towns and those operating within the National Bureau of Investigation itself. In large-scale investigations especially, a small investigative team is set up whose composition varies according to the kind of evidence to be collected (so that revenue and tax officers are included if necessary). In the past year there have been several cases (mostly drug offences and economic crimes) in which there has been effective cooperation among different national law enforcement agencies (investigators, public prosecutors and revenue officers)—not least as a result of cooperation projects undertaken to improve the exchange of information among these authorities. However, the situation is not ideal: traditionally, in fact, there have been communication problems between investigators and public prosecutors on the one hand, and the courts on the other. The result has been that a quite significant period of time (up to two years) has normally elapsed between the conclusion of investigations and the bringing of the case before a court. This has happened mainly in big cities, whereas smaller-sized ones have been less affected because of the lighter workload on law enforcement agencies and therefore the relative ease with which investigator and court schedules can be coordinated. Communication has recently improved, but there still remains much to be done.

Cooperation by banks is good; less so is that provided by other financial institutions. Non financial institutions are almost entirely uncooperative. Hopefully, the situation will improve following the recent amendment made to the Act on Preventing and Clearing Money Laundering by law no. 365 of 16 May 2003. As a result, since 1 June 2003 the reporting obligation applies to several new bodies, such as accountants, auditors, dealers and agents in precious goods and legal professionals if they participate in business transactions in the name of their customers or on behalf of them. The real estate sector and gambling houses came under the reporting obligation on 1 March 1998 and since then have sent reports to the FIU on yearly basis. Informants have contributed practically nothing to financial investigations, since their use in general is extremely rare.

With reference to the judicial phase, the provisions of law no. 875 of 2001 entered into force on 1 January 2002. Their application is therefore still rare and it is too early to assess their effects. However, some general comments relating to both the new and the old legislation can be made. The need for a conviction in order to confiscate is not perceived as a major obstacle against adoption of the measure, so that the implementation of confiscation provisions has to date been satisfactory. A problem that affects all criminal proceedings (and therefore also confiscation proceedings) is a shortage of human resources, especially of public prosecutors. Hence, although the latter are highly trained on the matter, their workloads are enormous. In general, much more training is given to public prosecutors than to judges. The training provision for public prosecutors focuses on civil and commercial law because of their importance in tracing the proceeds from crime and applying confiscation provisions.

The management of seized assets is satisfactory, also because of the administrators' good level of competence. An account is opened for shares and money, so that contractual interests are paid. With the exception of perishable goods, the assets may only be sold with the consent of the defendant and his/her creditors.

The disposal phase lasts seven and a half months on average. It is characterised by good cooperation between the offices involved and also by highly trained administrators. The human and material resources devoted to the enforcement of confiscation orders are both good; with reference to the latter, computer systems are being updated to facilitate the tracking of assets. As a rule, no significant problems arise.

By way of summary, Figure 4 shows the Investigative Phase Law in Action Index, the Judicial Phase Law in Action Index, and the Disposal Phase Law in Action Index for Finland. These Indexes quantify the law in action of the country by expressing on a scale from 0 to 100 the extent to which the law in the books is enforced in each phase. *The higher the index, the better the law in action of the phase.*

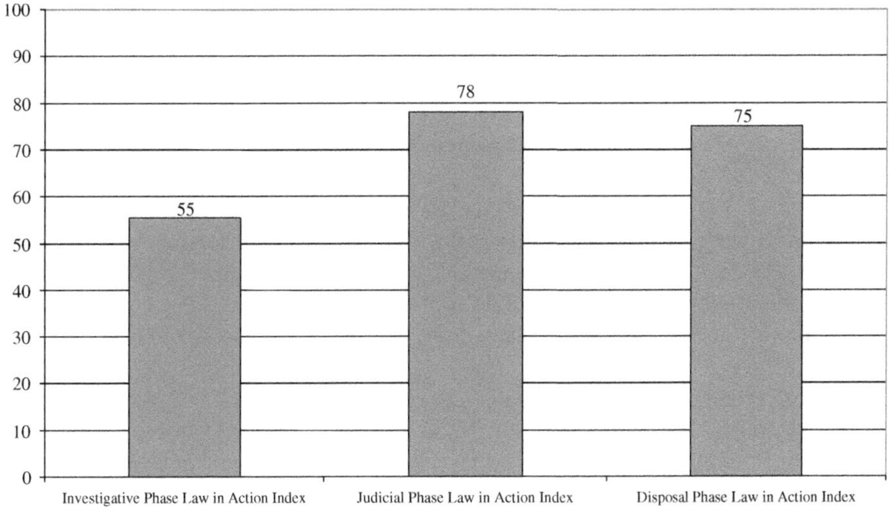

Figure 4. Law in Action Indexes of the Investigative, Judicial and Disposal Phases in Finland. Source: Author's elaboration of the national expert's replies to the questionnaire.

4.5 FRANCE

A) Law in the Books

Financial investigations are undertaken by the French FIU, the *Traitement du renseignement et action contre les circuits financiers clandestins* (TRACFIN), set up at the Ministry for the Economy, Finance and Industry on 9 May 1990. On the same day, another bureau devoted to financial investigations, the *Office Central pour la Répression de la Grande Délinquance Financière* (OCRGDF), was created at the Ministry of Interior. Such investigations may concern any person suspected of having benefited from crime or having received proceeds from crime as a straw man. The special investigative means foreseen for normal investigations may be used accordingly.

The national confiscation system was amended in 1994 when the new Penal Code came into force.[44] Other significant changes were made to the system in 1996 and 1999, and more recently in June 2001. Before 1994, French law differentiated between (1) *confiscation générale*, which deprived the offender of all his/her property, and (2) *confiscation spéciale*, which concerned only part of the offender's assets. The distinction was eliminated in the Criminal Code of 1994, and confiscation is now always regarded as *spéciale*.[45] The confiscation of the defendant's entire assets is exceptionally limited to certain offences, including the most serious cases of drug trafficking (article 222-49, paragraph 2).

The main provision on confiscation is article 131-21 of the Criminal Code, which defines the contents and the rules to be followed in application of the measure. First, the provision states at paragraph 1 that as a general rule the measure is optional, the only exception being items legally defined as dangerous, the confiscation of which is mandatory. Paragraph 2 of the article subjects to confiscation, among other things, the profits accruing from the criminal act (Desportes & Le Gunehec 1997, 627). The same article specifies that the measure cannot apply to objects "likely to be restituted". This expression should be taken to refer to the rights of *bona fide* third parties, that is persons who have not been prosecuted or sentenced, and whose ownership or holding is legal (Godefroy & Kletzlen 2000, 20).

Paragraph 3 of article 131-21 provides for value confiscation. Under this provision, if the goods to be confiscated have not been seized or are no longer available, confiscation of a sum of money equivalent to their value is ordered. The introduction of this provision allowing the use of value confiscation to the fullest possible extent has resolved previous judicial divergences on the matter (Desportes & Le Gunehec 1997, 627).

In the French system the public prosecutor must provide full proof that assets are of illegal origin. The only exception to the rule is provided by article 222-39-1 of the Criminal Code. Introduced on 13 May 1996, this article stipulates, besides a five-year period of imprisonment, payment of a fine by a person convicted for carrying on habitual relations with a drug trafficker or user. The fine is applied should the person be unable to demonstrate the legal origin of funds commensurate with his/her lifestyle.

According to paragraph 5 of article 131-21, confiscated assets devolve to the State, unless they are to be destroyed under specific provisions.[46]

[44] For analysis of the national confiscation system before 1994, see Godefroy & Kletzlen (1997).

[45] For detailed analysis of the *confiscation spéciale* see Matsopoulou (1995).

[46] Destruction is foreseen, for example in the case of counterfeited money (article 442–13 of the Criminal Code).

Special confiscation provisions contained in article 222-49 of the Criminal Code apply to goods connected with drug trafficking. Under paragraph 1 of the article, the proceeds originating from the offence are mandatorily removed from the offender and from any *mala fide* third party.

Seizure of assets to be confiscated is provided for by articles 97 and 99 paragraph 4 of the Code of Criminal Procedure. Furthermore, in relation to drug trafficking offences, conservative measures may be adopted under article 706-30 of the Code of Criminal Procedure in order to ensure that confiscation is executed.[47] On 15 June 2001 the application of article 706-30 was extended to the proceeds of persons charged with money-laundering offences.

Finally to be mentioned is the introduction by law no. 515 of 23 June 1999 of article 99-2 of the Code of Criminal Procedure. Under this article, the sale of personal assets subject to seizure may be ordered by the examining judge in certain circumstances: when the assets are no longer necessary to demonstrate the truth, or if they have become dangerous, or their owner is unknown, or are unclaimed, or have significantly decreased in value. The money obtained from the sale must be kept for ten years or until the final confiscation order.

B) Law in Action

With reference to the investigative phase, inquiries into the proceeds from crime are conducted systematically in organised crime cases and from a very early stage. They are completed in a short period of time, unless they involve other jurisdictions as well, in which case investigations are greatly delayed because international cooperation mechanisms are very slow and some countries are uncooperative on financial matters.

As said, these investigations are undertaken mainly by the TRACFIN (Ministry for the Economy, Finance and Industry) and by the OCRGDF (Ministry of Interior). The fact the these two agencies were established on the very same day "[...] reveals the well-known rivalry between police and custom's authorities in France, which makes inter-agency operations quite difficult. The two bodies have different cultures, methods and means" (Godefroy & Kletzlen 1997, 276). The national expert interviewed confirmed this point and emphasised that it implies that the benefits of a multidisciplinary approach to the tracing of illicit assets are rarely exploited. Furthermore, with the exception of the two bodies mentioned and of three other financial and economic pools, which must compulsorily be multidisciplinary in their composition, the combining of different competencies and skills in the same office is not usual in other law enforcement agencies.

Another defect of the French system is the training given to financial investigators, who follow a general programme which almost entirely neglects financial aspects. Also indicative of the low priority given to financial investigations is the scarce material and (above all) human resources allocated to them. Moreover, the conduct of investigations

[47] For an analysis of seizure provisions in France see Godefroy & Kletzlen (2000, 23–24).

is hampered by the reluctance of the non banking financial institutions and non financial institutions to cooperate with investigators. By contrast, satisfactory assistance is provided by the banking system. Cooperation from informants on the proceeds from crime is a rare occurrence, mainly because there is no protection system for informers, and because of the fear factor.

Like the investigative phase, the judicial one is significantly affected by the low priority given to removal of the defendant's assets; the main objective is to obtain a conviction. As a result, inadequate training in seizure and confiscation is given to public prosecutors and judges: a poorly organised course is held at the *Ecole de Magistrature*, so that most training is in fact received on the job. Consequently, although the human and material resources available are adequate, their effective employment in confiscation proceedings is hampered by their poor preparation.

Further obstacles against the implementation of seizure and confiscation measures in France are raised by the features of the legal system, which always requires conviction before the proceeds of crime can be confiscated and does not usually allow for reversal of the burden of proof. Experience shows that the fulfilment of both requirements is also made difficult by the money laundering techniques used by criminals. Its discretional character, furthermore, implies that the measure is not adopted even in cases where all the legal prerequisites have been met. Another problem concerns the implementation of value confiscation. Whilst property confiscation does not encounter particular problems, so that once the proceeds have been seized they are then usually confiscated, value confiscation has to date been applied in a very limited number of cases (with the sole exception of the customs sector). The main reason for this is that value confiscation is still an unfamiliar concept to French juridical culture.

The management of seized assets is largely neglected: there is only one provision aimed at minimising the deterioration in value of seized personal assets (i.e. article 99-2 of the Code of Criminal Procedure), and its range of application is limited to personal assets. More significantly, to date this provision has been rarely applied in practice.

This situation is exacerbated by the slowness, in criminal proceedings, of judicial procedure. As a consequence, and given that it is not usually possible to sell the assets seized before the final confiscation order, goods often significantly decrease in value before their confiscation.

With regard to the disposal phase, no problems arise if the confiscation order relates to money. Other assets derive to the Treasury and are usually sold. The sale procedure is at present overly complex and time-consuming (especially in the case of the disposal of real property; personal property is disposed of in a reasonable amount of time), and this often decreases the value of confiscated assets. This problem is also due to the department that manages confiscation orders (as well as all State properties), namely the *Domaines de l'Etat*, which has insufficient resources to ensure that assets are kept in good condition while confiscation orders are being enforced.

By way of summary, and in particular of the numerous problems highlighted by the national expert who completed the questionnaire, Figure 5 shows the Investigative

Phase Law in Action Index, the Judicial Phase Law in Action Index, and the Disposal Phase Law in Action Index for France. These Indexes quantify the law in action of the country by expressing, on a scale from 0 to 100, the extent to which the law in the books is enforced in each phase. *The higher the index, the better the law in action of the phase.*

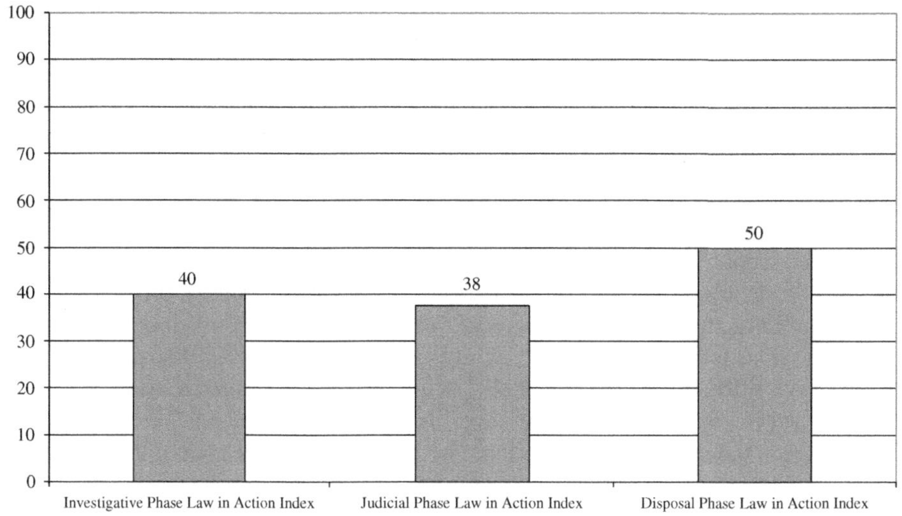

Figure 5. Law in Action Indexes of the Investigative, Judicial and Disposal Phases in France. Source: Author's elaboration of the national expert's replies to the questionnaire.

4.6 GERMANY

A) Law in the Books

In Germany, numerous specialised units, set up at both the Federal level (*Bundeskriminalamt*) and the individual State level (*Landeskriminalamt*), and whose operations are supervised by public prosecutors, are responsible for tracking down illicit property, investigating all circumstances concerning the origin of the defendant's assets, and executing seizures. Financial investigations must be conducted on any person suspected of having benefited from crime or of having received proceeds from crime as a straw man. A wide range of special investigative means are available.

The confiscation system has been significantly amended by the 'law to combat the illicit trafficking in narcotic drugs and other manifestations of organised crime' (the so-called Organised Crime Act) enacted on 15 July 1992. This law, which introduced the new offence of money laundering, also revised the confiscation regulations. As a result, the removal of illicit wealth from criminal organisations is pursued under section

43a (in force until March 2002, when it was declared unconstitutional)[48] and section 73 of the Criminal Code.

Proceeds from any crime are obligatorily confiscated under section 73 (*Verfall*), introduced in 1975. Before 1992, the term 'proceeds' referred only to the net profits generated by criminal conduct. The notion has been expanded by the Organised Crime Act to include gross products (Kilchling 2002, 30). The measure applies both to the benefits directly obtained from the crime and to those acquired through their transfer (section 73, subsection 2). If the assets are owned or are subject to a third party claim, they are confiscated both if this person has provided them for the commission of the crime and if s/he knew of their illicit origin (section 73, subsection 4). The sanction also applies to assets received by third parties on whose behalf the offender acted (section 73, subsection 3).

According to section 73a, the confiscation of an amount of money equal to the value of the unlawful profits may be ordered if the proceeds cannot be found.

Under section 73d, which provides for so-called 'augmented confiscation', it is possible to seize not only the proceeds directly linked to the criminal offence but also further profits acquired by the offender and presumed to arise from criminal activities. The provision, introduced in 1992, clearly facilitates the work of the public prosecutor, since full proof of the connection between the assets and the crime need not be provided (Fornari 1997, 194). However, as stated by the Federal Court of Appeals (*Bundesgerichtshof*), the measure cannot be based on mere suspicion. Proof beyond any reasonable doubt that the assets stem from crime is required (Benseler 1997, 207). To be noted is that augmented confiscation applies only in the case of serious crimes, usually committed by criminal groups.

It should be pointed out that confiscation applies independently of a conviction. According to section 76a, the removal of criminal assets may also take place if no person has been prosecuted or sentenced.

In 1992 the provisions regulating the removal of illicit wealth were reinforced by the introduction of section 43a. With reference to the same serious offences committed by criminal organisations to which augmented confiscation applies, the judge may inflict, in addition to imprisonment for life or for more than two years, a property fine, the maximum amount of which is equal to the entire assets of the convicted person. This section is no longer in force as it was declared unconstitutional in March 2002.

In order to minimise the deterioration of seized assets, the so called 'emergency sale' procedure is used. Once the public prosecutor has proved that it is necessary to prevent a significant decrease in value of the seized assets, this procedure becomes obligatory. It is managed by a registrar who works in the office of the public prosecutor or is employed by the court. The sale is the registrar's responsibility, but s/he must agree with the public prosecutor or with the court. The money raised by the sale is placed in a special account, and if the adoption of confiscation is refused it is returned to the defendant.

[48] Decision of the Federal Constitutional Court (*Bundesverfassungsgericht*) of 20 March 2002. For comments on this decision, see Kilchling (2004, 724).

Specialised employees (registrars) at the Department of Public Prosecution deal with finally confiscated assets. If the goods are specific assets, they become the property of the State when the deprivation order becomes final; they are then sold or used for social purposes. The order to pay the sum of money fixed by the order must be enforced in accordance with section 459, letters f and g, of the Code of Criminal Procedure.

According to section 111b, subsection 1, of the Code of Criminal Procedure, the seizure of assets may be ordered if the prerequisites for their confiscation exist.

B) Law in Action

As regards the way in which this legal framework is implemented, and starting with identification of the proceeds from crime, the law requires that financial investigations must be conducted at an early stage in organised crime cases.[49] This rule is invariably complied with. Investigations are always made on any person involved as a straw man, also because it is mandatory to do so, and special investigative means are always used in the case of more serious offences.

As seen, numerous specialised units carry out financial investigations. Revenue officers are seconded to these units, and financial analysts are used as well. Accountants are employed at the office of public prosecutors. Following a decision by the public prosecutor, made on the basis of the features of the case in question, a special investigative team is set up whose level of multidisciplinary composition varies, although in practice it is generally good. There is a very satisfactory level of inter-agency cooperation as well.

Also as a result of the emphasis placed on the importance of effective action against criminal wealth by recent initiatives (the best known being the Action Plan on Seizure and Confiscation adopted in North Rhine–Westphalia at the beginning of 2000),[50] the training of financial investigators has improved and is now satisfactory throughout Germany. Good human and material resources are now available. With reference to the latter, investigators often use electronic systems to determine the economic circumstances of a suspected criminal. One of these systems is particularly promising: the *ZIVED* (Central Information Exchange from External Databases), which is a special electronic search system developed by the Land of North Rhine-Westphalia and now used by investigators throughout the country. The system works very well and

[49] In Germany, the investigative phase divides into two stages: (1) the so-called 'undercover investigation', where the suspect does not know that s/he is being investigated, and (2) the so-called 'open investigation', in which the suspect is aware of being investigated. Financial investigations to identify the proceeds from crime always start from the very beginning, that is while the undercover investigation is in progress.

[50] The Action Plan on Seizure and Confiscation adopted in North Rhine–Westphalia has two main features:

1) the principle of separation, that is investigations to locate the proceeds of crime must be kept separate from those conducted in order to prove the defendant's guilt and undertaken by highly specialised teams of investigators;
2) on-going training, that is the highly specific and targeted training of the authorities involved in confiscation proceedings.

enables law enforcement agencies to obtain a complete picture of a defendant's financial situation in a relatively short time. Its sources are all accessible databases world-wide (i.e. more that 6,000 databases), and it uses the Internet as its medium.

With regard to the cooperation provided by external institutions, banks are obliged to furnish any relevant information, and they have special employees to deal with requests for cooperation from the law enforcement agencies. This has recently produced a very good level of cooperation, with an additional factor being the monitoring and search programmes used by banks to retrieve individual transactions and the details thereof. The legal obligation is the same for the other financial institutions, and also for non financial institutions (although in the latter case the regulations have been introduced more recently). However, cooperation by the other financial and non financial institutions is less satisfactory than that provided by banks, mainly because of the low level of training received by employees at those institutions, but also because they are sometimes reluctant to co-operate. Witnesses have a a duty to cooperate, and so have supergrasses, and their cooperation is satisfactory.[51]

To sum up, it would seem that at the law enforcement level confiscation is recognised as a significant objective, and that investigative efforts to locate the proceeds from crime are successful.[52]

Turning to the judicial phase, when the public prosecutors obtain a conviction—which is not particularly difficult in organised crime investigations, where great efforts are made by law enforcement agencies—in most cases a confiscation order ensues. Confiscation is most frequently ordered in relation to drug related offences, while the measure is still rarely applied in money laundering cases (Kilchling 2002, 38–40). The few data available show that seizures and confiscations significantly increased during the 1990s, especially in those *Länder* (such as Baden-Württemberg and North Rhine-Westphalia) where financial investigations were first introduced and are more deeply rooted in the culture. With the exception of the property fines foreseen, until March 2002, by section 43a, which have been applied in an insignificant number of cases, confiscations (section 73), as well as extended confiscations (section 73d), have become more frequent. In particular, value confiscation (section 73a), rarely employed until 1996, is now commonplace (Ibidem, 45–49). The provisions on value confiscation, in fact, are much easier to apply than those on property confiscation and extended confiscation. Indeed, property confiscation is not always applied to a satisfactory extent, largely because public prosecutors are unable to prove the assets/crime link in all cases. Extended confiscation is also difficult to implement, mainly because of the complexity of the relevant legal text, so that it has to date been applied in an insignificant number of cases. The provisions on the seizure and confiscation of crime proceeds from third parties are implemented to a quite satisfactory extent, although there are some cases in which it is impossible or extremely difficult to provide evidence that the third party has acted as a straw man.

[51] For the German legislation concerning supergrasses, see Mehrens (2000, 341–344).

[52] These findings confirm those by Kilchling (2002, 61).

A practice first applied in drug cases and still very frequently used in them is the so-called 'renunciation' (*Verzicht*). The offender is requested, informally, to renounce previously seized assets. In the case of agreement, which is usually reached shortly before conclusion of the trial, and is generally forthcoming from the offender with the intention (whether overt or covert) to obtain either a milder sentence or restitution of a portion of the seized assets, the court no longer orders the confiscation of the portion in question. Little information is available on the extent of this practice (Ibidem, 37–38). One of its advantages is that it markedly reduces the time needed to effect confiscation: when there is an agreement between the defendant and the public prosecutor, a confiscation order can be obtained very rapidly. In other cases (those of 'conflict defence'), in which there is no cooperation between the defendant and the public prosecutor, a great deal of time may elapse before the confiscation order is enacted, as the criminal proceedings continue until conviction of the defendant by the High Court.

The human and material resources allocated to the judicial phase are now good—especially as a result of recent initiatives to heighten awareness of the importance of an effective strategy against criminal wealth. Thus, for example, the proceeds from crime have recently been used to increase the number of prosecutors. Also good is the level of training given to public prosecutors and judges on these matters. Public prosecutors about to specialise in confiscation cases are trained together with investigators in police institutions, and in several areas. They generally receive training for a total period of about four weeks, while the other public prosecutors attend courses on three occasions for three days at a time. With reference to judges, they are working hard to catch up with the public prosecutors. In the past they were less well trained than public prosecutors, but now are at the very same level. They are trained together with 'other public prosecutors' (not the specialised ones). In general, however, they are still reluctant to order confiscation, and in many cases set the issue aside during the trial without any reasonable motive for doing so. The legal provisions on the management of seized assets are, as said, only intended to minimise their deterioration (not to maximise their value) by means of so-called 'emergency sales'. Most of the cases, generally involving computers and cars, are successful.

Adequate material and human resources (i.e. registrars employed at the public prosecutor service) are allocated to the disposal phase. The main problem arising if assets are sold at public auction is that the price obtained is often low: the market price is not always the best one. The assets disposed of for social purposes are not always in the best condition when given to the law enforcement agencies. No problems arise for confiscated cash, which is disposed of to a very satisfactory extent.

By way of summary, and in particular of the problems highlighted by the national expert who completed the questionnaire in the judicial and disposal phases, Figure 6 shows the Investigative Phase Law in Action Index, the Judicial Phase Law in Action Index, and the Disposal Phase Law in Action Index for Germany. These Indexes quantify the law in action of the country by expressing, on a scale from 0 to 100, the extent to which the law in the books is enforced in each phase. *The higher the index, the better the law in action of the phase.*

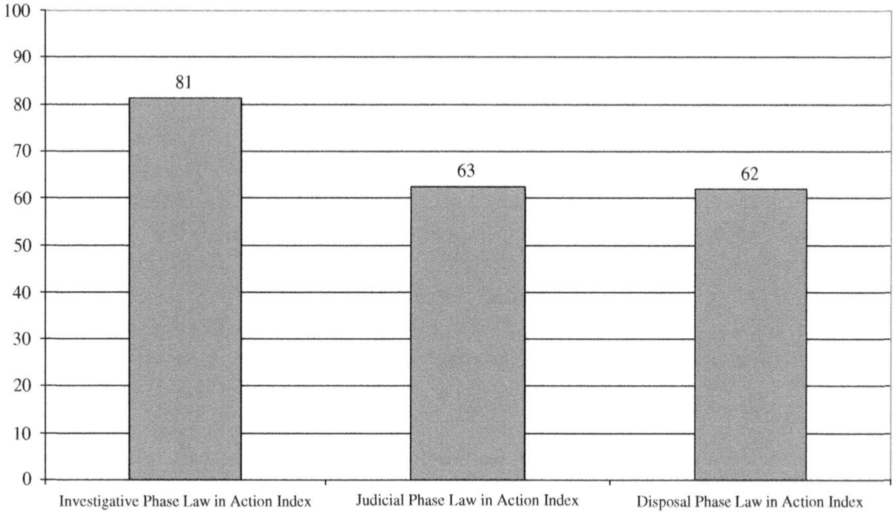

Figure 6. Law in Action Indexes of the Investigative, Judicial and Disposal Phases in Germany. Source: Author's elaboration of the national expert's replies to the questionnaire.

4.7 GREECE

A) Law in the Books

Investigations relative to the proceeds of crime are mainly undertaken by the Greek FIU, that is the Committee of Financial and Criminal Investigations (CFCI),[53] and by the Financial and Economic Crime Unit (SDOE).[54] Such inquiries may concern any person possessing ill-gotten gains, and special investigative means are available to those conducting them.

Confiscation can be enacted in Greece via both criminal and civil proceedings. The following analysis first concentrates on the dispossession of unlawful gains in the criminal context, and then describes civil confiscation.

Article 76 of the Penal Code provides at paragraph 1 for the compulsory confiscation of the articles—goods and proceeds—resulting from a felony or an intentional misdemeanour[55] and the assets acquired from their sale, and also of a sum of money equal to the value of such articles.

[53] The Greek FIU was created by article 7 of law no. 2331/1995.

[54] The Financial and Economic Crime Unit (SDOE) was created by law no. 2343 of 1995 and by Presidential Decree no. 218 of 1996. It is a special administrative unit with inspection, control and other functions aimed at preventing and dealing with a variety of economic crimes (e.g. tax evasion, trafficking in weapons, drugs, fraud against the financial interests of the European Union, etc.).

[55] The Criminal Code defines three grades of crime: petty offences, misdemeanours and felonies.

If the assets are dangerous to public welfare, confiscation applies both to any third party who may possess them and to the heirs if the defendant dies after the final confiscation order. Greece has a non conviction based confiscation system; the sanction, in fact, can also be enacted before conviction is passed or if prosecution has been impossible (article 76 paragraph 2).

In 1995, this traditional confiscation regime was updated by law no. 2331[56] which applies to more serious offences typically connected with the activity of criminal organisations. According to article 2 of this law, the proceeds from these criminal activities and the means used for their commission are obligatorily subject to confiscation. The measure also regards third parties if the criminal origin of the assets is known. The measure may also be adopted if there has been no criminal action or prosecution. If the criminal proceeds are no longer available among the defendant's assets, an order to pay a sum of money equal to their value is made.

Goods confiscated in the criminal context are sold at public auction unless the court decides that they are to be destroyed.

Seizure is provided for, in criminal proceedings, by article 260 of the Code of Criminal Procedure.

To be finally mentioned is a draft law currently under discussion that, if approved, will introduce in criminal cases, among other things, a sharing of the burden of proof between defendant and public prosecutor.

In addition to criminal confiscation, law no. 2331/1995 provides for the confiscation of the proceeds from crime in the civil framework.

Article 3 of this law states, at paragraph 1, that if a person has been sentenced to a prison term of at least three years for a serious crime, the State may request the civil courts to remove from the offender any property acquired by similar crimes. Civil action may also be taken if conviction has not been pronounced or prosecution has not been possible in relation to these analogous offences. Reversal of the burden of proof operates in civil confiscation, since all property acquired by the offender over the previous five years and until the verdict of his/her final conviction is presumed to derive from the mentioned offences. The onus of proving the licit origin of the assets consequently shifts to the defendant.[57] The term 'property', *ex* article 1 of the law, denotes "assets of every kind, incorporated or non incorporated, mobile or immobile, material or immaterial, as well as the legal deeds or documents which prove ownership of title or rights for the acquisition of such property assets". Property can also be confiscated from relatives of the defendant and from persons who have acquired it in bad faith during the criminal proceedings (article 3, paragraph 2).

Seizure is regulated, in civil proceedings, by articles 904-1046 of the Code of Civil Procedure.

[56] This law, together with law no. 2145/1993, implemented the EU Directive 91/308 on money laundering in Greece. On this see Zerey (1997) and Stefanou & Xanthaki (1999).

[57] On this see Konstantopoulos (1999, 9–10).

B) Law in Action

When discussing the practice of confiscation in Greece, it is obviously necessary to differentiate again between civil confiscation and criminal confiscation. With reference to the former, the discussion will be brief for the simple reason that to date there has been no proceeding instituted for the application of the measure, which has consequently never been used. This can be explained in terms of cultural opposition to civil confiscation. The institute is completely alien to the Greek legal tradition and has never been accepted. Hence, even if its constitutionality has been upheld by the Supreme Court, the measure has been strongly criticised as unconstitutional by academics and practitioners.

As regards the implementation of criminal confiscation, and starting with the investigative phase, financial investigations are generally begun at the very first stage of criminal proceedings. In practice their coverage is extremely wide, and careful investigation of third parties apparently involved as straw men is regularly made. Special investigative means are often used for any type of offence requiring technical investigation.

There is a high level of multidisciplinarity within the Greek FIU, which is made up of ten representatives and chaired by a High Court judge. The representatives are from all relevant bodies, such as: Ministry of Public Order, Ministry of Interior, Ministry of Commerce, Bank of Greece, police, SDOE and the courts. Although the various institutions involved in financial investigations do not cooperate as closely as they could, when acting within the FIU they are all directed by a single judge or public prosecutor, who obliges them to cooperate immediately. Human resources are entirely adequate. This is largely due to the multidisciplinary composition of the FIU and implies that any of the bodies involved participates with its personnel in the search for the proceeds from crime (so that, e.g. the SDOE has 4,000 investigators in every part of the country). Although there is sufficient personnel for investigations, however, they are not given adequate training in the tracing of criminal proceeds. They are able to conduct effective investigations when there is proof that a crime has been committed (i.e. in reactive investigations), but they are much less able to conduct proactive investigations. The material resources available to investigators are not entirely adequate, the main problem being a lack of software for the cross-comparison of data.

As regards cooperation by external institutions in tracing criminal profits, banks have a well organised and functional structure for the identification of suspicious transactions, also because of their legal obligation to appoint clerks for this purpose and to submit reports on suspicious transactions to the FIU. The other financial institutions, such as those that transmit money (e.g. Western Union), are less closely regulated: for example, in order to perform their functions, they simply need to submit a declaration to the Bank of Greece and obtain a license. Hence they are not obliged to co-operate and not subject to stringent prerequisites. In practice, however, these institutions cooperate to a satisfactory extent with investigators, and are sometimes more willing than banks to do so—perhaps because their links with their customers are weaker and less permanent than those between banks and their clients. They also have very advanced computerised systems, so that they can reconstruct paper trails very easily. The frequency of transactions can be readily identified as well. Non financial institutions cooperate to a significantly less satisfactory extent: for example, in the past year no reports at all have been made by life insurance companies. They sometimes provide investigators with information, but generally do so because of the checks made on them by the Ministry of Trade. Informants often provide investigators with information on criminal wealth, but it is not always of any great value, and in any case cannot be used officially.

In the judicial phase it is difficult to get a conviction, especially in organised crime cases. An extended confiscation regime has been put in place for money laundering cases, and because it facilitates the task of the public prosecutor, it is very successful in practice. Since confiscation is compulsory, the courts are obliged to confiscate the proceeds from crime when convicting a defendant. It may sometimes happen that the amount is reduced by the court, but this does not impair the general level of implementation of the measure, which is good. There are no particular probatory problems, especially because there is a specific crime to act as a starting point. Implementation of seizure and confiscation towards third parties is very satisfactory. It should be pointed out, however, that the training of public prosecutors and judges is in need of improvement and should be more closely focused on seizure and confiscation. Indeed, no specific training on such matters is provided. It can be said, however, that public prosecutors are better informed on confiscation provisions than are judges. Moreover, the human and material resources devoted to the phase are insufficient.

The management of seized assets is to be criticised. Generally speaking, there is no provision intended to prevent the deterioration in value of seized assets: they are simply retained until the procedure has concluded. The only exception is represented by cars, which are often sold before confiscation to minimise their decrease in value. Hence, with this limited exception, which works very well, the value of the assets normally diminishes. The situation is even worse when a conviction is a prerequisite for confiscation (i.e. in most cases) because of the long time required to obtain one.

The disposal phase is very rapid. The authorities involved are the judicial authorities and the administrators, to whom the final decision must be forwarded, and they generally cooperate well. There are good human resources in the administrators' offices. Because the law does not require it, however, administrators do not have any particular competence to increase the value of assets while managing and disposing of them, which usually causes a significant decrease in the value of the goods. Nor does the sale of confiscated assets at public auction seem to work particularly well: assets decrease in value and the sale procedure is affected by a lack of transparency.

By way of summary, and in particular of the problems highlighted by the national expert who completed the questionnaire in the judicial phase, Figure 7 shows the Investigative Phase Law in Action Index, the Judicial Phase Law in Action Index, and the Disposal Phase Law in Action Index for criminal confiscation in Greece. These Indexes quantify the law in action of the country by expressing, on a scale from 0 to 100, the extent to which the law in the books is implemented in each phase. *The higher the index, the better the law in action of the phase.*

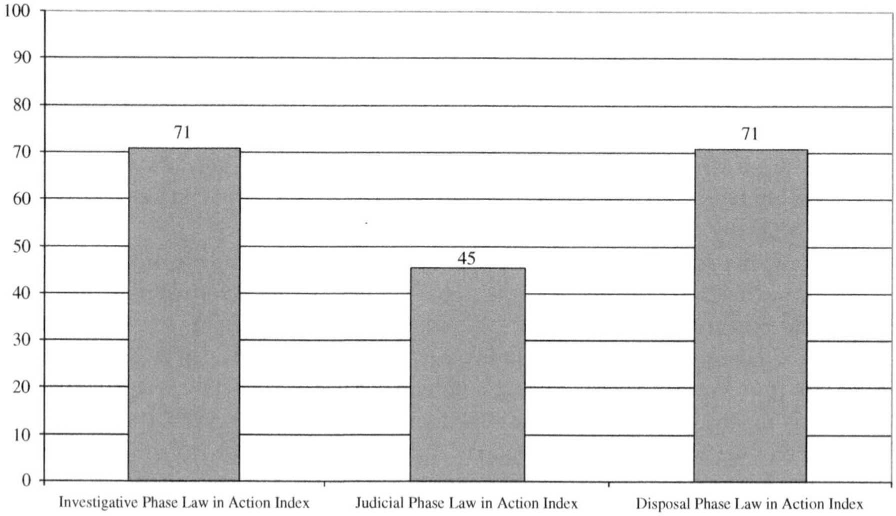

Figure 7. Law in Action Indexes of the Investigative, Judicial and Disposal Phases in Criminal Proceedings in Greece.
Source: Author's elaboration of the national expert's replies to the questionnaire.

4.8 IRELAND

A) Law in the Books

Until 1996 the deprivation of illicit wealth in Ireland could be achieved via criminal proceedings. In that year, a number of dramatic events linked to drug trafficking shocked Irish public opinion and led to revision of the national confiscation system.[58] In response to these events, the Proceeds of Crime Act was enacted on 4 August, 1996, and introduced the civil confiscation of the criminal proceeds into the Irish judicial system.

The confiscation of illicit wealth in criminal proceedings is regulated by the Criminal Justice Act of 1994, which the preamble defines as "an Act to make provision for the recovery of the proceeds of drug trafficking and other offences [. . .]". As highlighted by the preamble, the statute allows for the confiscation of both the proceeds of drug trafficking (section 4) and the proceeds of other offences (section 9).

An extended confiscation regime is foreseen only with reference to drug trafficking offences, since in this case the court must rely on certain assumptions, unless these are shown to be incorrect, or their employment would lead to a serious risk of injustice. First, any property transferred to the defendant in the six-year period before the conclusion of the proceedings instituted against him/her, and held by him/her after the conviction, are presumed to have been received as payment or reward in connection with drug trafficking. Furthermore, any expenditure by the defendant in the above-mentioned

[58] On 6 June 1996 Gerry McCabe, a detective of the *Garda Síochána* (the Irish police) was murdered. Some weeks later, on 26 June, Veronica Guerin, an investigative reporter for the *Sunday Independent* in Dublin, was killed.

six-year period is assumed to have been met out of payments received in connection with drug trafficking. For the purpose of valuing any property obtained (or assumed to have been obtained) by the defendant, it is assumed that s/he obtained it free of any other interests in it (section 5).

A conviction is required before a confiscation order can be made both in drug trafficking and non drug trafficking cases. To be noted is that different standards of proof are required for conviction of the defendant and for confiscation of his/her illicit profits, respectively. For the defendant to be convicted, s/he must be found guilty of the offence according to the criminal standard of proof, that is beyond reasonable doubt. For the proceeds of his/her crime to be confiscated, the civil standard of proof is sufficient; consequently, it is necessary to prove that the assets are proceeds from crime on the balance of probabilities. This difference in the standard of proof, which is clearly intended to facilitate the dispossession of unlawful gains, has nevertheless proved inadequate in attacking criminal assets. This act of confiscation could only be executed after the defendant had been sentenced; however, it may be very difficult to obtain the conviction of the leaders of criminal organisations. It has been rightly pointed out that "[. . .] in general, the proceeds of criminal activity lay in the hands of the principals of the various criminal gangs. Experience has shown that it was very difficult to successfully prosecute these persons due to a variety of reasons, including the way in which they conducted their criminal activity and the fear factor which deterred others from giving evidence against them" (Murphy & Galvin 1999, 21). The Proceeds of Crime Act was enacted in order to deal with this problem.

The Proceeds of Crime Act,[59] approved by Parliament in August 1996, is defined in its preamble as "an Act to enable the High Court, as respect the proceeds of crime, to make orders for the preservation and, where appropriate, the disposal of the property concerned and to provide for related matters".

The statute allows the High Court to order, with neither the need for a conviction nor the involvement of the defendant in criminal activities, measures aimed at depriving the defendant of assets suspected of being the proceeds of crime.

On request by an authorised officer of the Revenue Commissioners or by a member of the *Garda Síochána* (the Irish police) not below the rank of Chief Superintendent, the High Court may order the deprivation of the suspected illicit assets by means of three types of order: an interim order, an interlocutory order and a disposal order.

An interim order is granted by the High Court when the applicant proves that a person is in possession or in control of property which constitutes, directly or indirectly, proceeds of crime or property acquired with or in connection with property that represents, directly or indirectly, proceeds of crime.[60] Furthermore, the applicant must prove that the value of the assets is not less than £10,000 (around 30,000 euro) (section 2).

[59] For a comment on this Act, see Meade (1998).

[60] The meaning of the term 'proceeds of crime' is explained in section 1, subsection (1), according to which 'proceeds of crime' means any property obtained or received at any time (whether before or after the passing of this Act) by or as a result of or in connection with the commission of an offence. The term 'property' used in this definition includes, according to the same provision, money and all other property, real or personal, inheritable or moveable, including choses in action and other intangible or incorporeal property; moreover, any interest in property is included.

The standard of proof required is that typically found in civil proceedings, that is on the balance of probabilities (section 8). The order, during a period of twenty-one days from its issue, has the effect of prohibiting the defendant and other people who know about it from disposing of or otherwise dealing with the assets and from reducing their value. If the defendant or any person claiming ownership of any of the property proves that it does not represent proceeds from crime, or that its value is less than £10,000, the court may discharge or vary the order.

On expiry of the twenty-one-day period from its issue, the interim order lapses, unless the applicant makes application for an interlocutory order. In this case the interim order lapses on the decision of the High Court on the application for the interlocutory order or on the expiry of the term for bringing an appeal against this decision. In order to obtain an interlocutory order, the applicant must provide the court with the same elements as required for issue of an interim order. The High Court may then make an interlocutory order. This order has the same effect as the interim order, that is it freezes the relative property. An order cannot be made if there is serious risk of injustice, or if the defendant or any person claiming ownership of the property proves that its origin is not criminal or that its value does not exceed £10,000 (section 3). Once the interlocutory order has been made, the defendant and the third parties may obtain a discharge or variation of the order if they show the licit origin of the assets or the situation of injustice produced by the order. Otherwise, the interlocutory order "[...] can stay in place indefinitely" (Lavelle 1998, 11).

However, seven years after its making, the applicant may ask the High Court for the issue of another order, that is the disposal order (section 4). A disposal order operates to transfer the property to the State. It differs from the interim and the interlocutory order in that it definitively removes from the defendant any rights over the property. The goods pass to the Ministry for Finance or to another person, as the court decides, so that benefit of the property can be realised for the Central Exchequer. A disposal order cannot be made if the defendant proves that the origin of the property is legal; furthermore, any person with ownership claims to the assets has an opportunity to be heard in court. The order is not enacted if it might lead to serious risk of injustice.

As regards the management of assets, at any time when an interim or interlocutory order is in force, the High Court may appoint a receiver over all or part of the property. According to the directions of the court, the receiver will take possession of the assets and either manage them or sell them, depending on the particular circumstances of the case (section 7). The Proceeds of Crime Act also states that the court may make such orders that it considers necessary to enable the defendant to discharge reasonable living expenses and to carry on a business, trade or profession to which the assets relate (section 6). There are provisions whereby the Minister for Finance pays such compensation as the court directs where an interim order is made and a subsequent interlocutory order is not made concerning the same property, or an interim or interlocutory order is varied or discharged, provided the respondent is able to show that s/he has suffered loss and that the property does not represent the proceeds of crime (section 16).

In order to guarantee full implementation of the Proceeds of Crime Act, the Criminal Assets Bureau Act came into force on 15 October 1996. This Act created the Criminal Assets Bureau, the office specifically in charge of applying the Proceeds of Crime Act, for which reason it has been defined as "[. . .] the body that oversees and co-ordinates the drive against organised crime, money laundering and related crimes" (Reid 1997).

The Criminal Assets Bureau is an independent multi-agency statutory corporation with perpetual succession and the power to sue and be sued in its corporate name and to acquire, hold and dispose of any kind of property (section 3). The objectives of the Criminal Assets Bureau are: (a) to identify the proceeds of crime; (b) to take appropriate action under the law to deprive criminals of such illicit gains; (c) to investigate and undertake other preparatory work related to the proceedings arising from the objectives mentioned in letters (a) and (b) (section 4). One particular function of the Criminal Assets Bureau should be emphasised: taking all actions necessary for the confiscation, restraint of use, freezing, preservation or seizure of assets identified as deriving from criminal activity (section 5).

The Chief Bureau Officer heads the Criminal Assets Bureau, being chosen among members with the rank of Chief Superintendent of the *Garda Síochána*. S/he supervises the Bureau's administration and is accountable for its performance (section 7). The office is made up of members of the *Garda Síochána*, the Revenue Commissioners and the Ministry for Social Welfare (section 8). Furthermore, the staff also comprises the Bureau Legal Officer, who is normally selected by the High Court as the receiver of assets subject to interim or interlocutory orders (Criminal Assets Bureau 2002, 9) and professional and technical members who assist the bureau officers (section 9).

The officers of the *Garda Síochána*, of the Revenue Commissioners and of the Minister for Social Welfare continue to exercise the powers of their original office, to which they still belong. An exceptional power is provided by the Act for a member of the *Garda Síochána* not below the rank of Superintendent who, because of his membership of the Criminal Assets Bureau, may in urgent cases issue a search warrant valid for twenty-four hours. This power can be exercised only if there are reasonable grounds for believing that proof relative to criminal proceeds is to be found in a certain place (section 14).

The criminal and civil confiscation systems described so far were enhanced by the Proceeds of Crime (Amendment) Act, which was passed on 12 February 2005. Among other things, this Act extends the proceeds of crime legislation to cover corrupt enrichment as well as foreign criminality, when the proceeds of that criminality are in Ireland. The Act also bolsters the powers of the Criminal Assets Bureau and extends them to the proceeds of white-collar crime and corruption.

B) Law in Action

Because the Proceeds of Crime (Amendment) Act 2005 has only recently come into force, the discussion in this section refers to the implementation of the criminal and civil confiscation regimes in place before the amendment of the Criminal Justice Act 1994, the Proceeds of Crime Act 1996 and the Criminal Assets Bureau Act 1996 by this new piece of legislation. Any discussion of its operation in practice would be premature at this time.

With reference to criminal confiscation, financial investigations in criminal proceedings are normally conducted by the ordinary police. They are carried out systematically and from a very early stage in all cases; this strategy is in fact a necessary part of the proper police procedure, since, for investigations to be closed and the case passed to the Director of Public Prosecutions, financial investigations must have been already completed. Special investigative means are not frequently used and, when they are, it is mainly with reference to terrorism, but for preventive purposes rather than prosecution. The investigation of third parties, although theoretically possible, is in practice a rare occurrence, due to the fact that most offenders in criminal cases are able to avoid prosecution (so that their straw men evade it as well). The Irish police make minimal use of civil servants (e.g. no accountants are employed by the force), so that the knowledge and skills of officials with different and specific areas of expertise are rarely exploited, although the Garda Bureau Fraud Investigations Office is an exception in that it employs two accountants. With reference to the level of inter-agency cooperation, tension sometimes arises among the various agencies (police, tax, customs, revenue) involved in financial investigations. However, inter-agency cooperation has been improved by a series of Memoranda of Understandings. The informal, flexible and above all voluntary nature of this instrument has helped to reduce the tension and rivalry that characterised relations among the law enforcement agencies, and it has enabled their collaboration in a reciprocal position of parity, rather than of hierarchy.

Investigators receive excellent cooperation from financial and non financial institutions. The former employ specialised money laundering officials and, in general, take money laundering investigations very seriously and cooperate to a wide extent with the police. Non financial institutions cooperate closely even in the absence of stringent legal constraints to do so, in consideration of the fact that the Irish police have always enjoyed strong support in every part of the country. The contribution of informers in criminal cases is limited: the fear factor plays an extremely significant role in limiting their cooperation with investigators. In fact, for their statements to be acquired as evidence in criminal proceedings, they must be identified (anonymity is not possible) and then be placed on a protection programme. Their use is also limited because historically their evidence has been viewed with suspicion.

Very limited human and material resources are allocated to financial inquiries, the only exception being the Garda Bureau Fraud Investigations Office, as well as some small teams specialised in fraud and operating at the local police level. As a consequence, the Criminal Assets Bureau sometimes intervenes to support police activities, with a resulting overlap between the police and the Criminal Assets Bureau. By contrast, the level of training is good. Some policemen enter the force already in possession of good degrees, and there is a centralised body—a police college—where police are trained fairly well and which reaches excellent international standards, also thanks to visits by foreign institutions: for example, courses are held by foreign specialised agencies like the Federal Bureau of Investigation (USA) and the Serious Fraud Office (UK). Members from the Criminal Assets Bureau also cooperate in training activities, so that continuing training is ensured.

As regards the judicial phase, the impact of criminal confiscation has been low. To date the measure has been applied only in an insignificant number of cases, mainly due to the difficulty of obtaining the defendant's conviction, especially if s/he is the leader of a criminal group. Top criminals are able to insulate themselves against detection.

The same applies to the extended confiscation regime foreseen in drug cases, where all proceeds acquired in the six-year period before conviction are presumed to derive from crime. In practice, very few cases have come before the courts. Moreover, legal provisions are somewhat unclear. To date, there have been very few cases (no more than ten) in which reversal of the burden of proof has been applied (i.e. drug trafficking cases). It seems that the judges concerned did not fully understand the process, which consisted of *in personam* proceedings. It should be stressed, however, that some important cases have been successfully prosecuted, mainly because the lawyers and judges had a higher level of preparation and understanding of the law.

The judge must assess whether or not the person has profited from the crime. But ordering confiscation or otherwise is at his/her discretion. Although the few cases of criminal confiscation make it difficult to discern any clear trend, examination of court verdicts to determine how this discretion is used shows that, due to the inadequacy of the criminal process to confiscate, in about 30% of potential cases for criminal confiscation the Criminal Assets Bureau is asked to intervene, and the cases are consequently dealt with in civil proceedings. Given that the system is value based, value confiscation is the rule. However, value confiscation may turn into property confiscation, as a consequence of a court order, in the case of proactive receivership, that is in the following two instances: (a) when the convicted person fails to pay, and (b) when there is a risk that proceeds from crime will be removed. The confiscation has been implemented to only a moderate extent in the few cases in question, also because the judges have been unfamiliar with confiscation provisions and because the legal provisions lack clarity. There have been only two cases of confiscation from third parties, so that it is hard to detect a pattern.

With regard to the adequacy of human and material resources, until a few years ago only scant personnel and insufficient material resources were devoted to the judicial phase. In the last two years, however, changes have been made at the Department of Public Prosecutions and the situation has now improved—amongst other things because solicitors who previously worked for the Criminal Assets Bureau have moved to the Department of Public Prosecutions. With reference to training, junior and senior trial barristers have very good legal preparation (indeed of the highest quality), whilst judges refused to take any training until five years ago: they now attend seminars but are still unfamiliar with the topic.

The Department of Public Prosecutions is responsible for the management of seized assets, but it has only limited experience and there is no dedicated agency. Receivership is possible before or after the conviction and is mainly intended to prevent the removal of assets, rather than their deterioration, which is not frequent. The receiver is generally appointed rapidly.

The disposal phase is allocated sufficient resources (also because relatively few resources are needed at the end of the procedure), and there is close cooperation among the agencies involved: customs, police, the Department of Public Prosecutions and a receiver, who is usually supervised by the Criminal Assets Bureau. All property is sold and the proceeds are remitted to central funds (government account). Assets like cars, horses or houses are rapidly disposed of whenever a receiver is appointed. Little time is usually required to enforce confiscation orders, although in two cases delays have been caused by individuals trying to postpone confiscation as long as possible. In fact, confiscation proceedings are even slower than are routine criminal proceedings because the defendants and their lawyers seek to take advantage of any procedure that may delay the adoption and enforcement of confiscation (appeals, human rights claims, etc.).

By way of summary, Figure 8 shows the Investigative Phase Law in Action Index, the Judicial Phase Law in Action Index, and the Disposal Phase Law in Action Index of criminal confiscation in Ireland. These Indexes quantify the law in action of the country by expressing, on a scale from 0 to 100, the extent to which the law in the books is enforced in each phase. *The higher the index, the better the law in action of the phase.*

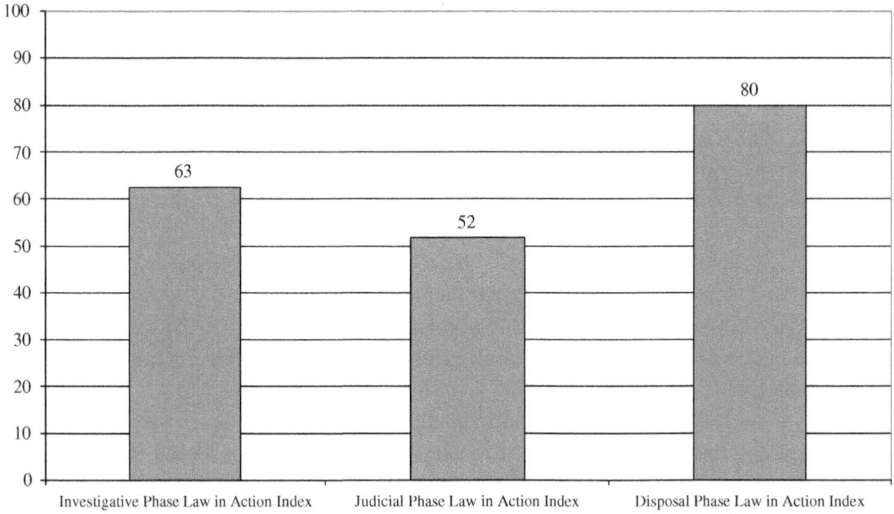

Figure 8. Law in Action Indexes of the Investigative, Judicial and Disposal Phases in Criminal Proceedings in Ireland.
Source: Author's elaboration of the national expert's replies to the questionnaire.

Turning to civil confiscation, many of the remarks already made with reference to criminal confiscation will be repeated here, given that there are several overlaps between the two regimes in the investigative phase. Normally, in fact, criminal investigations are conducted, and only when they have been completed does it become clear whether a criminal proceeding (if there is sufficient evidence to convict) or a civil proceeding will ensue. Consequently, special investigative means are rarely employed, with the sole exception of terrorism and organised crime, where phone tapping and electronic surveillance are occasionally used. In general, straw men emerge in about 25% of the cases under investigation.

The above-mentioned excellent cooperation by financial and non financial institutions with investigations applies to civil confiscation proceedings as well. Contrary to what happens in criminal proceedings, however, informers cooperate very closely with the Criminal Assets Bureau: in this case their attitude is entirely different because they do not have to give full evidence (a lower standard of proof applies in civil proceedings) and their anonymity is ensured (in criminal cases, on the contrary, they must enter the witness protection programme). Furthermore, they receive more favourable treatment (higher benefits in terms of less proceeds confiscated, or lower taxes to be paid on what they have illegally earned); in criminal cases this would be impossible to achieve, and the procedure is highly formalised.

With regard to the Criminal Assets Bureau, worth noting is its excellent multidisciplinary composition (computer technicians, forensic accountants, etc.), and there is an excellent level of cooperation between the Criminal Assets Bureau and the police.

A large amount of human and material resources are available. The Criminal Assets Bureau has unlimited resources, in fact, and this is probably one of the main factors in its success. Resources are invested to enhance the skills of its members (e.g. one million euro have recently been allocated to improving the IT system). Very good training is provided for the officials of the Bureau, who are home-trained by the Bureau Legal Officer. Then, depending on the case, representatives from the institutions involved (e.g. lawyers, bankers, etc.) are called in to provide Criminal Assets Bureau members with the necessary expertise. Hence the training is ongoing in nature, and in the first two years is supplemented with on-the-job training. Moreover, visits by foreign investigative agencies (e.g. US Marshall Service and British Serious Fraud Office) are arranged, so that the principle applied is that expertise is used wherever it can be found.

During the judicial phase of civil proceedings, although adoption of the measure is discretionary, it is generally applied if it is an appropriate remedy. There are essentially two cases in which the measure is not applied (a) when an informant is involved as a defendant (so that confiscation may not be applied in order to obtain the informant's cooperation); and (b) when the work is passed on to another agency (e.g. there is enough evidence to get a criminal confiscation). No problems at all arise in implementing civil confiscation; the success rate to date has been 100%. Receivership is exercised by the Bureau Legal Officer, who has an excellent preparation. All goods have always been sold, and rapidly (e.g. some time ago three houses were sold in six months in very competitive conditions). Sales are generally by auction, and very good prices are obtained.

As said, human as well as material resources are excellent, both within the Criminal Assets Bureau, whose officials—exceptionally well trained—request adoption of the measure in civil proceedings, and within the judicial authority that decides on civil confiscation cases. With reference to the training of judges, after enactment of the Proceeds of Crime Act and the setting up of the Criminal Assets Bureau, the Bureau Legal Officer requested the High Court to appoint a judge to deal exclusively with civil confiscation proceedings for at least a minimum period of time (generally two years), assisted by a special registrar and a special courtroom. This was in order to achieve consistency in rulings on civil confiscation. A stenographer has been employed since enactment of the Act to record the trials, the purpose being to accumulate materials useful both as consistent jurisprudence and as significant assistance for newcomer judges. This amounts to the training for judges in this field and they are supported by the Criminal Assets Bureau.

Worth mentioning is that some cases have dragged on a long time, and every available means has been exploited by lawyers to avoid confiscation (e.g. no lawyer available; appeals; sick defendant; etc.). Defendant's lawyers see delay as some sort of victory.

Sale by auction is foreseen for all kinds of assets and is completed in a timely and efficient manner. The offices involved in the disposal phase are the Criminal Assets Bureau, auctioneers (generally very competent) and the receiver (normally the Bureau Legal Officer). Cooperation among the actors mentioned is very satisfactory.

By way of summary, and in particular of the very good level of enforcement of civil confiscation provisions in all phases remarked on by the national expert who responded the questionnaire, Figure 9 shows the Investigative Phase Law in Action Index, the Judicial Phase Law in Action Index, and the Disposal Phase Law in Action Index of civil confiscation in Ireland. These Indexes quantify the law in action of the country by expressing, on a scale from 0 to 100, the extent to which the law in the books is enforced in each phase. *The higher the index, the better the law in action of the phase.*

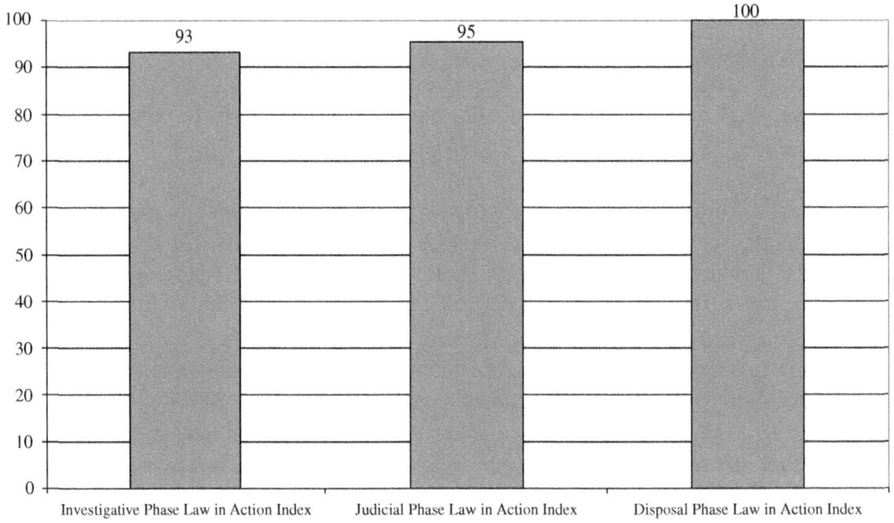

Figure 9. Law in Action Indexes of the Investigative, Judicial and Disposal Phases in Civil Proceedings in Ireland.
Source: Author's elaboration of the national expert's replies to the questionnaire.

4.9 ITALY

A) Law in the Books

In Italy, investigations to locate the proceeds from crime are undertaken by different units: (1) the *Direzione Investigativa Antimafia* (DIA); (2) the *Raggruppamento Operativo Speciale* (ROS) set up within the *Carabinieri*; (3) the *Comando Investigazioni Economico Finanziarie* (CIEF) recently established within the *Guardia di Finanza*: within the CIEF, financial inquiries are conducted mainly by the *Nucleo Speciale Polizia*

Valutaria and by the SCICO; (4) the *Servizio centrale operativo* (SCO) of the *Polizia di Stato*. Investigations may concern not only suspected criminals but also any persons suspected of acting as straw men for them.

As regards confiscation provisions in particular, Italy has developed a complex confiscation system in order to attack the financial bases of organised crime. Since the 1980s, new confiscation measures specifically related to criminal organisations have been added to the traditional form of confiscation granted under article 240 of the Penal Code.

Article 240 of the Italian Criminal Code provides, at paragraph 1, amongst other things, for the optional confiscation of the profit obtained from a crime; conviction is a prerequisite for execution of the measure. Paragraph 2, no. 1, of the article states that the price obtained by the offender for commission of the crime is mandatorily confiscated if a conviction has been passed. In both cases, confiscation cannot take place if the assets belong to persons other than the defendant.

In 1982, law no. 646 supplemented the Criminal Code with article 416-*bis*, which criminalises participation in a Mafia-type organisation. In the case of conviction for this offence, the price, the proceeds of the crime or the use thereof are mandatorily confiscated (article 416-*bis*, paragraph 7).

Another special criminal confiscation measure was introduced in 1994 by law no. 504, which added article 12-*sexies* to law no. 356/1992. This special form of confiscation applies to persons convicted for offences typically related to the activity of criminal groups. In the case of conviction, assets at the disposal of the convicted person and out of proportion to his/her income or to his/her economic activity are confiscated. It is worth noting that the measure applies if the defendant has not been able to prove the licit origin of his/her property.

For all the various kinds of confiscation enacted within criminal proceedings, seizure is ordered *ex* article 321, paragraph 2, of the Code of Criminal Procedure, according to which "the judge can also provide for the seizure of the items subject to confiscation".

The above-mentioned law no. 646 of 1982 significantly amended statute no. 575 of 1965. Article 2 of law no. 575 extended the *misure di prevenzione personale* (literally preventive personal measures) concerning special surveillance for public security and obligatory residence to persons suspected of participating in a criminal organisation and deemed socially dangerous. In addition to these personal measures, law no. 575, as amended in 1982, allows for the application of financial measures, that is civil confiscation as a preventive measure (the so called *confisca di prevenzione*), to the above-mentioned category of dangerous persons. To be noted is that personal and financial preventive measures (*ante* or *praeter delictum*) are intended to prevent certain individuals considered to be socially dangerous from committing offences. The commission of previous offences is not a consideration when a decision is rendered and a preventive measure is issued. However, it is worth noting that a confiscation order normally follows the adoption of a preventive personal measure. According to article 2-*bis* of law no. 575/1965, the sources of income of those suspected of being criminals are to be assessed in terms of their lifestyle, financial means, property and economic activities. The provision allows investigation not only of suspected criminals but also of their spouses, children and cohabitees during the previous five years. Furthermore, any natural or legal persons, companies, societies or associations at the direct or indirect disposal of the criminal are subject to such financial investigations. Seizure and confiscation are permitted by article 2-*ter* of the law. During the proceeding for application of a personal measure, the court may order seizure of the defendant's assets. Two conditions are required for seizure. The first is that the assets must be directly or indirectly at the disposal of the presumed criminal. The second condition is integrated with either (1) the disparity between the defendant's wealth and his/her income or level of economic activity, or (2) the existence of sufficient evidence that the assets are the proceeds of crime or the use thereof. Together with adoption of the personal measure, the court orders confiscation of seized assets whose lawful origin has not yet been demonstrated by the defendant.

With reference to the disposal phase, assets subject to confiscation *ex* articles 240 and 416-*bis* are sold or destroyed. The regulations on the disposal of confiscated assets *ex* article 12-*sexies* of law no. 356/1992 and in civil proceedings are laid down by law no. 109/1996. This law, which amended law no. 575/1965, allows the use of confiscated assets for social purposes. Under a complex procedure, real property passes: (1) to the State, which uses it for judicial, public order or civil protection purposes, or (2) to the local authority, which uses it for institutional or social purposes. Business assets pass to the State and are sold, liquidated or rented. Personal property and shares are sold and the money obtained from the sale is placed, together with money from the sale, rent or liquidation of business assets, in a special Fund used to finance social programmes (article 2-*undecies*, paragraph 1, and article 2-*duodecies*, paragraphs 1 to 3).

B) Law in Action

When discussing the practice of confiscation in Italy, it is obviously necessary to differentiate between criminal confiscation and civil confiscation.

Starting with criminal confiscation, and looking at the investigative phase, first to be pointed out is that special investigative means (undercover operations, for instance) are not frequently employed. Nor are potential straw men systematically investigated. One may therefore conclude that financial investigations are not methodically conducted in Italy. Furthermore, when they are carried out, it is often too late, that is after charges have been brought, and this may compromise their fruitful development. With the exception of the specialised investigative units mentioned above, exploitation of the diverse skills and competencies needed to locate the proceeds from crime is not satisfactory and mainly takes the form of cooperation among the public prosecutor, the judicial police, and various consultants and financial analysts. Also requiring improvement is the level of inter-agency cooperation.

Cooperation by financial and non financial institutions is generally poor. Regarding the former, whose cooperation is regulated by law no. 197 of 1991, although compliance is improving, it is still not satisfactory. Even less satisfactory is collaboration by other financial institutions. Non financial institutions are entirely uncooperative, so that the relative regulation, that is decree no. 12 of 1999, remains merely 'on the books'. The contribution by informers to identification of ill-gotten gains is in most cases limited, because they are viewed with suspicion, and also because informers do not always have detailed knowledge of the criminal organisation's wealth.

Inadequate material and human resources are allocated to the investigative phase. The training given to financial investigators is rather poor: there is no *ad hoc* preparation, and courses are run by the *Guardia di Finanza* and by the most experienced public prosecutors. Although the situation is improving, this inadequate training provision is a major obstacle against identification of the proceeds from crime. Money laundering schemes designed to reduce the risk of confiscation are constantly evolving, and consequently grow increasingly complex and difficult to uncover. Criminal organisations have learnt to diversify the allocation of their money, which is now invested not only in real property but also in more volatile assets like shares. Investigators are instead better able to locate real property, that is the more visible part of criminal wealth, because financial inquiries are conducted indiscriminately with no previous 'study' of the suspected criminal, his/her business relationships and movements (Turone 1994, 49; Nanula 1999, 32).

As regards the judicial phase, one may conclude that the various confiscation measures provided by the Italian legal system have to date had only modest impact on the illicit gains of criminal organisations. Articles 416-*bis* and 12-*sexies* were introduced to overcome the limited impact of article 240 of the Penal Code, regarded as entirely inadequate in any effective fight against organised crime. Although practice shows that the measure, although discretional, is always applied, the article requires the existence of a direct link between the goods to be confiscated and the offence. As a consequence, laundered assets and proceeds cannot be confiscated under the provision. Moreover, the article closely protects the rights of third parties, so that property in the possession of 'dummies' cannot be attacked. Lastly, the optional regime provided by article 240 for the confiscation of the proceeds from crime seems utterly unreasonable. Nevertheless, it does not seem that confiscation provisions tougher than article 240 are working much better.

Confiscation *ex* article 416-*bis* is hampered by the enormous difficulties faced by public prosecutors in obtaining convictions for the Mafia-type association offence (Commissione Parlamentare Antimafia 2002, 7). Furthermore, confiscation under this article has a much more limited area of application than originally foreseen (Fiandaca 1983, 268). Under the prevailing interpretation, it applies only to the means used to commit a Mafia-type association offence and to the price, products and proceeds from such an offence. It does not apply to the price, products and proceeds acquired by the criminal association from the crimes committed and from management of economic activities, although these profits are generally much higher than those deriving from Mafia-type association crimes (Ibidem). With reference to the article 12-*sexies*, in order to apply the measure it is necessary to prove the disproportion between the defendant's entire wealth and his/her legitimate sources of income. In practice, this proof is very difficult to provide, mainly because a burdensome—and sometimes unrealistic—workload is placed on law enforcement agencies. The situation is exacerbated by the not very abundant resources—human and material—allocated to the judicial phase.

The level of training of public prosecutors and judges is good, also as a result of their close cooperation with the *Procure Distrettuali Antimafia* in organised crime cases.

The management of seized assets encounters problems with firms, as well as with personal property (in particular cars). With reference to the former, their management is a particularly complex and delicate undertaking: on the one hand, active management is required to ensure that the firm remains competitive; on the other, credit channels are closed after seizure, and in any case administrators prefer to be cautious because they are accountable for the firm's management. This has negative consequences, the worst being closure of the firm. Regarding cars—assets which are particularly perishable by their nature—they are literally abandoned in depots which charge high tariffs. Thus, although the State is paying high costs for their conservation, these assets greatly decrease in value—also as a result of the low accountability of the administrators and their scant competence (the job is unattractive and most experienced personnel avoid it).

The disposal phase is excessively slow, also in consideration of the inadequate resources allocated to the enforcement of confiscation orders. This results in further depreciation in the value of confiscated assets.

By way of summary, and in particular of the many problems highlighted by the national expert who completed the questionnaire, Figure 10 shows the Investigative Phase Law in Action Index, the Judicial Phase Law in Action Index, and the Disposal Phase Law in Action Index for criminal confiscation in Italy. These Indexes quantify the law in action of the country by expressing, on a scale from 0 to 100, the extent to which the law in the books is enforced in each phase. *The higher the index, the better the law in action of the phase.*

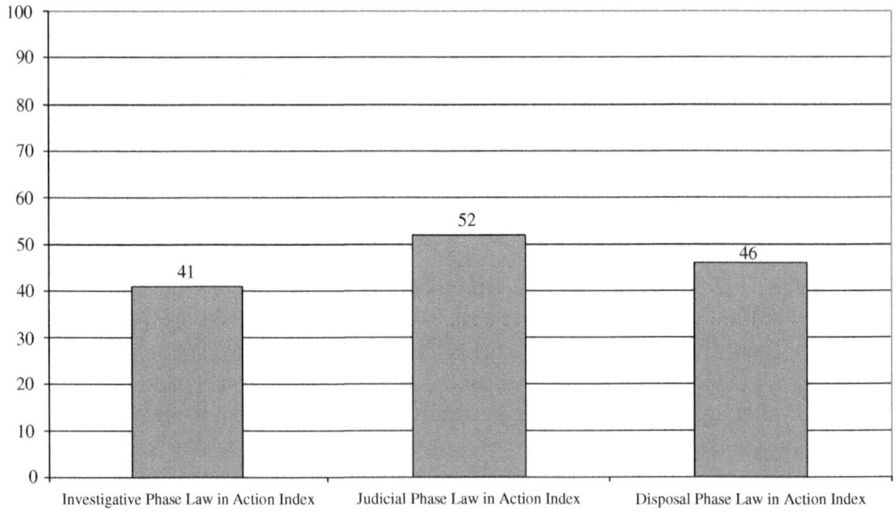

Figure 10. Law in Action Indexes of the Investigative, Judicial and Disposal Phases in Criminal Proceedings in Italy.
Source: Author's elaboration of the national expert's replies to the questionnaire.

As regards civil confiscation, most of the comments already made on criminal investigations again apply, since there is usually an overlap between the two procedures in the investigative phase—with the consequence that only after investigations have been concluded does it become clear whether criminal or civil confiscation will be requested. The only difference exhibited by investigations in civil confiscation cases is their more frequent employment of special investigative means, owing to the larger number of institutions involved—in particular, the *Direzione Investigativa Antimafia*, which encourages the use of the investigative means mentioned. Financial investigations are conducted systematically, with location of the proceeds from crime given much more importance than in criminal cases. However, since the main concern is adoption of a preventive personal measure, the use of financial inquiries is generally delayed.

Turning to the judicial phase, it seems that the impact of civil confiscation has to date been rather modest, for several reasons. The first is the symbolic and overemphatic use of seizure, which is often adopted without careful consideration of whether the necessary prerequisites exist (Commissione Parlamentare Antimafia 1999, 16; Lomonte 1997, 238–239). As a consequence, seizure is often not converted into confiscation. Another reason for the scant effectiveness of this potentially very aggressive measure is the lengthiness of the procedure. The average amount of time elapsing between seizure and confiscation has been estimated at 1413 days (Presidenza del Consiglio dei Ministri, Ufficio del Commissario straordinario del Governo per la gestione e la destinazione dei beni confiscati alle organizzazioni criminali 2000, 81–84). In the meantime, assets often decrease in value, which is also due to the generally low competence of the administrators managing the seizures. Hence, the same problems regarding the management of seized assets mentioned when discussing criminal confiscation arise in civil confiscation. The only difference is that, since the judicial phase in civil proceedings normally lasts less than in criminal cases, the seized assets may deteriorate to a slightly lesser extent.

When straw men have been employed by the defendant, it is extremely difficult for the public prosecutors to prove that the goods are actually at their disposal.[61] Reversal of the burden of proof is not particularly effective: practice shows, in fact, that criminals are becoming extremely adept at justifying their possession of any kind of asset, and they rarely make use of assets whose (fictitious) licit origins cannot be proven.[62] Finally, experience shows that criminal organisations frequently avoid confiscation by killing any of their members whose assets (which, in reality, belong to the organisation) are about to be confiscated (Commissione Parlamentare Antimafia 1997, 11–12); the death of the defendant makes it impossible to continue the proceedings and to confiscate assets from the defendant's heirs.

The human and material resources allocated to the judicial phase are inadequate. The level of specialisation in financial matters of the few magistrates employed within the court sections dealing with civil confiscation cases (*sezioni di prevenzione*) is not

[61] On this point, see also Maugeri (1996, 886) and Fallone (1995, 631).
[62] On this point, see also Stea (1998, 313–314).

particularly high: in fact, they do not receive *ad hoc* training, but only a general preparation from courses organised by the CSM (*Consiglio Superiore della Magistratura*).

The main problem with the disposal of confiscated assets system introduced by law no. 109 of 1996 is the excessive lengthiness of the procedure, the great complexity of which prolongs the disposal phase for far too long. On average, 2023 days elapse between the confiscation and disposal orders (Presidenza del Consiglio dei Ministri, Ufficio del Commissario straordinario del Governo per la gestione e la destinazione dei beni confiscati alle organizzazioni criminali 2000, 84). Moreover, the administrators are sometimes incompetent in the management of the assets, and as a result their value decreases.

By way of summary, and in particular of the many problems highlighted by the national expert who completed the questionnaire, Figure 11 shows the Investigative Phase Law in Action Index, the Judicial Phase Law in Action Index, and the Disposal Phase Law in Action Index for civil confiscation in Italy. These Indexes quantify the law in action of the country by expressing, on a scale from 0 to 100, the extent to which the law in the books is enforced in each phase. *The higher the index, the better the law in action of the phase.*

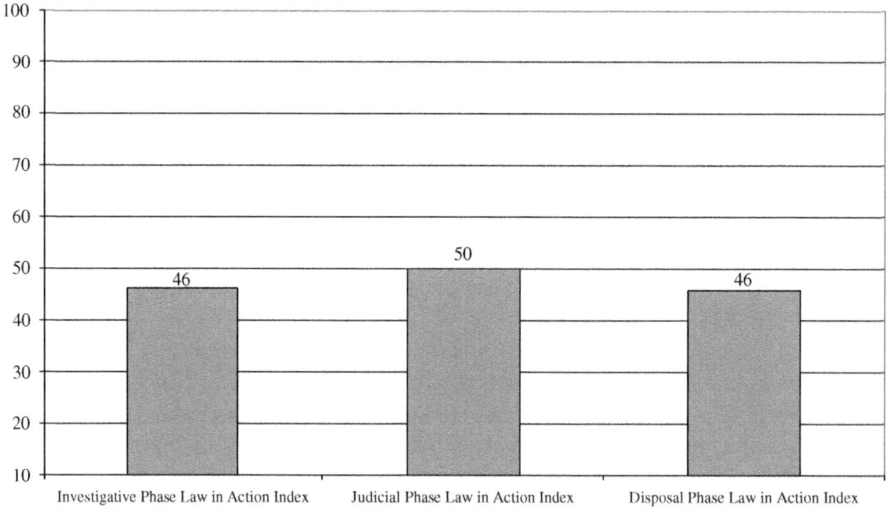

Figure 11. Law in Action Indexes of the Investigative, Judicial and Disposal Phases in Civil Proceedings in Italy.
Source: Author's elaboration of the national expert's replies to the questionnaire.

4.10 LUXEMBOURG

A) Law in the Books

In Luxembourg, financial investigations are conducted as part of the general investigation into the offence(s) and the perpetrator(s) by the following specialised units set up within the *Service de Police Judiciaire*: the *Section Criminalité Organisée*, the *Section Anti-blanchiment* and the three sections of the Economic and Financial Crime Division. Special means of investigations can be used only in exceptional circumstances, that is in cases concerning offences defined as felonies (i.e. conduct punishable with imprisonment for a period of time longer than five years) or misdemeanours (conduct punishable with imprisonment for a period of time up to five years), when other means of investigations are not profitable. This the judge must expressly recognise in his/her order. When there is evidence that certain third parties may be involved as straw men, the investigative magistrate and police officers are empowered to investigate them.

Regarding confiscation, the law enacted on 13 June 1994 revised the existing legislation by introducing special confiscation (*confiscation spéciale*), which according to article 31 of the Criminal Code applies, amongst other things, to the proceeds obtained from the criminal act and their substitute assets. If these goods are no longer available, the judge orders the payment of a sum of money equal to their value (*amende subsidiaire*).

Ex article 32, special confiscation is mandatory for felony; it is optional for misdemeanour. When minor offences (*contraventions*) have been committed, the measure can only be applied in the cases specified by law.

The seizure of goods which may then be confiscated (*tout ce qui est susceptible de confiscation*) is provided by article 31 of the Code of Criminal Procedure.

Special provisions on the confiscation of assets in drug cases are contained in the legislation on narcotics (law of 19 February 1973), as modified by the statute enacted on 17 March 1992 and more recently by the law of 11 August 1998. According to article 8-2 of this legislation, in addition to confiscation *ex* article 31 of the Penal Code, in drug cases also subject to confiscation are (1) the real and personal property of the convicted person acquired by means of the proceeds from crime or whose value is equal to the proceeds from crime and (2) the earnings originating from the mentioned assets. It is worth noting that, according to article 18 of the law of 19 February 1973, confiscation in relation to drug cases may be ordered even without conviction. Furthermore, the measure applies to narcotic substances owned not only by the defendant but also by non authorised third parties. The same applies to goods acquired with the ill-gotten gains or to goods of corresponding value.

In money laundering cases, article 32-1 of the Penal Code applies. The provision, introduced by article 10 of the law of 14 June 2001, states that in such cases the *confiscation spéciale* covers the object, product, profit of the crime and the assets into which they were converted. Value confiscation is also included in the above-mentioned provision.

As regards the management of seized assets, there exists only one legal provision, applicable to traffic offences, which allows the public prosecutor to request the sale of the seized vehicle, if the owner has not asked for its restitution within three months. The Ministry of Justice intends to extend this possibility to all penal cases and all kinds of seized assets.

Confiscated assets go to the State: specifically, they pass to a subdivision of the Ministry of Finance, that is the State Property Office, which receives a copy of the judicial order. In the case of real estate, a further division of the same department (*Administration de l'enregistrement—Bureau des hypothèques*, responsible for the transfer of real property) is involved in the procedure and transcribes the sale of the property. Unless the destruction of confiscated assets or their use for social purposes has been ordered, they are rapidly sold and the money obtained is paid into the public exchequer. The law of 17 March 1992 provides for the special disposal of proceeds from drug offences. According to article 5 of this law, such profits are placed in a special Fund (*Fonds de lutte contre le trafic des stupéfiants*) and used to support and implement anti-drug measures.

Finally to be mentioned is a bill of law, currently under discussion by the Council of State, which scrutinises all bills before they are presented to Parliament. This bill will (1) make value confiscation applicable in all penal cases, and (2) allow *exequatur* of foreign confiscation decisions as a general legal assistance measure. At present these two possibilities concern only drug and money laundering cases.

B) Law in Action

Moving to the law in action, and commencing with the investigative phase, financial investigations are not employed systematically. If it is clear from preliminary inquiries that large sums of money have been earned, financial investigations are conducted from an early stage. But their use essentially depends on the amount of money involved (and there are relatively few cases of large-scale organised crime in Luxembourg). It more often happens that dirty money from foreign organised criminal groups is present in the country, and in these cases what really matters is the assistance provided to foreign authorities, as well as provisions to give effect to their final judgements on confiscation. Special investigative means are infrequently used, owing to the narrow formulation of legal provisions. The latter, as seen, state that the surveillance of communications can be made only in exceptional circumstances. When there is evidence that certain third parties are involved as straw men (e.g. money has been transferred to them by the defendant), they are investigated.

The *Service de Police Judiciaire* has a satisfactory multidisciplinary composition: officers with degrees in auditing, accounting, financial analysis and law are employed, and engineers and technicians assist them. The tax authorities have to date cooperated with the prosecution service and the police, providing them with information on taxes, albeit in only few cases. There is in fact a long tradition in Luxembourg that the police should deal with criminal cases, while the tax authorities have administrative powers to investigate tax cases. The two aspects are therefore clearly distinguished and kept separate.

With regard to training issues, investigators attend training seminars and lessons held by senior colleagues. There is no specific training in financial investigations, although investigators employed in specialised sections receive further training, which also includes visits to foreign police schools. With reference to the human and material resources devoted to financial investigations, the main problem is that it is impossible to investigate all cases satisfactorily. There is insufficient personnel at the policing and judicial levels for all investigations to be carried out. This shortage of investigators causes delays in investigation and prosecution and places too heavy a workload on too few people. This is a widely recognised problem, which the Ministry of Justice (operational aspects) and the Ministry of Interior (material aspects, e.g. equipment, buildings, personnel) are endeavouring to solve. For example, the Ministry of Justice enacted in June 2001 a five-year plan to increase the number of judges and prosecutors, and on the police side, the number of judicial police officers. It is planned to increase the number of personnel devoted to investigations over the next few years, for example from 140 to 200, and to improve their training. Some progress has been made, but of course there are budgetary considerations to be taken into account.

With regard to the amount of cooperation that investigators receive from external institutions/people, financial and non financial institutions cooperate to a satisfactory extent. This is a sort of 'forced cooperation', since these entities are obliged by the anti-money laundering law to cooperate fully when legally requested to do so, and to report suspicious transactions to prosecutors. They also have an obligation of professional secrecy, however. In cases other than money laundering, a warrant for search and seizure is issued by the investigating judge. It may happen that a perpetrator or a witness provides investigators with useful information. They generally do so, at least in case of co-perpetrators, in order to obtain certain benefits. However, the level of such cooperation is low, and it is hampered by the perpetrator/witness's fear of reprisals.

The confiscation system in the judicial phase is, as already seen, conviction based. The very few exceptions to this rule (e.g. article 18 of Drug Legislation and money laundering cases, where it is possible to confiscate even in the case of the defendant's death and prescription) have never been applied in practice. Furthermore, it is necessary to prove the direct crime/proceeds link. The only exceptions are drug legislation and anti money laundering legislation, where value confiscation applies; however, in these cases, too, it is necessary to obtain a conviction and to prove the perpetrator's gain. When the measure is discretionary (i.e. for misdemeanours), it is generally applied. However, there are some cases in which the measure is not pronounced because it would be disproportionate (in a recent case of illicit cigarette sales, e.g., the necessary licence was not obtained. The prosecutor asked for the the money gained from the illicit activity to be confiscated, but the judge refused because the punishment would have been excessive). Value confiscation is infrequently used, because only few cases of major importance come before the courts. In any event, no special problems arise in its application. Nor do they arise in application of the measure towards third parties. As regards the human and material resources devoted to the phase, however, difficulties do occur, but less so than in the investigative phase. This also depends on the fact that investigators must do most of the work, under the supervision of the investigating magistrates. Some progress has been achieved since the above-mentioned five-year plan was launched in June 2001 by the Ministry of Justice to increase the number of judges and public prosecutors. Nor is the training of public prosecutors and judges fully satisfactory. No specific training is provided, only general instruction consisting of seminars and visits to foreign institutions.

With reference to the management of seized assets, the almost complete lack of regulation entails that no active administration takes place. In most cases, seized assets consist of money held in bank accounts seized and then managed by the bank so that interest is generated under the supervision of the investigating magistrate or the Treasury of the State.

The disposal phase is usually completed rapidly. Cash amounts and bank accounts balances are immediately transferred to the State Treasury, which also receives the money realised from the sale of real and personal property (cars, jewellery, etc.), although to date there have been no cases in which real estate has been disposed of (just one case of seizure of a house). No problems arise with sales. The only risk is the price obtained by public auction, which may be very high if there are numerous bidders or, on the contrary, very low. Use for social purposes is theoretically possible, but there have been very few cases to date (e.g. very sophisticated walkie-talkies were given to the police in one case; weapons are sometimes put in the police force collection and the technical training of junior officers). No problems of resources arise at this stage, also because there are relatively few cases. Also because of the short time taken to dispose of assets, there is no active management of them; the goods are already available and the phase is simply seen as a bureaucratic procedure.

By way of summary, and in particular of the problems in the investigative and judicial phases highlighted by the national expert who completed the questionnaire, Figure 12 shows the Investigative Phase Law in Action Index, the Judicial Phase Law in Action Index, and the Disposal Phase Law in Action Index for Luxembourg. These Indexes quantify the law in action of the country by expressing, on a scale from 0 to 100, the extent to which the law in the books is enforced in each phase. *The higher the index, the better the law in action of the phase.*

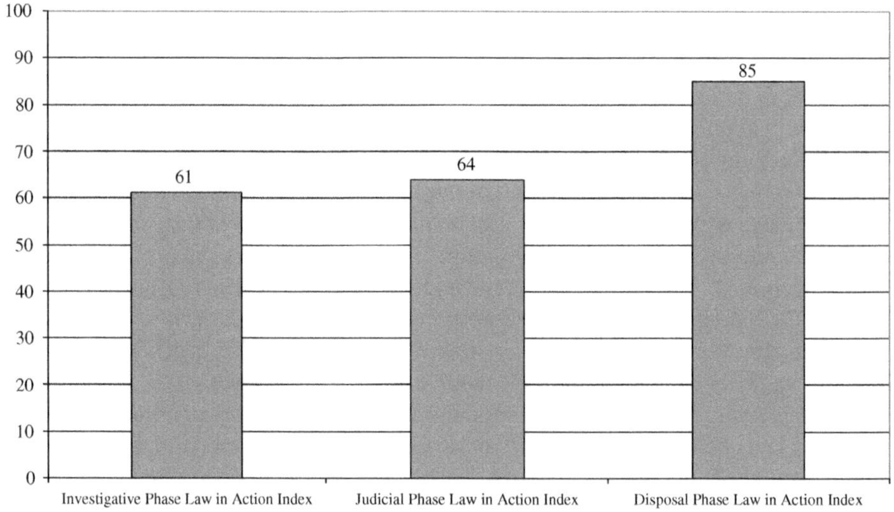

Figure 12. Law in Action Indexes of the Investigative, Judicial and Disposal Phases in Luxembourg.
Source: Author's elaboration of the national expert's replies to the questionnaire.

4.11 THE NETHERLANDS

A) Law in the Books

Deprivation of the proceeds from crime has been possible in the Netherlands since 1983, but "[. . .] in such a limited way that this instrument was hardly used" (Lodder 2001, 1).[63] The Dutch system was revised by the statute of 10 December 1992, which came into effect on 1 March 1993. This statute significantly amended the existing regime aimed at depriving criminals of their illicit profits.[64] Not only confiscation provisions but also criminal investigations and seizure rules were renewed in order to create the system described below, which was further strengthened by the law of 1 September 2003.

The main provision regarding confiscation is article 36e of the Criminal Code. After the amendment of 1993, this article allows, at paragraph 1, for the optional issue of an order to pay a sum of money. For the purpose of removing the proceeds of crime from a person convicted of a serious offence, four different categories of illicit gains can be attacked, viz.

1) the profits directly arising from the offence for which the conviction was enacted;
2) the profits from similar offences for which a fifth category fine (i.e. a fine of more than NLG 100,000-around 45,000 euro) may be imposed if sufficient evidence exists that the offender is guilty;
3) the profits from offences for which a fifth category fine may be applied if sufficient evidence exists that they were committed by the offender;
4) the profits in any way obtained from other criminal offences; conditions for their confiscation are the conviction of the person for an offence for which a fifth category fine may be imposed and a criminal financial investigation.[65]

Since article 36e requires 'sufficient evidence', the standard of proof prescribed by the law for the confiscation of illicit profits is slightly lower than the criminal standard.

To be noted is that the confiscation proceedings run separately from the proceedings of the main case; during the latter, the public prosecutor may in fact ask the court for the adoption of confiscation in a separate decision (article 511b of the Code of Criminal Procedure). The reason for this distinct procedure is "[. . .] to prevent the trial of the main case being slowed down by investigations that normally take up considerable

[63] Among the reasons for the scarce use of confiscation before 1993 were the following: the need to prove a direct link between assets to be confiscated and a judicially ascertained crime; the scant time that could be devoted to financial investigations, because confiscation proceedings had to take place during the session of the criminal case itself; the impossibility of making precautionary seizure of the defendant's assets, which resulted in the unsatisfactory execution of the subsequent confiscation; the short duration of the alternative imprisonment term (six months) imposed in case of non-payment.

[64] For information on the confiscation regime in force in the Netherlands before 1993, see Groos (1993).

[65] In this case, "[. . .] the link between the act for which the suspect stood trial and the proceeds to be confiscated has been relinquished further". See Engee, van Schendel & van der Zee (2000, 49). More detailed analysis of the four categories of criminal proceeds subject to confiscation can be found in the same report.

time" (Daams & van der Reyt 1997, 309). The amount to be confiscated is assessed by the judge, who also takes the costs and savings into consideration.

Article 511c of the Code of Criminal Procedure has given public prosecutors new powers with regard to confiscation. Under this provision, the public prosecutor may agree in writing with the defendant as to payment of a sum of money equal to the value of the criminal assets. As a consequence of this agreement, the defendant is released from the confiscation claim; legal responsibility for prosecution remains.

A new type of inquiry, the criminal financial investigation, introduced in 1993 and regulated by articles 126 to 126f of the Code of Criminal Procedure, facilitates setting the amount of the proceeds to be confiscated. These investigations may be authorised by the examining judge, on suspicion of a serious offence for which a fifth category fine can be imposed and which might generate relatively high profits. In this case the public prosecutor and the police officials have "[...] broader powers and a longer period of time in which to perform the investigation" (Engee, van Schendel & van der Zee 2000, 47). To be noted is that financial inquiries are undertaken by specialised units—the Financial Support Bureaux (FSBs)—whose sole task is to apply the provisions on confiscation and coordinate the action of the various offices involved in confiscation proceedings. They can make use of a wide range of special investigative means such as electronic surveillance, undercover operations, infiltration, house searches, phone tapping.

Article 94a of the Code of Criminal Procedure provides for the seizure of assets to be confiscated.[66]

Public prosecutors possess a more powerful device in confiscation cases, in that since 1993 they have been able to use a typical civil law instrument: the revocatory action or *actio pauliana*. By means of this power, public prosecutors may act before the civil courts and obtain annulment of the legal acts committed by the defendant in prejudice of the State's right to confiscation.

Under article 117 of the Criminal Procedure Act, seized objects cannot be alienated unless authorisation has been obtained. This authorisation may be given by the Public Prosecutor's Service as regards objects (a) which are not suitable for storage; (b) whose storage costs bear no relation to their value; (c) which can be replaced and the counter value of which can easily be determined. Once the alienation decision has been taken, the person involved will first be given the opportunity to recover the objects against production of a surety. A period of one month is set for that purpose. Failure to pay will result in alienation of the object. With regard to the management of seized and confiscated assets, a major role is played in the Public Prosecution Service by the Criminal Assets Deprivation Bureau (BOOM). This office, which is staffed by various experts (three public prosecutors, two penal judicial advisors, two civil law specialists and four accountants), assists public prosecutors in confiscation cases, also with reference to the above-mentioned management, and backs up the National Execution

[66] For detailed examination of the provisional measure, see Engee, van Schendel & van der Zee (2000, 54).

Bureau.[67] The seizure is signalled automatically to the BOOM and the office will take all the necessary precautions as rapidly as possible; these precautions may be: stalling, the return or sale of the seized goods, and accepting bail so that profits are maximised and costs are minimised.

The law of 1 September 2003 amended the above legal framework, doing so among other things:

- by extending the public prosecutor's authority in respect of urgent searches;
- by replacing the alternative imprisonment imposed beforehand by article 24d of the Criminal Code—which provided for detention not exceeding six years if the convicted person did not comply with the confiscation order—with retrospective committal for non compliance through civil action. This imprisonment can be ordered by the public prosecutor for a maximum term of three years and does not replace the State's claim against the person involved;
- above all, by providing for the precautionary seizure of objects belonging to a person other than the defendant and that can be seized under special conditions, viz.: (a) the object originates directly or indirectly from the crime as a result of which the fine or deprivation measure can be imposed (*origin requirement*), and (b) there is sufficient evidence that the object became the property of the third party for the purpose of obstructing or preventing its recovery (*recovery frustration requirement*), and (c) the third party knew or could reasonably suspect that the object originated from a crime (*knowledge requirement*).

B) Law in Action

Moving to the law in action and dealing first with the investigative phase, financial investigations are systematically employed in organised crime cases, generally at an early stage, and special investigative means such as electronic surveillance, undercover operations, infiltration, house searches and phone tapping are frequently used. A multidisciplinary approach to the search of the proceeds from crime, as well as to gathering evidence in criminal cases, is standard practice. The Financial Support Bureaux are characterised by well-developed multidisciplinarity, given that accountants and tax officers work together with investigators. Furthermore, depending on the competencies needed in each case, agreements are reached in order to enhance either the multidisciplinary composition or the level of cooperation received from other law enforcement agencies. They may take the form of either contracts (in order to recruit private experts) or agreements with specific agencies. In practice, inter-agency cooperation is satisfactory: it involves tax authorities, police, revenue agencies and special units for economic crimes.

[67] Other tasks of the Criminal Assets Deprivation Bureau are collecting and disseminating legal and judicial sources on the deprivation of criminal proceeds and advising the General Prosecutor on policies to be followed in this field.

Whereas the material resources devoted to financial investigations are adequate, the human ones are not so. Too few financial specialists are employed in investigative units and, furthermore, there is still insufficient training provision for financial investigators.[68] Training is particularly important for the application of a confiscation regime like the Dutch one, which mixes civil and criminal rules. At present, the training provided is fragmentary and does not cover all the relevant subjects, although the main topics (such as aspects of civil and financial law, banking law and international law) are taught. Generally, a week of training is given on each subject. The problem is that no assessment is made of the effective level of preparation reached by single individuals after the courses, the only requirement being mere attendance on the course. In order to improve this situation, the entire education programme was overhauled in 2004. An intensive modular training programme has been organised for the first two-year period, and the structure of the programme consists of two/three-week courses followed by on-the-job training, and then again courses, and so on. Mechanisms have been put in place to monitor progress: there are assignments for each module, and a final examination has to be passed.

As regards cooperation by financial and non financial institutions, that by banks reaches a satisfactory level. In the past, the reluctance of banks to cooperate was due to the regulations on banking secrecy, which made them afraid of liability claims by their clients. This obstacle has been removed at the legal level by article 96 of the Code of Criminal Procedure. There is also good cooperation with the Dutch Association of Banks, with which a civil agreement on their cooperation with financial investigations was signed in at the end of the 1990s. This agreement was necessary because, following amendment of confiscation provisions in 1993, banks were alarmed by the heavy workload that they would be required to assume. The problem of client privacy protection arises for the other financial institutions as well. Although there are special laws which oblige them to provide the information required, these institutions are less cooperative than banks. Non financial institutions are not very co-operative as a rule. The cooperation of informants is rather rare occurrence, also because of the fear factor. One rare example concerns a lawyer working for a criminal organisation, who cooperated satisfactorily with investigators.

During the judicial phase it is not usually difficult to confiscate. In fact, given the existence of an extended confiscation regime, it is sufficient to obtain a conviction for any of the further crimes from which it is suspected that the offender has benefited. Although adoption of the measure is discretionary, in organised crime cases it is almost always applied. Seizure is extensively used and proves very useful in obtaining evidence for proceedings both on the criminal wealth and on the main offence. Some problems arise, however. Material resources allocated to this phase are insufficient, and the training of both public prosecutors and judges in this field is poor. However, increased human resources have been made available over the past few years. Most courts now

[68] This finding confirms that of a 1998 report requested by the Ministry of Justice and prepared by its Research and Documentation Centre (WODC), according to which "[. . .] within the training programmes, insufficient attention is being paid to the proceeds-based approach" (Nelen & Sabee 1998).

have specialised chambers for confiscation matters and there are four specialised prosecutors at the BOOM, who assist local public prosecutors in the most serious criminal cases. Most prosecutors and judges are still generalists and not specialised in confiscation matters. There is also constant job rotation, especially for judges, who also show little interest in the matter. There are few opportunities to receive specific training: the country has only one training centre, where courses on proceeds of crime confiscation are held only twice a year, for about eighty people at a time, with personnel from the BOOM usually acting as the teachers. It would seem that the proceeds-based approach finds more support in society than it does in the law enforcement agencies, which are still culturally distant from this strategy and concentrate on putting criminals behind bars. Another unsatisfactory aspect is the ten-case standard, that is the target of ten confiscation requests per year which every public prosecutor must fulfil according to instructions from the Public Prosecution Service. This standard should be abandoned, because it is often used merely to fulfil the quota, being applied to minor cases with no concern for the quality of the cases prosecuted.[69] Finally, implementation of the confiscation regulations has been hampered until recently by the use made by criminals of corporate bodies and straw men to prevent their dispossession of illicit gains. In these cases, "[. . .] due to jurisprudence of the Dutch Supreme Court, the possibilities for dismantling constructions which conceal the ownership of criminal assets turn out to be less promising than expected" (Nelen & Sabee 1998).[70] This obstacle has recently been removed by the law of 1 September 2003, which permits the seizure and confiscation of crime proceeds owned and/or held by a third party in the case of so-called apparent constructions. The preliminary results of practical application of this recent provision are very promising.

As for the management of seized assets, after seizure these are registered in a computerised system and their management passes to the BOOM. At the local level, in fact, there is scarce competence in this area. Seized assets are administered by a single central unit located within the BOOM, namely the CEBES (an acronym for attachment and enforcement restraint system) which manages seized assets nationwide, supported by a computer system. The office is very good at maximising the value/minimising the deterioration of the goods, doing so, for example, by selling them as soon as possible and thereby reducing storage costs (from €600,000 to €250,000 yearly). This at least reduces the risk of assets deterioration, which is particularly high if one considers the long time—six to seven years, and sometimes ten years—usually necessary to complete the entire procedure. This slowness is due mainly to the fact that many defendants use every opportunity to lodge appeals and delay the procedure, also because the law is still relatively recent and its provisions are not particularly amenable to clear interpretation.

[69] On the shortcomings of the 10-case standard see the document entitled *Minister of Justice Introduces Package of Detection and Prosecution Measures Designed to Improve Seizure of Criminal Profits*, 27 October 1998 [http://www.minjust.nl:8080/c_actual/persber/pb0338.htm]. See also the article entitled *WODC Evaluation: Implementation of Seizure Legislation still at Inadequate Stage of Development*, 27 October 1998 [http://www.minjust.nl:8080/c_actual/persber/pb0339.htm].

[70] On this point, see also Financial Action Task Force on Money Laundering (1998, 15).

The disposal phase is very rapid (lasting three months on average), so that assets are sold as soon as is possible. Good (although still not optimal) are the number of human resources at the BOOM and the quality of its material resources (e.g. a good computer system). The Public Property Department of the Ministry of Finance acts as an important partner with BOOM in this phase, and the two offices cooperate to a satisfactory extent. However, BOOM always has freedom to choose the most appropriate instance for storing or selling goods like motorcycles, cars, etc. (e.g. cars are stored at the Public Property Department, but the selection of the most appropriate department depends on the case and on the type of assets).

By way of summary, and in particular of the problems in the investigative and judicial phases highlighted by the national expert who completed the questionnaire, Figure 13 shows the Investigative Phase Law in Action Index, the Judicial Phase Law in Action Index, and the Disposal Phase Law in Action Index for the Netherlands. These Indexes quantify the law in action of the country by expressing, on a scale from 0 to 100, the extent to which the law in the books is enforced in each phase. *The higher the index, the better the law in action of the phase.*

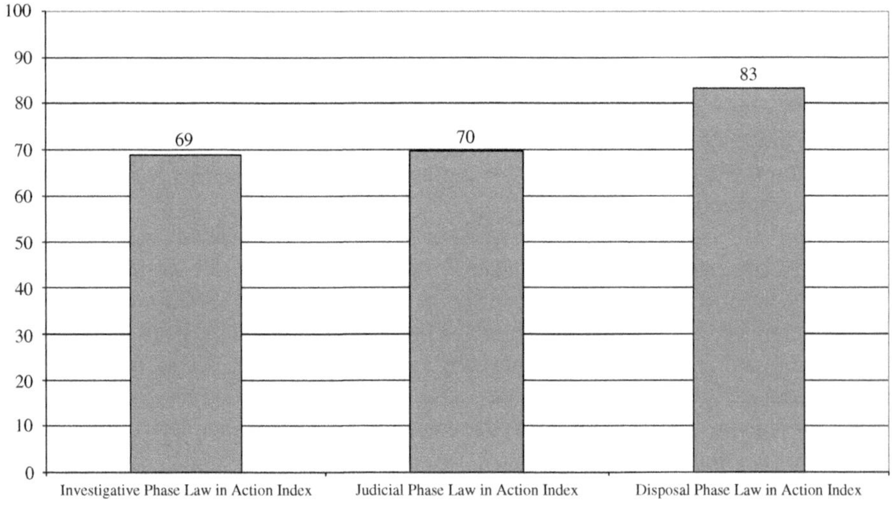

Figure 13. Law in Action Indexes of the Investigative, Judicial and Disposal Phases in the Netherlands.
Source: Author's elaboration of the national expert's replies to the questionnaire.

4.12 PORTUGAL

A) Law in the Books

Financial investigations are mainly undertaken by the Portuguese FIU, the *Brigada de Investigação de Branqueamento de Capitais*, which is a specialist unit set up within the Anti-Drug Trafficking Department of the judicial police.

In the Portuguese legal system, confiscation is regulated by article 111 of the Criminal Code.[71] The confiscation system was substantially amended by decree-law no. 48 of 15 March 1995[72] and, more recently, by law no. 5 of 11 January 2002.

According to article 111, the measure covers the price obtained by the offender for commission of the crime (paragraph 1). The sanction also covers all property, rights and profits directly obtained from commission of the crime and which represent a financial advantage of any type (paragraph 2). Items or rights acquired by means of a transaction or an exchange for assets directly obtained by means of the crime are also to be confiscated (paragraph 3). The measure cannot prejudice the rights of the victims or of *bona fide* third parties.

If the above-mentioned categories of financial advantage cannot be confiscated, the defendant must pay to the State a sum of money equal to their value (paragraph 4). According to article 112, paragraph 2, when ordering value confiscation the judge must take consideration of the defendant's economic circumstances. Consequently, if the measure appears to be too severe, the judge must reduce the amount to be paid.

Law no. 5 of 2002 has introduced a reversed burden of proof in specified circumstances. Under article 7 of this law, in the case of conviction for certain serious offences (i.e. drug trafficking, terrorism, trafficking in weapons, passive corruption and embezzlement, money laundering, criminal association, contraband, etc.), the difference between the value of the patrimony of the convicted person and that which is congruent with his/her lawful income is presumed to have derived from criminal activities. The concept of 'patrimony' includes the assets owned or controlled by the criminal at the time of his/her constitution as defendant. In addition, the notion also covers goods acquired by the defendant in the five years prior to such constitution, or transferred by him/her to third parties at no cost to the latter over the same period of time. These disproportionate assets are consequently subject to confiscation under article 111 of the Criminal Code, unless the offender proves, *ex* article 9, that the proceeds resulted from incomes of a lawful nature, or were owned by the defendant for at least five years previous to the moment of the constitution as defendant.

Specific provisions relating to confiscation are set out in the anti-drug legislation contained in decree-law no. 15/1993, as amended by law no. 45/1996. Article 36 of this decree-law allows for the confiscation of both the price of the drug crime and the assets, rights and gains directly and indirectly obtained from such an offence. The regulation provides for value confiscation as well. Article 37 states that if the assets, rights and gains have been transformed into other goods, the measure regards the latter. According to article 38, also interests and other benefits derived from assets to be confiscated are to be removed. Article 36A protects the rights of *bona fide* third parties.

Seizure of assets to be confiscated is provided by the Code of Criminal Procedure, articles 178 to 186.[73]

[71] For an exhaustive commentary, see Maia Gonçalves (1999, 374–386).

[72] For an examination of the Portuguese confiscation system before the revisions of 1995, see De Figueiredo Dias (1993, 613–639).

[73] For a comment on seizure provisions see Maia Gonçalves (1999, 393–399).

B) Law in Action

Moving from the law in the books to the law in action, and starting with the investigative phase, the use of special investigative means is rare, and mainly relates to drug cases. Also, financial investigations have a limited coverage in practice, since, with the sole exception of trafficking related offences, third parties suspected of acting as straw men for defendants are not systematically subjected to these inquiries. Furthermore, with the exception of the *Brigada de Investigação de Branqueamento de Capitais*, whose composition must compulsorily be multidisciplinary, the idea of combining different competencies and skills in the same office is not usual in other law enforcement agencies. Only in complex cases are investigative teams set up, and their composition varies according to the kind of evidence to be collected. Even in these cases, however, the integration of officials with different skills, such as police and revenue officials, is not satisfactory, owing to their tendency to see their tasks as reciprocally autonomous and separate.

With reference to the level of cooperation from financial and non financial institutions, that by banks and other financial institutions is unsatisfactory; and that by the non financial institutions even more so. Witnesses and informers collaborate to negligible extent in the location of the proceeds from crime.

The overall impression is that the systematic investigation of the financial situations of criminals is not regarded as a priority, so that in general financial investigations are not conducted systematically in organised crime cases, even though the latter usually generate huge profits. This is largely because training on the subject is poor (the time devoted to it is marginal), and scant resources, both human and material, are allocated to financial investigations.

With reference to the judicial phase, the results produced to date by the legislation in terms of finally confiscated assets seem to be poor.[74] There are various reasons for this unsatisfactory performance of the Portuguese confiscation system. First, public prosecutors and judges are not aware of the possibilities offered by the legislation to confiscate the proceeds from crime. Indeed, there are no opportunities to gain specialisation in this field, and no specific training is provided. Also because of this lack of training and this lack of awareness of the possibilities offered by the legislation, it may happen that, insofar as the measure is discretionary, the issue is put aside during the trial even if the standard of proof has been met.

A particularly weak point is the condition of seized assets, which is far from satisfactory. There is no systematic registration of assets at the so called *Conservatorias do Registo Predial*. This gives rise to a chaotic situation where it may be extremely difficult to track seized assets down. Moreover, because it is not possible to sell seized assets before the final confiscation order has been issued, and owing to the low level of competence and responsibility of the people in charge of administering the goods, these (e.g. cars) are often completely abandoned and vandalised. The situation is exacerbated by the excessively long duration of criminal proceedings, which results in the serious depreciation of the value of seized assets.

[74] On this point, see also the Financial Action Task Force on Money Laundering (1999, 21), which pointed out a significant gap between the amount of proceeds seized and the amount of those confiscated.

The disposal phase, like the judicial one, is excessively lengthy, so that assets further depreciate. Furthermore, both the ability of the receivers to administer confiscated assets and the level of cooperation between the offices involved in the procedure are inadequate and require improvement. Confiscated assets are usually sold at public auction, but this does not function properly. The market price is not always the best price so that, at the end of a very long procedure, with the relative high costs sustained by the State, the amount of money gained by the latter from the sale of confiscated assets is in many cases insignificant.

By way of summary, and in particular of the many problems highlighted by the national expert who completed the questionnaire, Figure 14 shows the Investigative Phase Law in Action Index, the Judicial Phase Law in Action Index, and the Disposal Phase Law in Action Index for Portugal. These Indexes quantify the law in action of the country by expressing, on a scale from 0 to 100, the extent to which the law in the books is enforced in each phase. *The higher the index, the better the law in action of the phase.*

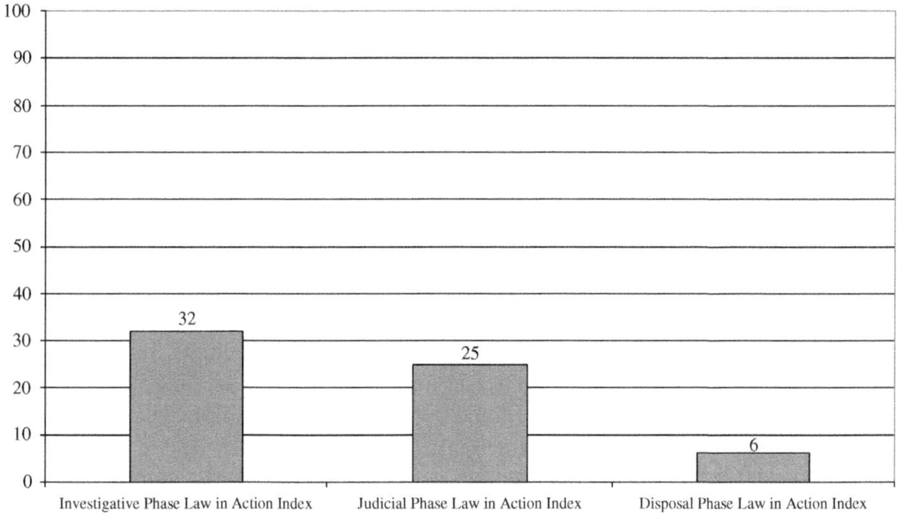

Figure 14. Law in Action Indexes of the Investigative, Judicial and Disposal Phases in Portugal.
Source: Author's elaboration of the national expert's replies to the questionnaire.

4.13 SPAIN

A) Law in the Books

In general, financial investigations can be conducted with regard to all offences. Hence, proceeds from crime are normally searched for in the course of the investigation concerning the main offence. Inquiries to locate the proceeds of crime are conducted by a variety of specialised units: the Spanish FIU, that is the *Servicio Ejecutivo de la Comisión de Prevención del Blanqueo de Capitales e Infracciones Monetarias—Banco de España* (SEPBLAC); the *Brigada de delinquencia económica y financiera* (BDEF); the *Brigada de investigacion delitos monetarios* (BIDM); the *Unidad central estupefacientes*; the *Unidad adscrita a la fiscalia general del Estado* (UAFGE); the *Unidad adscrita a la fiscalia especial para delitos economicos*; the *Unidad central investigacion fiscal y antidrogas* (UCIFA). Special investigative means, such as electronic surveillance, undercover operations and telephone tapping, can be employed.

As regards proceeds from crime confiscation, the measure was only introduced in 1995 (Mapelli Caffarena 1998, 49) with enactment of the new Spanish Criminal Code of 1995. It is regulated by articles 127 and 128, contained in book 1—title VI of the Penal Code, which deals with the *consecuencias accesorias* of a crime.[75] Article 127 states that, in addition to the penalty for a *delicto* or *falta dolosos*[76] confiscation of the profits derived from the offence (*las ganancias*), independently of the changes that they may have undergone, is ordered.

There are two restrictions on application of the measure. The first concerns *bona fide* third parties who have legally acquired the goods, to whom confiscation according to article 127 paragraph 2 cannot apply. The second restriction, set out in article 128, derives from the principle of proportionality. According to the article, if the value of the ill-gotten gains is disproportionate to the seriousness of the offence, confiscation is not ordered or may regard only part of the assets. To be noted is that the prerequisites for application of this provision are that the goods are commercially available and that payment has been made for the civil responsibilities arising from the crime. With reference to the management of seized assets, the only relevant provision is article 129 paragraph 1 letter e), where it is foreseen that, in order to protect the interests of employees and creditors, the judge may order the management of the company.

With reference to drug offences, confiscation is possible under a special provision, article 374 of the Criminal Code, which allows for the confiscation of the proceeds directly or indirectly gained from the offence. According to paragraph 3 of the article, the assets confiscated pass to the State, their subsequent disposal being specified by law no. 17 of 29 May 2003. This statute—which further develops rules originally contained in law no. 36 of 1995 (the so-called *Ley del Fondo*), abrogated by the same text—has established a Fund financed out of the assets confiscated in drug cases, as well as in drug contraband, and to be used, according to article 2 of the law, (1) to finance programmes for drug addiction prevention, assistance to drug addicts and their social and occupational rehabilitation; (2) to promote and improve measures to prevent, investigate, prosecute and repress drug related crimes; (3) to promote international cooperation on such matters.

A provisional measure can be adopted under article 334 of the Code of Criminal Procedure. The management of seized assets, their sale or destruction is then decided in accordance with the rules contained in article 338.

[75] For analysis of the confiscation procedures before 1995 see Manzanares Samaniego (1983, 251–289). For a comment on the confiscation regime that came into force in 1995, see Alcaraz & Lanzas (1999, 108–117), and López Garrido & García Arán (1996, 81–83).

[76] The distinction between *delictos* and *faltas* is contained in article 10 of the Spanish Penal Code.

B) Law in Action

Moving to the law in action, financial investigations, which may be conducted on any offence, are used unsystematically because the priority of law enforcement agencies is investigation of the predicate offence. Another reason for the limited use of financial investigations is that they are extremely time-consuming (investigators must acquire and process a huge mass of information, and, in addition, it takes time to obtain information from financial and non financial institutions because there are numerous procedural steps to follow) and, of course, there are other priorities (e.g. everyday crimes). Since financial investigations can be conducted on any third party in some way related to the defendant (e.g. family, friends, assistants, companies, etc.), when these inquiries are undertaken, they are very frequently directed against third parties, especially family members. Special investigative means are also frequently employed during the search for the proceeds from crime: for example, telephone tapping is used in almost all investigations into the principal crime, which remains the main priority.

The multidisciplinary composition of the SEPBLAC, where officials from the police, the Central Bank and tax authorities cooperate together, is not fully exploited in practice. The main obstacle in the past was the general prohibition on using tax information in a criminal investigation. This obstacle against the use of all available information to trace the proceeds from crime has been only very recently removed by law no. 19 of 4 July 2003. Another aspect that warrants closer attention is the inadequate amount of human and material resources devoted to the location of the proceeds from crime. Generally good, by contrast, is the training provided to investigators, mainly in the form of courses, of which there are usually two or three per year, lasting for one or two weeks. They deal with money laundering and other economic crimes, as well as with financial investigation techniques and how to link the proceeds with the crime from which they originate. In addition, investigators are trained on the job by more experienced colleagues.

With reference to the level of cooperation of financial and non financial institutions, under the anti money laundering regulations all the entities mentioned must furnish information on cash flows to the SEPBLAC. They may also be required to disclose relevant information following an order issued by the investigating magistrate. Banks are very cooperative both with the FIU and the investigating magistrate, and provide them with all information needed. Other financial and non financial institutions have much less contact with the law enforcement agencies than do banks. This implies that they are often unaware of what investigators require; an unfamiliarity which makes their cooperation less satisfactory than that by banks. Only a very minor contribution is made by informants to financial inquiries. Despite the existence since 1994 of a law disciplining the protection of witnesses, few informers are willing to provide investigators with information on the financial position of a suspected criminal, mainly because they are afraid of reprisals.

With regard to the judicial phase, especially in the case of certain serious crimes (e.g. money laundering), and also in consideration of the broad guarantees afforded to defendants and third parties, it is difficult to obtain convictions. This evidently hampers the adoption of confiscation, given that the system is value based. However, when a conviction is passed, no particular problems arise in applying property confiscation, not even with regard to third parties acting as straw men. A weakness is the inadequate human and material resources devoted to the phase. Nor is the level of training given to public prosecutors and judges particularly good. Only public prosecutors working in special prosecution offices (e.g. those for drug and money laundering) receive special training. There is no similar specialisation for judges, who are given only very general preparation.

With reference to the management of seized assets, as already mentioned, the judge may appoint an administrator of seized companies in order to keep them in operation. In practice, however, this provision is rarely applied, and when it is, it does not work well, because the task is a very delicate one and people are consequently loath to assume it. Because those appointed are generally unwilling, they merely effect a 'passive administration'.

The provisions on disposal work relatively well, including those relative to the use of assets for social purposes. Some problems arise with cars (some judges require very good car insurance before they assign confiscated cars to the police). Goods are sold at public auction, sometimes realising good prices, sometimes not. Although a simpler and more rapid procedure for the sale of confiscated goods at auctions was introduced in January 2001, the system does not work properly in that confiscated assets are often sold at too low prices. It may also happen that the criminals are able to buy them back.

By way of summary, Figure 15 shows the Investigative Phase Law in Action Index, the Judicial Phase Law in Action Index, and the Disposal Phase Law in Action Index for Spain. These Indexes quantify the law in action of the country by expressing, on a scale from 0 to 100, the extent to which the law in the books is enforced in each phase. *The higher the index, the better the law in action of the phase.*

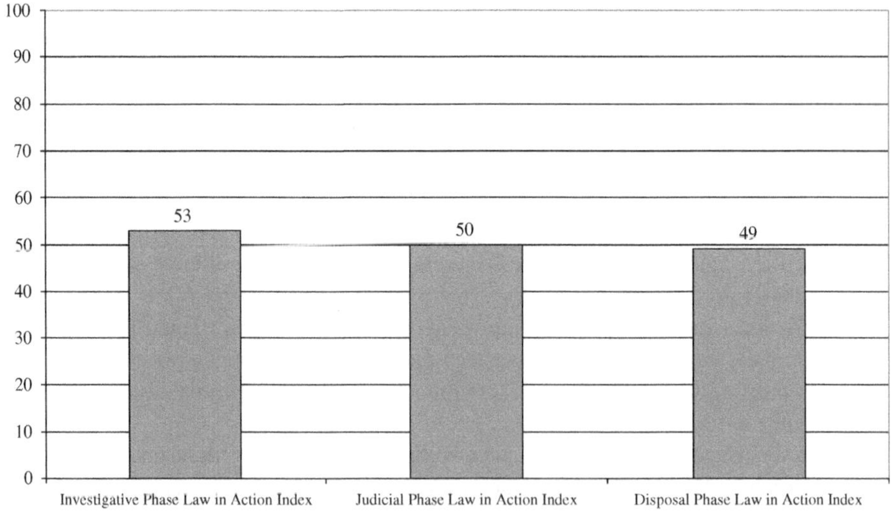

Figure 15. Law in Action Indexes of the Investigative, Judicial and Disposal Phases in Spain. Source: Author's elaboration of the national expert's replies to the questionnaire.

4.14 SWEDEN

A) Law in the Books

In Sweden, investigations on the proceeds from crime are conducted by ordinary police forces while they investigate the main offence. In the case of most serious crimes, investigations are carried out by the Economic Crime Bureau, which is a prosecutorial bureau set up on 1 January 1998. Special investigative means such as camera surveillance and phone tapping are allowed when very grave crimes are being investigated (i.e. aggravating crimes punishable with at least two years of inprisonment).

As regards confiscation, the country still has a rather traditional system, which was revised in the 1980s with some minor amendments made in the 1990s. The relevant provisions are contained in chapter 36 of the Criminal Code.

According to section 1 of the chapter,[77] the proceeds of a crime must be confiscated unless this seems grossly unjust. The regulation allows for the confiscation of assets given to a third party as payment for costs sustained in commission of a crime. A sum of money equal to the value of the assets may be confiscated instead. In addition to the offender and his/her accomplices, property may also be removed from third parties. Their position is clarified by section 5, according to which assets may be confiscated from the following categories of persons: those who acquired the assets in awareness of their criminal origin and persons who obtained them by means of a division of jointly held marital property, inheritance or gift.[78]

Confiscation of drugs and related proceeds is regulated by section 6 of the Narcotic Drugs Act of 1968,[79] whose section 6 establishes that any gains accruing from such offences shall be declared confiscated if this is not manifestly unjust.

Seizure is provided for by chapter 27, section 1 of the Code of Judicial Procedure. There are also provisions intended to minimise the deterioration in value of seized assets. Thus, for example, it is prescribed that money must be placed in bank accounts so that it earns interest, and that cars must be maintained so as to reduce their deterioration in value.

The disposal of confiscated assets is regulated by law no. 1066 of 1974, as amended by law no. 1700 of 1995. The goods are sold unless their destruction is ordered.

B) Law in Action

The Swedish investigative system focuses on the crime, rather than on the proceeds from crime. When an aggravated crime has been committed, special investigative means (in particular telephone tapping) are normally employed to clarify the circumstances of the crime and to collect evidence. However, it is important to point out that the use of these special investigative means is mainly intended to collect proof of the crime committed. Hence their benefit for confiscation is only indirect, because obtaining evidence on the crime increases the likelihood of obtaining a conviction, which is generally a prerequisite for confiscation. One of the main problems of the Swedish investigative

[77] This section was last modified in 1986 by law no. 1007.
[78] This section was last modified in 1987 by law no. 791.
[79] This section was last modified in 1983 by law no. 363.

system is that the focus is on the crime, and secondarily on the proceeds from it. In most serious cases, however, when the Economic Crime Bureau, rather than the ordinary police forces, is involved, financial investigations are carried out on a regular basis and always from a very early stage. Third parties are not systematically investigated, mainly because investigators and prosecutors have long experienced enormous difficulties in proving to courts that these third parties have acted as straw men. Indeed, they tend to avoid wasting resources on what they regard as an almost hopeless task.

As regards cooperation with financial investigations by financial and non financial institutions, these are required to report suspicious transactions to the police under the anti money laundering regulations introduced in 1993. Banks were initially rather uncooperative. Subsequently there was substantial improvement and they now customarily inform the Intelligence police as soon as a suspicious transaction is noted. Although other financial institutions are not as cooperative as banks, they nevertheless contribute to the conduct of financial investigations to a satisfactory extent. Less cooperation is forthcoming from non financial institutions. As regards cooperation by informants, this is almost non existent, due to their fear of reprisals.

With reference to the handling of information on an individual's financial situation, it is worth noting that the marked multidisciplinary composition of the Economic Crime Bureau—where public prosecutors, police officials, accountants, economists and financial analysts work closely together—has led to significant success in locating the proceeds of crime. The Bureau also cooperates with external financial experts and accountants. When the case is not being dealt with by the Economic Crime Bureau, the level of multidisciplinary composition is lower because an ordinary prosecutorial authority is involved and usually has to find external experts or ask for assistance from the Economic Crime Bureau. Public prosecutors, custom and social services cooperate together to a satisfactory extent.

The human and material resources available to the Economic Crime Bureau are adequate, but only if cases are prioritised. Otherwise, without prioritisation, the means would be insufficient to cover any case at all. The level of training in the Bureau is good. Courses and seminars on bookkeeping and other topics related to financial investigations are held for both public prosecutors and police officers. The courses last some weeks.

In the judicial phase, although confiscation is always discretionary, as long as the court ascertains that it is not adopted unreasonably, the measure is very often applied once the prosecutor has requested it. However, closer inspection of the implementation of both property and value confiscation shows that problems arise in practice because of the high level of proof required. The public prosecutor must, in fact, provide the court with full proof that the proceeds stem precisely from the crime for which conviction is requested. This also hampers confiscation from third parties. In a recent case, for example, a drug seller was found with a bag full of money (about 30,000 euro) at home, but avoided confiscation by declaring that he had received the money from his mother. In the absence of proof that the money had derived from the specific drug affair to which the prosecution referred, confiscation did not occur. In cases like this one especially—that is where a person gains wealth from a criminal activity unlikely to be committed on a one-off basis—the law as it stands is an obstacle against confiscation.

The human and material resources devoted to the judicial phase are adequate if a case is important, that is if different priority is given to it because of the amount of ill-gotten gains potentially involved. Owing amongst other things to a lack of adequate and specialised training, public prosecutors and judges have scant awareness of the importance of confiscation in fighting criminal organisations. Consequently, there is some sort of cultural opposition to confiscation.

With reference to the management of seized assets, although provisions exist to minimise deterioration before confiscation, their application by the police is imperfect because of the intricacy of the task. Moreover, in some cases damage occurs to seized goods and is then compensated by the State.

The implementation of disposal provisions by enforcement offices is often hampered by lengthy procedures, so that a long time elapses before the phase is concluded. The enforcement offices have generally adequate resources; the problem, however, is that they do not try to realise the maximum monetary yield from confiscated assets. One gains the impression that confiscation is not a priority for them and is implemented as a merely administrative procedure—probably because officials in the enforcement offices lack specific training.

By way of summary, and in particular of the problems highlighted in the judicial and disposal phases by the national expert who completed the questionnaire, Figure 16 shows the Investigative Phase Law in Action Index, the Judicial Phase Law in Action Index, and the Disposal Phase Law in Action Index for Sweden. These Indexes quantify the law in action of the country by expressing, on a scale from 0 to 100, the extent to which the law in the books is enforced in each phase. *The higher the index, the better the law in action of the phase.*

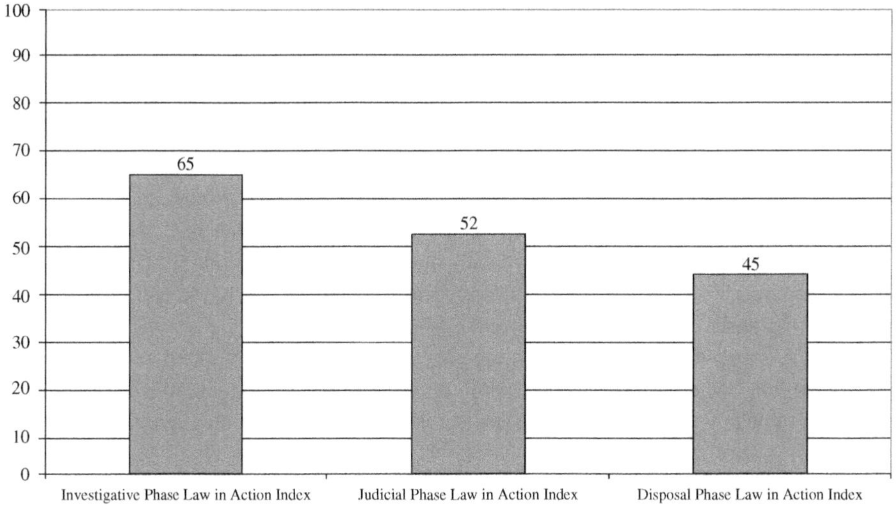

Figure 16. Law in Action Indexes of the Investigative, Judicial and Disposal Phases in Sweden. Source: Author's elaboration of the national expert's replies to the questionnaire.

4.15 THE UNITED KINGDOM

A) Law in the Books

The Proceeds of Crime Act of 2002[80] (henceforth PCA) completely renewed the law on proceeds from crime confiscation in the United Kingdom, which was previously contained (a) in the Drug Trafficking Act of 1994 as regards the proceeds from drug trafficking offences, and (b) in Part VI of the Criminal Justice Act of 1988 as regards the proceeds from non drug trafficking offences (limited to indictable offences and certain summary offences).[81] As a result of this Act, confiscation can be now made either (a) in criminal proceedings, normally following a conviction or (b) in civil recovery proceedings.

Starting with criminal confiscation, the PCA has unified the rules on drug trafficking and non drug trafficking offences and has made it possible to adopt the measure in relation to any offence. Under section 6 of the Act, in the case of conviction for any offence, the public prosecutor may ask the Crown Court to proceed with the confiscation procedure. The court may initiate the procedure also in the absence of the prosecutor's request. The court must first ascertain whether the defendant has a criminal lifestyle, which is established in case of conviction (a) for an offence unlikely to be committed on a one-off basis (like drug trafficking, money laundering, people trafficking, arms trafficking, etc.) (schedule 2), (b) for a conduct forming part of a course of criminal activity and for an offence committed over a period of at least six months, if the benefit is higher than £5,000 (section 75). If the court decides that the defendant has a criminal lifestyle it must decide whether s/he has benefited from his/her general criminal conduct. In doing so, the court must rely on certain assumptions, unless these are shown to be incorrect, or their employment would lead to a serious risk of injustice. First, any property transferred to the defendant in the six-year period before the beginning of the proceedings, and held by him/her after the conviction, are presumed to derive from crime. Furthermore, any expenditure by the defendant in the above-mentioned six-year period is assumed to derive from the proceeds of such an offence. For the purpose of valuing any property obtained (or assumed to have been obtained) by the defendant, it is assumed that s/he obtained it free of any other interests in it (section 10). If the court instead decides that s/he does not have a criminal lifestyle it must decide whether s/he has benefited from his/her particular criminal conduct. In this case, the court must calculate the benefit that the defendant has obtained from the offence for which s/he has been convicted. To be noted is that the standard of proof applied to the entire procedure is the civil standard (i.e. on the balance of probabilities).

In both cases, once the amount of the proceeds obtained (or presumed to have been obtained) has been ascertained, the court will calculate the recoverable amount, that is the amount payable by the defendant. As a general rule, the recoverable amount is

[80] For in-depth analysis of the Proceeds of Crime Act of 2002, see Gumpert, Kirk & Bojarski (2003), Rees & Hall (2003) and Alldridge (2003).
[81] For a complete analysis of the previous discipline, see Mitchell, Taylor & Talbot (2002).

equal to the defendant's benefit from the conduct concerned; however, if this amount is no longer available in the defendant's wealth, it is reduced accordingly (section 7).

Foreseen in order to prevent property-dealing before confiscation is the adoption of a restraint order, whose effect is to prohibit any specified person from dealing with any realisable property held by him/her (section 41).

A confiscation hearing may be held before the defendant has been sentenced in regard to the offence for which s/he has been convicted, or the hearing may be postponed for a maximum period of two years from the date of conviction (section 14). The amount ordered to be paid is owed on the making of the confiscation order, unless the court allows payment to be made in a specified period because the defendant shows that s/he needs some time to pay (section 11). In the case of non payment, the court fixes a term of imprisonment to be served (section 38). Furthermore, interest on the sum to be paid is due.

It is worth noting that confiscation may also be ordered when the defendant has absconded either before his/her conviction or after being charged but prior to trial if the prosecutor requests it and if the Crown Court finds the request appropriate (section 27). If the defendant absconds prior to conviction, and once two years have elapsed since the day s/he absconded, confiscation can be ordered on the request of the prosecutor (section 28). If, after the confiscation order has been made, the defendant ceases to be an absconder and is then convicted, s/he can, in the twenty-eight-day period after conviction, ask the Crown Court to alter the order if the amount subject to confiscation is believed to be excessive (section 29). If, instead, the defendant is acquitted at a later stage, the court must discharge the order on application of the person concerned (section 30).

A significant organisational innovation introduced by the PCA has been the creation of a national confiscation agency, the Assets Recovery Agency (henceforth ARA). This is an independent government department whose staff bring together a wide range of competencies, that is financial investigators, casework administrators, lawyers, forensic accountants, etc. Some are employed directly by the Agency, while others are seconded from other agencies. The main functions of ARA are to support the police, customs and other agencies in financial investigations by setting up a system for accreditation and training as regards financial investigations (section 3);[82] to investigate cases leading to post-conviction confiscation orders and/or applying for such orders (part 8); to enforce certain confiscation; to sue in the High Court for the civil recovery of the proceeds of unlawful conduct.

The use of the above-mentioned power of civil recovery allows the Agency to commence civil proceedings before the High Court to recover property obtained by a person by or in return for unlawful conduct, that is the so called recoverable property, as well as any other associated property (including, among items listed under section 245, any interest in the recoverable property), whether this is his/her own conduct or another's (section 242). Both before or after the initiation of proceedings, and even

[82] For this purpose, the Financial Investigation Centre of Excellence operates within the Agency and provides training for investigators specialised in tracing criminal assets.

without prior notice to the person concerned,[83] the Director of the Agency may ask the High Court to issue an interim receiving order. This is an order for the detention, custody or preservation of the mentioned property categories and for the appointment of an interim receiver. The order prohibits any person to whose property the order applies from dealing with it (section 252) and may require the person subject to the order to place the property at the disposal of the receiver and to take any action required by the receiver for the preservation of the property (section 250). The receiver's powers are particularly broad and include the following: the power to seize the property covered by the order; to obtain information (regardless of any restriction applicable to the disclosure) and to require a person to answer any question; to search any property to which the order applies; to manage any property through the sale of perishable goods and carrying on, if needed, trade or business (schedule 6), plus a general power to take any other steps the court deems appropriate (section 247). If the court is satisfied that the property is recoverable, it must make a recovery order whose effect is to vest the property in the trustee for civil recovery. The trustee is appointed by the court and acts under the direction and on behalf of the Director of the ARA. S/he gives effect to the recovery order, and in so doing seeks to maximise the amount finally payable to the Director. The standard of proof is the typical civil one (i.e. on a balance of probabilities); no reversal of the standard of proof applies (section 241).

Civil recovery proceedings cannot be initiated if twelve years have elapsed from the date on which the property was unlawfully obtained (section 288). Second, if a victim claims to the court that property alleged to be recoverable property belongs to him/her and the court accordingly makes a declaration, the property cannot be subjected to a recovery order. Furthermore, civil recovery proceedings cannot be commenced unless the Director has reasonable grounds to believe that the aggregate value of the recoverable property exceeds £10,000 or more (section 287).

Finally worth mentioning is a special civil recovery system foreseen by the PCA and replacing the one previously regulated under Part II of the Drug Trafficking Act,[84] which exclusively applied to cash intercepted at borders and suspected of deriving from the proceeds of drug trafficking or intended for use in such activity. Under this special system, if the recoverable property consists of cash[85] found at any place in the United Kingdom, the civil proceedings take place in a Magistrates' Court. Upon authorisation by a justice of the peace or a senior officer, a police or customs officer who has reasonable grounds for suspecting that cash which is recoverable property or is intended by any person for use in unlawful conduct is on a premise or transported by someone, and whose value is not less than £5,000 (section 303), may search for the cash (sections 289 and 290) and seize it (section 294). An application for its forfeiture

[83] ARA can only apply *ex parte* for an interim receiving order if giving notice would prejudice the ARAs right to obtain a recovery order, for example the assets are likely to be dispersed, etc.

[84] For detailed analysis of the previous discipline, see Mitchell, Taylor & Talbot (1997, 219–222) and Home Office, Organised and International Crime Directorate (1997, 61–64).

[85] Cash is defined so as to include postal orders, cheques (including traveller's cheques), bankers' drafts, bearer bonds/shares as well as currency (section 289).

may be made to a Magistrates' Court by the commissioners of customs and excise or by a constable, and the court may order the forfeiture of the cash or any part of it if satisfied that the cash is recoverable property or is intended for use in unlawful conduct. The civil standard of proof applies.

The Proceeds of Crime Act has also enhanced investigatory powers in financial investigations. The instruments available are the following: production order, search warrant, disclosure order, customer information order and account monitoring order.[86] These instruments are available to the appropriate officers. Financial investigations are undertaken by various law enforcement agencies: the police service, the National Crime Squad (NCS), the customs, the Serious Fraud Office (SFO), the Inland Revenue, the Department of Social Security (DSS) and the Department of Trade and Industry.

B) Law in Action

Before dealing with the practice of proceeds from crime confiscation it should be noted that, because the new regime described in the previous letter only recently came into force, any discussion of its operation in practice is premature. The discussion in this section consequently refers mainly to a changing reality in which old rules are dispensed with and new ones only begin to have effect.

First, it is necessary to differentiate between criminal confiscation and civil confiscation.

Discussion of the practice of the new civil recovery scheme is premature because the Assets Recovery Agency became operational in February 2003 and the police are only now beginning to use the powers provided by the Act. Some broad comments can be made on implementation of the powers now foreseen for the PCA under a special civil recovery system, since these powers are a continuation of the cash forfeiture regime previously regulated by Part II of the Drug Trafficking Act of 1994. In exercising these powers customs & excise have co-operated with the police to a satisfactory extent, and vice versa. Numerous police/customs and excise officers have been available to seize cash, but only a few qualified lawyers. In general, cash forfeiture has been applied successfully, also in consideration of the fact that no great expertise is required to enforce cash confiscation.

With more general reference to the practice of criminal confiscation, and starting with the investigative phase, to be noted is that production orders are frequently used; and so are searches, if appropriate. Possible straw men are systematically investigated, and with particular regard to 'gifts' received by them. The level of cooperation by banks is good, although that by other financial and non financial institutions is less satisfactory. Also good is the collaboration of informers with financial investigations; in fact, if an informer is prepared to co-operate s/he will usually assist with regard to assets as well.

Some of the findings of a report produced in 2000—that is that "[...] financial investigation is underused, undervalued and underresourced in the UK. There is also a

[86] For detailed analysis of the enhanced investigatory powers, see Rees & Hall (2003, 61–83).

shortage of people with the right skills and little cross-agency cooperation or sharing of best practice" (Cabinet Office, Performance and Innovation Unit 2000, 51)—are still largely valid. The human and material resources devoted to the phase are inadequate; although they have recently been improved, still more is required. Another aspect to be mentioned is the delayed onset of financial investigations, especially in the police service. In 1998, for example, financial inquiries began after charges in 45% of cases (Ibidem, 53). This was confirmed by the expert interviewed, who offered the explanation that no power to restrain pre charge was available until 2003. Finally, although in practice all agencies seek to assist each other if it is possible for them to do so, communication and information sharing among the various investigative units is frustrated by a lack of strategic coordination (Ibidem, 46–47). By contrast, the level of training of financial investigators has recently been improved, since ARA has accredited a number of investigators and will continue to do so.

With regard to the judicial phase in criminal proceedings, the main impediment until recently was the existence of the two different regimes mentioned above: the former applying to non drug trafficking offences; the latter, which was more severe, to drug trafficking ones. This complexity often caused "[. . .] uncertainty and confusion, and dissuades practitioners from using the powers" (Cabinet Office, Performance and Innovation Unit 2000, 64). Besides this aspect, which has been dealt with by the new law, the statutory assumptions on the defendant's assets—generally applied unless there is a serious risk of injustice—have to date worked well. Also the 'gift' provisions aimed at removing the proceeds from crime from *mala fide* third parties are used. Not so successful is the use of the reversed burden of proof. The case law states that judges should look for cogent evidence of legitimacy from the defendant, but they often seem too easily satisfied that assets have derived from legitimate sources—especially if a wife declares that 'she' purchased the matrimonial home. Also in those cases where discretion is applicable, some judges will always exercise their discretion in favour of the defendant. To be stressed is the inadequate preparation of practitioners: prosecutors receive some training, but possibly not enough, and judges receive very little, perhaps a one-hour lecture on the topic. Also needing improvement is the amount of human and material resources.

Although the level of competence of receivers is usually good, problems have arisen in the management of restrained assets since a court case of 1999 made it more difficult to sell a depreciating asset prior to conviction unless the defendant agreed, thereby reducing the receiver's effective management powers.

More human and material resources have recently been allocated to the disposal phase. The level of inter-agency cooperation in the phase varies, although it must be acknowledged that the new legislation has fostered cooperation among Crown Courts, prosecutors, Magistrate Courts, etc. To be noted, however, is that only a small part of the amount confiscated is subsequently collected. There are various reasons for this unsatisfactory collection rate. First, confiscation orders are sometimes set too high, that is above the value of realisable property. Furthermore, a significant proportion of the confiscated assets cannot be recovered because it is used to pay the high fees charged by receivers and lawyers (Cabinet Office, Performance and Innovation Unit 2000, 70).

Another factor explaining the small amount collected is the excessively long time that judges often give defendants to pay. Although receivers are highly competent, it is inevitable that the value of the assets diminishes in the meantime.

By way of summary, Figure 17 shows the Investigative Phase Law in Action Index, the Judicial Phase Law in Action Index, and the Disposal Phase Law in Action Index for criminal confiscation in the United Kingdom. These Indexes quantify the law in action of the country by expressing, on a scale from 0 to 100, the extent to which the law in the books is enforced in each phase. *The higher the index, the better the law in action of the phase.*

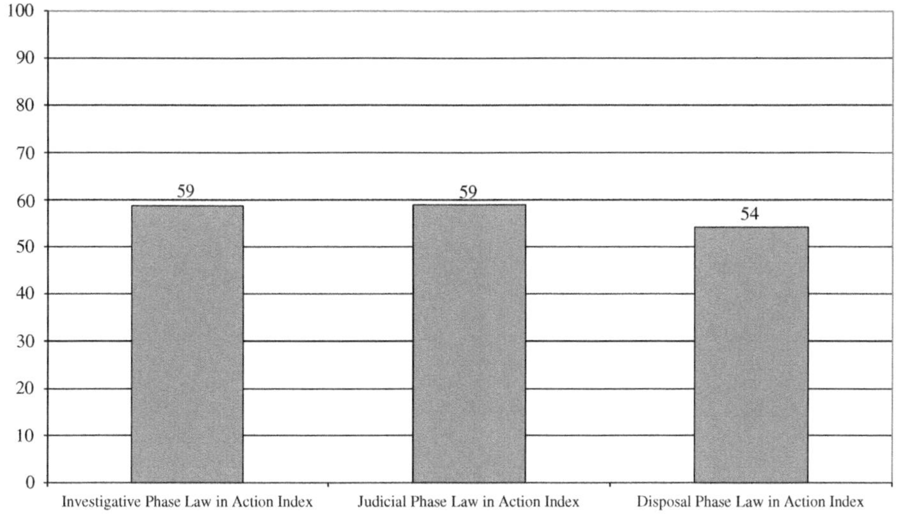

Figure 17. Law in Action Indexes of the Investigative, Judicial and Disposal Phases in Criminal Proceedings in the United Kingdom.
Source: Author's elaboration of national expert's replies to the questionnaire.

CHAPTER 5

MAPPING THE MAIN PROBLEMS AND HIGHLIGHTING THE BEST PRACTICES: A HORIZONTAL ANALYSIS

This chapter provides an overview of the enforcement of proceeds of crime confiscation in the EU framework. On the basis of the country-by-country analysis conducted in the previous chapter, this one carries out a horizontal analysis of the original fifteen EU Member States, the purpose being to sum up the main problems in the practice of proceeds from crime confiscation (section 1) and the best practices (section 2). Some concluding remarks are finally drawn (section 3).

5.1 MAIN PROBLEMS IN THE PRACTICE OF PROCEEDS OF CRIME CONFISCATION

The main problems hampering the full enforcement of confiscation provisions in the European Union are presented in a logical order that follows the development of confiscation proceedings from the investigative phase to the judicial phase and finally to the disposal phase.

Special means of investigations to locate the ill-gotten gains are still rarely employed

A first finding is the generally infrequent use made of special investigative means to locate the proceeds from crime. This is due to a variety of factors. In Luxembourg, for example, it is related to a narrow formulation of legal provisions that makes their use possible only in very exceptional circumstances. However, in most countries—emblematic in this respect being Italy and Sweden—the main reason for the limited use of these means to locate the proceeds from crime is that the system is focused on offenders rather than on their wealth. The use of special investigative means is mainly aimed at collecting evidence on the crime committed (author, circumstances, etc.). Consequently, their benefit for confiscation is only indirect, and to the extent that obtaining evidence on the crime increases the likelihood of a conviction, which is generally a prerequisite for confiscation. This mechanism is well exemplified by Italy, when one compares the use in that country of special investigative means in criminal and civil proceedings. In the latter, where the location of the proceeds from crime is much more important than in criminal cases and the commission of previous offences is not a consideration when rendering a decision and issuing a preventive measure, special investigative means are more frequently employed, also because of the involvement in the proceedings of institutions (i.e. the *Direzione Nazionale Antimafia*) whose financial culture is higher than average.

The degree of cooperation by non-financial institutions is low

Another problem is the generally low level of cooperation by non-financial institutions with financial investigations. The key factor seems to be a strictly legal one, namely the recent extension to these institutions of the obligation to cooperate with investigators. Linked to this is the absence of a system of disciplinary supervision (and related sanctions) as good as the one developed in the financial—and especially banking—sector. As a result, the measures undertaken by non-financial institutions in order to identify money laundering operations have been more limited than those undertaken by the financial institutions. This is reflected, for example, in the internal organisation of non-financial institutions, which is weak in terms of the training of employees to deal with suspicious operations. Moreover, because these institutions have had fewer contacts with law enforcement agencies than have financial institutions, they often do not know what investigators need; this unfamiliarity further contributes to making their cooperation with investigators less satisfactory than that of banks.

The cooperation of informers/witnesses with financial investigations is extremely limited

A finding common to all the EU Member States analysed here is their inability to exploit witnesses, and above all informants, to shed light on a criminal organisation's wealth.

As regards witnesses, this depends closely on the personal interests involved, and on whether or not the witness is afraid of the suspect.

As regards informers, it depends on various factors, some related to the legal framework, some to the ability and willingness of law enforcement agencies to use this source of information on criminal wealth, and yet others to the informer/witness him/herself. First, the legal framework. Not all Member States have protection programmes (e.g. Belgium and France), so that the fear of retaliation greatly restricts cooperation with investigators. Even when a protection programme is in place, however, it would seem—for easily understandable reasons—that cooperation by informers is reduced by the formalised path to be followed if their statements are to be acquired as evidence in criminal proceedings: these individuals must be identified, because anonymity is not possible, they must enter a protection programme and they must abide by the strict rules that discipline it. This mechanism is well exemplified by Ireland, where the level of cooperation by informers is an aspect on which criminal and civil confiscation proceedings differ greatly. Contrary to what happens in criminal proceedings, the level of cooperation by informers in civil proceedings is excellent. They have a completely different attitude to cooperation because they do not have to give full evidence (a lower standard of proof applies in civil proceedings) and their anonymity is ensured. Furthermore, they normally receive more favourable treatment (higher benefits in terms of fewer proceeds confiscated, or lower taxes to be paid on illegal earnings) made possible by the more flexible procedure. In criminal cases this would be impossible because the procedure is highly formalised. Other reasons for the very rare use made of informers is the suspicion with which they are generally viewed, and the fact that in some cases they can only provide a limited amount of information, owing to their lack of detailed knowledge of the distribution of wealth in criminal organisations.

Some inconveniences arise with reference to inter-agency cooperation, especially owing to the scant contribution to financial investigations by tax authorities

With reference to inter-agency cooperation, a major problem is the scant contribution made by tax authorities to the location of the proceeds from crime. The contribution of these authorities could instead be particularly useful, considering that tax records help determine a person's legitimate income—an element to be ascertained, for example, when request is made for extended confiscation, given that the measure is based on a disproportion between a person's licit income and his/her total income. The main reasons for this unsatisfactory cooperation by tax authorities are legal and cultural.

With reference to the former, in some EU countries (e.g. Belgium, Spain) tax authorities are not permitted to disclose any tax-related information to prosecutors and there is a general prohibition on the use of tax information in criminal investigations.

With reference to the latter, in some countries, such as Belgium, France, Luxembourg, Ireland and Portugal, there is tension and rivalry among the various law enforcement agencies potentially involved in financial investigations, and in particular a tendency to view criminal investigations and tax inquiries as clearly distinct and to be kept separate.

Human and material resources have been recently increased in most EU countries, but they are still inadequate

Greater material and human resources have recently been allocated to tracing the proceeds from crime in most of the EU Member States. However these resources, especially human ones, still largely fall short of requirements, although they are needed in particular by financial investigations, which are extremely time-consuming. Investigators must recover and process a huge mass of information, and it also takes time to obtain information from financial and non-financial institutions. Since a few people must assume a heavy workload, not all cases can be investigated. Consequently, in practice, investigators adopt various criteria to prioritise cases, one of the most relevant being the amount of proceeds involved.

Financial investigation training is on the rise, but still much remains to be done

The analysis conducted has shown that in general the culture of financial investigations has grown in the past few years, and that training has been improved as a consequence. However, it should be stressed that, in almost half of the original fifteen EU Member

States, the training provided to investigators is still far from being satisfactory, taking the form of general instruction which almost entirely neglects financial aspects. Also relevant is the absence of checks on how much trainees have effectively learnt from courses, because what is required is mere attendance on them.

The potential of the reversal of the burden of proof is not fully exploited

In the majority of the countries providing for a reversal of the burden of proof—namely Austria, Italy, Ireland and the United Kingdom—problems arise when provisions are implemented. On the one hand, criminals are becoming very adept at providing justification for any assets in their possession, and they rarely make use of assets whose (fictitious) licit origins cannot be proven. On the other hand, judges seem too easily satisfied that assets have been earned from legitimate sources. This attitude by judges is linked to another factor, namely their poor understanding and interpretation of the reversal of proof mechanism.

The training for public prosecutors and, above all, for judges on confiscation is low, and they have a cultural attitude against confiscation

A feature common to the EU Member States is the low level of training given to public prosecutors and judges on confiscation issues. Most prosecutors and judges are still not specialised in confiscation matters; and even when some training is arranged, little time is allocated, so that most of the training is delivered on the job.

This links to another problem. Owing to the lack of adequate and specialised training and to continual job rotation, public prosecutors and judges have little awareness of, or interest in, the importance of confiscation in the fight against criminal organisations. There exists some sort of cultural prejudice against seizing and confiscating the proceeds from crime, so that public prosecutors and judges are often loath to apply the legislation designed to deprive criminals of their illicit profits. As a result they may set the issue aside during the trial without any reasonable motive for doing so, as happens in Germany. In other cases, Belgium and Portugal for example, the discretionary nature of the measure means that in practice it is often not applied, even though the criminal standard of proof has been met.

It is interesting to note that the situation is less serious for public prosecutors than for judges. This mainly depends on the circumstance that, whilst some specialised prosecution offices have been established and work in close contact with financial investigators, the task of judges by its nature normally covers any kind of offence, either profit-generating or not.

The management of seized assets is neglected and their active administration is not encouraged

One of the most problematic aspects during the judicial phase throughout Europe is the management of seized assets. Because of an extremely poor legal framework—few provisions are normally devoted to the matter and prescribe passive administration, i.e.

the mere storage of the goods—the idea of the active management of these assets is not well-established. Also in consideration of the low competence and scarce responsibility of administrators—the job is unattractive and most experienced personnel avoid it—the result is a significant decrease in the value of seized assets. In Belgium, Italy and Portugal, for example, cars are abandoned in depots which charge high tariffs, so that although the State sustains high costs for their conservation the assets greatly decrease in value. In Italy and Spain, unsatisfactory too is the administration of firms: their management is a particularly complex and delicate matter and very few people—ones who are already not particularly motivated—are available for the task. This situation is exacerbated by the long duration of the judicial procedure in confiscation cases (see below).

Dilatory tactics and the long duration of the judicial procedure

Another problem is the long duration of proceedings in confiscation cases. Of course, this is a problem that affects criminal proceedings in every European country. However, it would seem that in confiscation cases, precisely because large economic interests are at stake, dilatory tactics (appeals, human rights claims, etc.) are more frequently used by defendants and by their lawyers to delay the procedure than in normal cases—as if defendants fear deprivation of their finances more than deprivation of their liberty. These tactics are also encouraged by the fact that the legislation is still relatively recent and often of unclear interpretation. Thus in the Netherlands, for example, cases may drag on even for ten years. Nor is the problem confined to criminal confiscation, if one considers that in Italy the average amount of time elapsing between seizure and final confiscation in civil proceedings has been estimated at 1413 days.

Some problems arise in the sale of confiscated assets and, above all, in their disposal for social purposes

A problem generally affecting the enforcement of the legal provisions of relevance in the disposal phase is its long duration, also as a consequence of the sometimes inadequate resources devoted to it. While the enforcement of confiscation orders generally encounters few problems when the orders relate to money—an asset that by its nature allows rapid conclusion of the procedure at low costs—the enforcement of orders relative to other types of assets like real and personal property is more problematic.

In most cases these assets are sold at public auction, where the prices realised are usually very low. It may also happen that criminals are able to buy their assets back. The sale procedure is sometimes overly complex and lengthy, especially when real property is being disposed of.

The provisions on the sale of confiscated assets work better than those on their use for social purposes foreseen in a number of countries. The latter provisions are either rarely applied (Belgium and Luxembourg), or when they are applied, the procedure is excessively complex and time-consuming, and the assets are not always in the best condition when given to the recipients—which are normally law enforcement agencies.

5.2 BEST PRACTICES IN PROCEEDS OF CRIME CONFISCATION

The main best practices in the implementation of confiscation provisions are now presented in a logical order that follows the development of confiscation proceedings from the investigative phase to the judicial phase and finally to the disposal phase.

Looking for financial investigation training wherever it is available

One best practice with regard to proceeds from crime investigations comes from Ireland, where the Criminal Assets Bureau was established in 1996 to locate ill-gotten gains and to request their civil confiscation. Very good training is given to officials at the Bureau, who are home trained by the Bureau Legal Officer. Then, depending on the case, representatives from the institutions involved (e.g. lawyers, bankers, etc.) are called in to provide Criminal Assets Bureau members with the necessary expertise. Hence the training is ongoing in nature, and in the first two years on-the-job training is provided. Moroever, visits from foreign investigative agencies (e.g. US Marshall Service and British Serious Fraud Office) are arranged, so that the principle applied is that expertise is used wherever it can be obtained.

Enhancing inter-agency cooperation by means of memoranda of understanding

Another best practice from Ireland is the enhancement of inter-agency cooperation by means of Memoranda of Understanding. The informal, flexible, and above all voluntary nature of this instrument has helped to reduce the tension and rivalry that characterised relations among the various agencies involved in acquiring information on the financial situations of suspects, and it has made their collaboration possible in a reciprocal position of parity, rather than of hierarchy.

Employing electronic systems to locate the proceeds from crime

Another best practice in the investigative phase comes from Germany, where investigators often use electronic systems to determine the economic circumstances of a suspected criminal. One of these systems is particularly promising: the *ZIVED* (Central Information Exchange from External Databases), which is a special electronic search system developed by the Land of North Rhine-Westphalia and now used by investigators in the entire country. The system works very well and enables law enforcement agencies to obtain a complete picture of a defendant's financial situation in a relatively short time. Its sources are all accessible databases world-wide (i.e. more that 6,000 databases), and it uses the Internet as its medium.

The idea of boosting electronic systems and databases for financial investigation purposes has been regarded as important elsewhere: for example, in Ireland, where the Criminal Assets Bureau, also in consideration of the unlimited resources available to the Bureau to develop its activity, has allocated one million euro to improving its IT system.

Distributing handbooks to improve public prosecutors training and to help them solve single cases

A best practice from Denmark concerns the training of public prosecutors in confiscation—a problematic issue as seen above. Specialised books and manuals are distributed to Danish public prosecutors in order to support them with concrete cases. These handbooks provide very useful guidance, illustrating the most recurrent problems and how to handle them. They are also an important tool for their training on the topic.

Striking a balance between the private and public interest in the management of seized assets

Another best practice in the judicial phase relates to the management of seized assets—a particularly delicate and problematic issue, as we have seen. Again, this best practice comes from Denmark, where defendants are allowed to suggest the arrangements necessary to manage the seized assets in order to maximise their value/minimise their deterioration. Such suggestions are met if reasonable—as they generally are.

In this way the system strikes a good balance between the public and private interest, thus enriching the public point of view with the private and more 'entrepreneurial' one.

Heightening judges' awareness of confiscation by reducing judge rotation and improving their preparation by recording trials

A best practice related to the training of judges—an aspect, as seen, that represents a significant problem in implementing confiscation provisions in all European countries—comes from Ireland. After enactment of the legislation on civil confiscation and the setting up of the Criminal Assets Bureau to ensure its enforcement, specific organisational measures were taken to ensure the full participation of judges in the application of the new provisions. The Bureau Legal Officer of the Criminal Assets Bureau immediately requested the High Court to appoint a judge to deal exclusively with civil confiscation proceedings for at least a minimum period of time (generally two years), assisted by a special registrar and a special courtroom. This was in order to improve judges' awareness of civil confiscation, as well as to achieve consistency in their rulings on the matter. Also, since enactment of the Act, a stenographer has been employed to record trials, the purpose being to collect materials useful both as consistent jurisprudence and as a significant basis for the preparation and training of newcomer judges.

Setting up ad hoc offices to manage seized assets efficiently and to fasten their disposal

A best practice from the Netherlands is the establishment of a centralised and specialised office, namely the Criminal Assets Deprivation Bureau (BOOM), which assists public prosecutors in confiscation cases also with reference to the management of seized assets and backs up the National Execution Bureau in the enforcement of confiscation orders. The reasons for the success of this office's action are the high competence of its officials, its exclusive focus on the management of seized and confiscated assets and the enforcement of confiscation orders, and its endowment with an excellent computerised system to register and track assets. The two basic principles inspiring the Bureau's action are the minimisation of management costs and the preservation of the value of assets.

As for the management of assets, after these have been seized they are registered in a computerised system and administered by a single central unit within the BOOM, namely the CEBES (an acronym for attachment and enforcement restraint system), which manages seized assets nationwide. The office is very good at maximising the value/minimising the deterioration of the goods, doing so, for example, by selling them as soon as possible and thereby reducing their storage costs (from €600,000 to €250,000 yearly). Also the disposal phase benefits from BOOM's activity. Its duration is very short (lasting three months on average), so that assets are sold as soon as is possible.

The idea of establishing an office devoted to the management of seized assets and the disposal of confiscated assets has recently been taken up by other EU countries, such as Belgium (with COSC, established in March 2003) and the United Kingdom (with ARA, operational since February 2003).

Reducing the length of the procedure and the related costs in terms of human and material resources by seeking an agreement with the defendant

A German practice, first applied in drug cases and still very frequently used in them, and which seems promising—although further research is needed before reaching a definitive conclusion—is so-called 'renunciation' (*Verzicht*). The offender is requested, informally, to renounce previously seized assets. In the case of agreement, which is usually reached shortly before conclusion of the trial and is generally forthcoming from the offender with the intention (whether overt or covert) to obtain either a milder sentence or restitution of a portion of the seized assets, the court no longer orders confiscation of the portion in question. When such an agreement is reached, a confiscation order can be obtained very rapidly, whereas a very long time normally elapses before a confiscation order is enacted, also because of appeals.

A portion of the seized assets is the 'price' to be paid by the State; however, in the vast majority of cases, if one considers that literally years of process can be avoided, this 'price' will be off-set by significant savings in terms of human and material resources.

5.3 CONCLUSIONS

The aim of this work has been to enrich knowledge of proceeds from crime confiscation in the European Union—knowledge which is generally limited to the law in the books—by adopting a practical approach which sheds light on the law in action, i.e. on how legal provisions on the matter are applied in practice in the original fifteen Member States. How can the findings of this endeavour be finally summed up?

An overall verdict on the enforcement of confiscation provisions in the EU framework based on the knowledge acquired by this study cannot be optimistic. Although signs of increased awareness of the importance of attacking the financial basis of criminal organisations have recently been shown by some EU Member States, where more resources and training have been devoted to the issue, implementation of the law is still far from perfect.

Of course, the budgetary restraints imposed on the activity of institutional actors entails that the very idea of the full enforcement of laws—including confiscation laws—smacks of Utopia, and in all public sectors. Moreover, as seen, judicial procedures are the necessary but not ideal setting for settling disputes over the origin—licit or illicit—of assets. The very long time normally taken by these proceedings and unfamiliarity with managerial principles by definition impact negatively on the assets involved in confiscation proceedings. Consequently, the judicial 'search for the truth' seems extremely difficult to reconcile with the entrepreneurial management of assets.

Even if the above considerations are taken into account, however, the general impression on conclusion of this study is that the 'tough on criminal wealth' philosophy is far from being deeply rooted in the everyday practice of law enforcement agencies, especially judicial ones. Confiscation is a challenge against the conventional wisdom on crime that prevails in most EU Member States. Putting criminals behind bars is still the main aim of the system, and most of the scarce resources available are devoted to achieving it. The fact that in most legislations confiscation continues to require prior conviction obviously further accounts for the infrequent use made of the measure. Many EU Member States exhibit the symptoms of what can be called a 'vicious cycle': few resources are devoted to the enforcement of confiscation laws; this implies (amongst other things) poor training provision for institutional actors; this produces scarce awareness of the importance of, and interest in, proceeds from crime confiscation; this may lessen the pressure on policy makers, so that they give it low priority; which means that few resources are devoted to it; and so on.

This study has started to build knowledge on this neglected and low profile subject by highlighting the obstacles against the implementation of confiscation provisions on which action should be taken, and pointing out the best practices that could be emulated by other countries. These findings make it even clearer than before that there is a need to collect reliable statistics on the enforcement of proceeds from crime confiscation, thereby further developing what this study has tentatively sought to do. These statistics should concern, for example, the number and value of seized, confiscated and disposed of assets; the time taken to confiscate and dispose of assets; the expenses sustained in confiscation proceedings both by the State and by the individuals involved in such proceedings. Also to be stressed is that future national efforts to collect these data should be coordinated at the European Union level, so as to standardise data collection procedures and thus enable the production of comparable data in all the European Union Member States. This would in fact be of further assistance when identifying where obstacles are concentrated, and in what they consist, and where, instead, good practices are flourishing and what they are. Only when this information is available will it be possible to evaluate the effectiveness and efficiency of confiscation policies in the European Union. And, after comparing the costs of confiscation for the State and for society as a whole against its benefits, 'knowledge based' discussion will finally be able to begin on whether or not such a stringent measure is really worth including in the national legislation.

BIBLIOGRAPHY

Adamoli, S., Di Nicola, A., Savona, E. U., & Zoffi, P. (1998). *Organised Crime around the World*, Publications Series No. 31. Helsinki: Heuni.

Albanese, J. (1985). *Organized Crime in America*. Cincinnati: Anderson Publishing Co.

Albrecht, H.-J. (1998). Money Laundering and the Confiscation of the Proceeds of Crime—A Comparative View on Different Models of the Control of Money Laundering and Confiscation. In T. G. Watkin (Ed.), *The Europeanisation of Law. United Kingdom Comparative Law Series* (Vol. 18, pp. 166–207). Oxford: Alden Press.

Alcaraz, N. C., & Lanzas, G. U. (1999). El comiso en el nuevo Código Penal de 1995: llamamiento urgente a la nueva jurisprudencia y doctrina. *Revista de Ciencias Penales*, *2*(1), 108–117.

Alexander, R. (1998). Do the UK's Provisions for Confiscation Orders Breach the European Convention on Human Rights? *Journal of Financial Crime*, *5*(4), 374–381.

Alldridge, P. (2003). *Money Laundering Law. Forfeiture, Confiscation, Civil Recovery, Criminal Laundering and Taxation of the Proceeds of Crime*. Oxford: Hart Publishing.

Baldwin, F. N. (2000). United States and Civil in Rem Forfeiture: the History and its Ancient Roots. *Journal of Money Laundering Control*, *3*(3), 204–213.

Bell, R. E. (1999). Civil Forfeiture of Criminal Assets. *The Journal of Criminal Law*, *63*(4), 371–384.

Bell, R. E. (2000a). An Evolving Series of Proceeds of Crime Models. *Journal of Financial Crime*, *8*(1), 21–31.

Bell, R. E. (2000b). The ECHR and the Proceeds of Crime Legislation. *The Criminal Law Review*, October, 783–800.

Bell, R. E. (2003). UK Part IV: Confiscating the Proceeds of Crime. In T. Graham (Ed.), *Butterworths International Guide to Money Laundering Law and Practice* (2nd ed., pp. 90–109). London: Butterworths.

Benseler, J. (1997). Forfeiture Legislation in Germany: Legal Basis and Prosecution Practice. *European Journal of Crime, Criminal Law and Criminal Justice*, *3*, 203–209.

Blumenson, E. D., & Nilsen, E. S. (1998). Policing for Profit: the Drug War's Hidden Economic Agenda. *University of Chicago Law Review*, *65*, 35–114.

Blumenson, E. D., & Nilsen, E. S. (1999). Contesting Government's Financial Interest in Drug Cases. *Criminal Justice*, *13*(4), 4–10.

Broadbridge, S., & Blair, C. (2001). *Proceeds of Crime Bill: Bill 31 of session 2201-2002*, House of Commons Library Research Paper 01/79.

Cabinet Office, Performance and Innovation Unit (2000). *Recovering the Proceeds of Crime*. http://www.cabinet-office.gov.uk/innovation/2000/crime/crime.pdf.

Cassella, S. D. (2001). The Civil Asset Forfeiture Reform Act of 2000: Expanded Government Forfeiture Authority and Strict Deadlines Imposed on All Parties. *Journal of Legislation, 27*, 97–151.

Clarke, B. (2001, December). Confiscation of Proceeds of Crime: Australian Response. Paper presented at the Investigation on Crime Conference, Durban. http://www.tsa.ac.za/conf/criminal/papers/clarke.pdf.

Commissione Parlamentare Antimafia (1997a). *Resoconto Stenografico della seduta del 6 maggio*, Rome.

Commissione Parlamentare Antimafia (1997b). *Resoconto Stenografico della seduta del 1° luglio*, Rome.

Commissione Parlamentare Antimafia (1998). *Resoconto Stenografico della seduta del 20 gennaio*, Rome.

Commissione Parlamentare Antimafia (1999). *Resoconto Stenografico della seduta del 25 maggio*, Rome.

Commissione Parlamentare Antimafia (2002). *Resoconto Stenografico della seduta del 29 gennaio,* Rome.

Corbetta, P. (1999). *Metodologia e tecniche della ricerca sociale*. Il Mulino: Bologna.

Council of Europe (2001). *Confiscation of Proceeds of Crime in South-Eastern Europe*. Strasbourg.

Council of Europe, European Committee of Crime Problems, Group of Specialists on Criminal Law and Criminological Aspects of Organised Crime (1997, June). *Criminal Financial Investigation. A Strategic and Tactical Approach in the European Dimension*. Strabourg.

Council of Europe, European Committee of Crime Problems, Group of Specialists on Criminal Law and Criminological Aspects of Organised Crime (2000). *Reversal of the Burden of Proof in the Confiscation of the Proceeds of Crime: a Council of Europe Best Practice Survey (Best Practice Survey No. 2)*. Strasbourg.

Council of the European Union (1998, November). *Draft Report of the Informal Money Laundering Experts Group (CRIMORG 173)*. Brussels.

Council of the European Union (1999, May). *The Production of European Union (EU) Statistics on Aspects of Money Laundering & Asset Seizure (CRIMORG 65)*. Brussels.

Council of the European Union (2000, May). *Proposal Regarding the Implementation of Recommendation 8.6 of CRIMORG 173—Dealing with the Expertises Required for Applying Sophisticated Financial Investigative Techniques (CRIMORG 51)*. Brussels.

Criminal Assets Bureau (2002). *Annual Report 2001*. Dublin.

Criminal Assets Bureau (2003). *Annual Report 2002*. Dublin.

Daams, C. (2002). Landesbericht Niederlande. In M. Kilchling (Ed.), *Die Praxis der Gewinnabschöpfung in Europa* (pp. 297–313). Freiburg: Kriminologische Forschungsberichte aus dem Max-Planck-Institut für ausländisches und internationales Strafrecht.

Daams, C., & van der Reyt, I. (1997). 'Strip-them' Legislation in the Netherlands: Measures Concerning Confiscation of Illegally Obtained Profit in the Dutch Law. *European Journal of Crime, Criminal Law and Criminal Justice, 3*, 308–313.

De Figueiredo Dias, J. (1993). *Direito penal português, parte geral. II. As consequências jurídicas do crime*. Lisbon: Editorial Notícias.

Desportes, F., & Le Gunehec, F. (1997). *Le noveau droit pénal. Tome 1—Droit pénal général*. Paris: Economica.

Dhiri, S., & Brand, S. (1999). *Crime Reduction Programme. Analysis of Costs and Benefits: Guidance for Evaluators*. London: Home Office—Research, Development and Statistics Directorate.

Donato, L., & Masciandaro, D. (1997). *Criminalità e intermediazione finanziaria. Economia e diritto*. Rome: Edibank.

Ehlers, S. (1999). *Policy Briefing: Asset Forfeiture*. Washington, DC: The Drug Policy Foundation.

Engee, J., van Schendel, J., & van der Zee, S. (2000). *International Legal Manual on Money Laundering & Confiscation of Illegal Assets* (Vol. 1). Zoetermeer: National Criminal Intelligence Division and Europol.

Europol (2000, March). *A European Design for Financial Investigation*. The Hague.

Fallone, A. (1995). Luci ed ombre del procedimento di prevenzione patrimoniale. *Documenti Giustizia, 4*, 599–638.

Fiandaca, G. (1983). Commento all'art. 1 legge 13/9/1982 No. 646. *Legislazione Penale, 2*, 257–268.

Financial Action Task Force on Money Laundering (1997a). *Evaluation of Laws and Systems in FATF Members Dealing with Asset Confiscation and Provisional Measures*. Paris.

Financial Action Task Force on Money Laundering (1997b). *Annual Report 1996–1997*. Paris.

Financial Action Task Force on Money Laundering (1998). *Annual Report 1997–1998*. Paris.

Financial Action Task Force on Money Laundering (1999). *Annual Report 1998–1999*. Paris.

Financial Action Task Force on Money Laundering (2001). *Review of FATF Anti-Money Laundering Systems and Mutual Evaluation Procedures 1992–1999*. Paris.

Financial Action Task Force on Money Laundering (2003). *The Forty Recommendations*. Paris.

Fisse, B. (1992). Confiscation of Proceeds of Crime: Discretionary Forfeiture or Proportionate Punishment? *Criminal Law Journal, 16*(3), 138–159.

Fornari, L. (1997). *Criminalità del profitto e tecniche sanzionatorie—Confisca e sanzioni pecuniarie nel diritto penale 'moderno'*. Milan: Cedam.

Friedman, D. (2001, November). Disguising the Elephant: Civil Recovery and the End of Criminal Law. Paper presented at the Matrix Seminar on Confiscations and the Proceeds of Crime. http://www.matrixlaw.co.uk/seminars/documents/15%20Nov%2001/DF%20paper.pdf.

Gallant, M. (1999). Money Laundering, Criminal Assets and the 1998 Proposed Reforms. *Journal of Financial Crime, 6*(4), 323–332.

Godefroy, T., & Kletzlen, A. (1997). Confiscation and Anti-Money-Laundering Regulations under French Law. *European Journal of Crime, Criminal Law and Criminal Justice, 3*, 273–280.

Godefroy, T., & Kletzlen, A. (2000). *Blanchiment et confiscation. La situation française vue à travers l'analyse de dossiers*. Guyancourt: CESDIP.

Godefroy, T., & Kletzlen, A. (2002). Landesbericht Frankreich. In M. Kilchling (Ed.), *Die Praxis der Gewinnabschöpfung in Europa* (pp. 135–237). Freiburg: Kriminologische Forschungsberichte aus dem Max-Planck-Institut für ausländisches und internationales Strafrecht.

Groos, W. F. (1993). Squeeze'em: from Legislation to Confiscation. In Dutch Ministry of Justice (Ed.), *Translations of Dutch Legislation on Money Laundering and Illegally Obtained Advantage.*

Gumpert, B., Kirk, J., & Bojarski, A. (2003). *Proceeds of Crime Act 2002: a Practical Guide*. Bristol: Jordans.

Gupta, D. (2002). Republic of South Africa's Prevention of Organised Crime Act: a Comparative Bill of Rights Analysis. *Harvard Civil Rights-Civil Liberties Law Review, 37*, 159–183.

Hawkins, C. W. (1999). Civil Forfeiture in Law Enforcement: an Effective Tool or Cash Register Justice? An Effective Tool. In J. D. Sewell (Ed.), *Controversial Issues in Policing* (pp. 23–28). Boston: Allyn and Bacon.

Her Majesty's Inspectorate of Constabulary for Scotland (2000). *Making Crime Pay: Confiscation of Criminal Assets in Scotland*. Edinburgh.

Home Office, Organised and International Crime Directorate (1997). *Confiscation and Money Laundering: Law and Practice. A Guide for Enforcement Authorities*. London: The Stationery Office.

Home Office Working Group on Confiscation (1998). *Third Report: Criminal Assets*. http://www.homeoffice.gov.uk/oicd/jcu/wgconf.htm.

Howard League for Penal Reform (1984). *Profits of Crime and Their Recovery: the Report of a Committee Chaired by Sir Derek Hodgson*. London: Heinemann Educational Books Ltd.

Hyde, H. (1995). *Forfeiting Our Property Rights: is Your Property Safe from Seizure?* Washington, DC: Cato Institute.

Jakhian, G. (1991). L'infraction de blanchiment et la peine de confiscation en droit belge. *Revue de droit pénal et de criminologie, 71*(8-9-10), 765–788.

Jensen, E. L., & Gerber, J. (1996). The Civil Forfeiture and the War on Drugs: Expanding Criminal Sanctions while Reducing Due Process Protections. *Crime and Delinquency, 42*(3), 421–434.

Joint Committee on Human Rights (2001, 30 November). *Third Report.*

Joint Committee on Human Rights (2002, 11 February). *Eleventh Report.*

Kathrein, U. (1999). Austria. The Criminal Justice Systems Facing the Challenge of Organised Crime. *International Review of Penal Law, 70*, 365–379.

Keyser-Ringnalda, F. (1992). European Integration with Regard to the Confiscation of the Proceeds of Crime. *European Law Review, 17*, 499–515.

Kilchling, M. (2002). Die Praxis der Gewinnabschöpfung bei Geldwäsche und Anderen Formen Organisierter Kriminalität in Deutschland. In M. Kilchling (Ed.), *Die Praxis der Gewinnabschöpfung in Europa* (pp. 19–81). Freiburg: Kriminologische Forschungsberichte aus dem Max-Planck-Institut für ausländisches und internationales Strafrecht.

Kilchling, M. (2004). Organised Crime Policies in Germany. In C. Fijnaut, & L. Paoli (Eds.), *Organised Crime in Europe. Concepts, Patterns and Control Policies in the European Union and Beyond* (pp. 717–762). Dordrecht: Springer.

Konstantopoulos, V. L. (1999, October). *Seminario internazionale "Eucos" sulle organizzazioni criminali dell'Unione Europea—Il quadro legislativo greco per la lotta alla criminalità organizzata e le varie tecniche investigative utilizzate dalle forze dell'ordine*. Rome.

Lavelle, K. (1998). The Criminal Assets Bureau. *Agon, 18*, 9–11.

Levi, M. (1997). Evaluating the 'New Policing': Attacking the Money Trail of Organised Crime. *The Australian and New Zealand Journal of Criminology, 30*(1), 1–25.

Levi, M., & Osofsky, L. (1995). *Investigating, Seizing and Confiscating the Proceeds of Crime*, Crime Detection & Prevention Series, Paper 61. London: Home Office Police Research Group.

Levy, L. W. (1996). *A License to Steal: the Forfeiture of Property*. Chapel Hill and London: The University of North Carolina Press.

Liberty (The National Council for Civil Liberties) (2001a). *Proceeds of Crime: Consultation on Draft Legislation*. London.

Liberty (The National Council for Civil Liberties) (2001b, May). *Opinion of Counsel on Part II of the Draft Bill—Criminal Confiscation*. London.

Liberty (The National Council for Civil Liberties) (2001c, May). *Opinion of Counsel on Part V of the Draft Bill—Civil Confiscation*. London.

Lodder, A. (2001, 4 October). *Lecture on Deprivation Legislation* (unpublished).

Lomonte, E. (1997). Gli interventi sui patrimoni mafiosi: uscire dall'ambiguità dell'enfasi simbolica per immaginare percorsi capaci di coniugare effettività e tutela dei diritti individuali. *Critica del Diritto, 4*, 236–240.

López Garrido, D., & García Arán, M. (1996). *El Código Penal de 1995 y la voluntad del legislador. Comentario al texto y al debate parlamentario*. Madrid: Eurojuris.

Löschnig-Gspandl, M. (1997). Fight against Organised Crime: Recent Changes to the Catalogue of Statutory Offences and the Confiscation System in Austrian Criminal Law. *European Journal of Crime, Criminal Law and Criminal Justice, 3*, 210–219.

Löschnig-Gspandl, M., & Kilchling, M. (2002). Landesbericht Österreich. In M. Kilchling (Ed.), *Die Praxis der Gewinnabschöpfung in Europa* (83–133). Freiburg: Kriminologische Forschungsberichte aus dem Max-Planck-Institut für ausländisches und internationales Strafrecht.

Lusty, D. (2002). Civil Forfeiture of Proceeds of Crime in Australia. *Journal of Money Laundering Control, 5*(4), 345–359.

Maddocks, R. (2000, 15 April). Another Kind of Asset Forfeiture. *Le Québécois Libre, 60*. Montreal.

Maia Gonçalves, M. (1999). *Código penal português*. Coimbra: Almedina.

Manzanares Samaniego, J. L. (1983). *Las penas patrimoniales en el Código Penal Español*. Barcelona: Bosch.

Mapelli Caffarena, B. (1998). Las consecuencias accesorias en el nuevo Código Penal. *Revista Penal, 1*, 43–54.

Masciandaro, D. (1994). *Banche e riciclaggio. Analisi economica e regolamentazione*. Rome: Edibank.

Matsopoulou, H. (1995). La confiscation spéciale dans le nouveau Code pénal. *Revue de science criminelle et de droit pénal compare, 2*, 301–317.

Maugeri, A. M. (2001). *Le moderne sanzioni patrimoniali tra funzionalità e garantismo*. Milan: Giuffrè.

Maugeri, A. M. (1996). La sanzione patrimoniale fra garanzie ed efficienza. *Rivista Trimestrale di Diritto Penale dell'Economia, 3*, 817–903.

Maxfield, M. G., & Babbie, E. (2000). *Research Methods for Criminal Justice and Criminology* (3rd ed.). Wadsworth: Thomson Learning.

Meade, J. (1998). The Proceeds of Crime Act, 1996: an Overview. *Irish Law Times, 16*(4), 52–54.

Mehrens, S. (2000). La disciplina tedesca sui collaboratori di giustizia per i reati commessi in forma organizzata (art. 5 l. sui collaboratori di giustizia). In V. Militello, L. Paoli, & J. Arnold (Eds.), *Il crimine organizzato come fenomeno transnazionale—Forme di manifestazione, prevenzione e repressione in Italia, Germania e Spagna* (pp. 341–344). Milan: Giuffrè.

Ministero della Giustizia, Dipartimento per gli affari di giustizia, Direzione generale della giustizia penale, Ufficio I (2002). *Consistenza, destinazione, utilizzo dei beni sequestrati o confiscati e stato dei procedimenti di sequestro e confisca (legge 7 marzo 1996, No. 109)*. Rome.

Mitchell, A. R., Taylor, S. M. E., & Talbot, K. V. (1997). *Confiscation and the Proceeds from Crime* (2nd ed.). London: Sweet & Maxwell.

Mitchell, A. R., Taylor, S. M. E., & Talbot, K. V. (2002). *Confiscation and the Proceeds from Crime* (3rd ed.). London: Sweet & Maxwell.

Murphy, F., & Galvin, B. (1999). Targeting the Financial Wealth of Criminals in Ireland: the Law and Practice. In J. P. McCutcheon & D. P. J. Welsh (Eds.), *The Confiscation of Criminal Assets. Law and Procedure* (pp. 9–35). Dublin: Round Hall Sweet & Maxwell.

Murphy, S. (1999). Tracing the Proceeds of Crime: Legal and Costitutional Implications. In J. P. McCutcheon & D. P. J. Welsh (Eds.), *The Confiscation of Criminal Assets. Law and Procedure* (pp. 39–50). Dublin: Round Hall Sweet & Maxwell.

Nagarajan, N., & Vanheukelen, M. (1997). *Evaluating EU Expenditure Programmes: a Guide. Ex Post and Intermediate Evaluation*. http://europa.eu.int/comm/budget/evaluation/keydocuments_en.htm.

Nanula, G. (1999). *La lotta alla mafia. Strumenti giuridici, strutture di coordinamento, legislazione vigente*. Milan: Giuffrè.

Naylor, R. T. (1999). *Follow-the-Money Methods in Crime Control Policy*. http://www.ncjrs.org/nathanson/washout.html.

Naylor, R. T. (2000, 29 August). Copping a Profit: Civil Forfeiture in the US Led to Police Profiteering and the Miscarriage of Justice. *Toronto Globe and Mail*. Toronto.

Nelen, J. M., & Sabee, V. (1998). *Het vermogen te ontnemen; evaluatie van de ontnemingswetgeving—eindrapport (The Deprivation of Criminal Assets. Evaluation of New Dutch Legislation—Final Report)*. Summary available at http://www.minjust.nl:8080/b_organ/wodc/summaries/ob170sum.htm.

Paoli, L. (1997). Seizure and Confiscation Measures in Italy: an Evaluation of Their Effectiveness and Constitutionality. *European Journal of Crime, Criminal Law and Criminal Justice*, *5*(3), 256–272.

Paoli, L. (2002). Landesbericht Italien. In M. Kilchling (Ed.), *Die Praxis der Gewinnabschöpfung in Europa* (pp. 239–295). Freiburg: Kriminologische Forschungsberichte aus dem Max-Planck-Institut für ausländisches und internationales Strafrecht.

Payne, T. E. (1999). Civil Forfeiture in Law Enforcement: an Effective Tool or Cash Register Justice? Cash Register Justice. In J. D. Sewell (Ed.), *Controversial Issues in Policing* (pp. 28–33). Boston: Allyn & Bacon.

Pieth, M. (2002). Financing of Terrorism: Following the Money. In M. Pieth (Ed.), *Financing Terrorism* (pp. 115–126). Dordrecht: Kluwer Academic Publishers.

Pound, R. (1910). Law in Books, Law in Action. *American Law Review*, *44*, 12–18.

Presidenza del Consiglio dei Ministri, Ufficio del Commissario straordinario del Governo per la gestione e la destinazione dei beni confiscati alle organizzazioni criminali (2000, 25 July). *Relazione al Signor Presidente del Consiglio del Commissario straordinario del Governo per la gestione e la destinazione dei beni confiscati alle organizzazioni criminali*. Rome.

Redpath, J. (2000, May). Asset Forfeiture: Some International Comparisons with South African Legislation. Paper presented at the ISS Seminar on Civil Asset Forfeiture: SA's New Weapon in the Fight against Organised Crime? Pretoria.

Rees, E., & Hall, A. (2003). *Blackstone's Guide to the Proceeds of Crime Act 2002*. New York: Oxford University Press.

Reid, P. (1997). Ireland. In A. Keltie & N. Pearson (Eds.), *International Tracing of Assets*. London: FT Law & Tax.

Salsich, P. W. (1995). A Delicate Balance: Making Criminal Forfeiture a Viable Law Enforcement Tool and Satisfying Due Process after United States v. James Daniel Good Real Property. *Saint Louis University Law Journal*, *39*, 585–618.

Sarantakos, S. (1998). *Social Research* (2nd ed.). South Yarra: Palgrave Macmillan.

Savona, E. U. (1996). European Money Trails. *Transnational Organized Crime*, *2*(4), 1–20.

Schönteich, M. (2000). The Asset Forfeiture Unit. Performance and priorities. *Nedbank ISS Crime Index*, *4*(3). http://www.iss.co.za/Pubs/CRIMEINDEX/00VOL4NO3/Assetforfeitu-re.html.

Scott, C. (1993). *Asset Confiscation Legislation and Methodology in the USA, Canada, the UK and Hong Kong*. http://members.ozemail.com.au/~themis/churchill/index.html.

Shelley, L. (2000). The Disposal of Seized Laundered Assets. In A. Jones, B. Rider, G. Saltmarsch, & L. Shelley (Eds.), *Killing Development: Money Laundering in the Global Economy* (pp. 45–53). Centre for Post-Collectivist Studies.

Stea, P. A. (1998). Le misure di prevenzione patrimoniali. L'esperienza applicativa. *Le misure di prevenzione patrimoniale: teoria e prassi applicativa* (pp. 301–326). Bari: Cacucci.

Stefanou, C., & Xanthaki, H. (1999). Greece: Money Laundering. *Journal of Money Laundering Control*, *3*(2), 161–172.

The Australian Law Reform Commission (1999). *Confiscation that Counts*, Report No. 87. Canberra.

The Law Reform Commission of Ireland (1991). *Report on the Confiscation of the Proceeds of Crime*. Dublin. http://www.lawreform.ie/publications/data/volume8/lrc_60.html.

Thomson, L. (2000). *Confiscation. A Practical Guide to Confiscating Crime Proceeds*. Edinburgh: W. Green & Son.

Thornton, J. (1990). Confiscating Criminal Assets: the New Deterrent. *Current Issues in Criminal Justice*, *2*(2), 72–89.

Transcrime (2001a). *L'uso delle sanzioni patrimoniali contro le organizzazioni criminali*. Trento: Transcrime.

Transcrime (2001b). *The Seizure and Confiscation of the Proceeds from Crime in the European Union Member States: What Works, What Does Not and What is Promising, Final Report (Part 1)*. Trento: Transcrime.

Turone, G. (1994). Le strategie di contrasto dell'economia criminale (dall'indagine patrimoniale alla confisca dei valori ingiustificati). *Questione Giustizia*, *1*, 42–91.

US Department of Justice, Criminal Division, Asset Forfeiture and Money Laundering Section (1998). *Asset Forfeiture Law and Practice Manual*. Washington, DC.

Vandermeersch, D. (1997). La loi du 20 mai 1997 sur la coopération internationale en ce qui concerne l'exécution des saisies et de confiscations—L'introduction en droit belge de la saisie immobilière pénale. *Revue de droit pénal et de criminologie*, *77*, 691–704.

Verbruggen, F. (1997). Proceeds-oriented Criminal Justice in Belgium: Backbone or Wishbone of a Modern Approach to Organised Crime? *European Journal of Crime, Criminal Law and Criminal Justice*, *3*, 314–341.

Vermeulen, G., De Ruyver, B., & Vander Beken, T. (1997). Belgium. In A. Keltie & N. Pearson (Eds.), *International Tracing of Assets*. London: FT Law & Tax.

Vettori, B. (2003). Sequestro e confisca dei proventi della criminalità organizzata nell'ordinamento italiano: linee evolutive, problemi applicativi e prospettive di riforma. In M. Barbagli (Ed.), *Rapporto sulla criminalità in Italia* (pp. 373–395). Bologna: Il Mulino.

Wadham, J. (2000, 30 November). *Confiscating the Assets of Those only Suspected of Involvement in Crime*. London: Liberty.

Walsh, J. P. (2000). Driven Criminal Justice: the Politics of Civil Asset Forfeiture. *Bloomington Bugle, Journal for Social Problems related to Crime, Law, and Justice*, *1*(2). http://www.indiana.edu/~thebugle/walsh.htm.

Williams, H. E. (2002). *Asset Forfeiture: a Law Enforcement Perspective*. Springfield, IL: Charles C. Thomas.

Worrall, J. L. (2001). Addicted to the Drug War. The Role of Civil Asset Forfeiture as a Budgetary Necessity in Contemporary Law Enforcement. *Journal of Criminal Justice*, *29*, 171–187.

Zerey, J. C. (1997). Greece. *Journal of Money Laundering Control*, *1*(2), 189–194.

ANNEX 1

THE QUESTIONNAIRES

This Annex contains the two questionnaires prepared for the development of the study.

The first was designed to explore the practice of proceeds of crime confiscation in criminal proceedings. The second examined the practice of proceeds of crime confiscation in civil proceedings for those countries whose legislations envisage it (i.e. Greece, Ireland, Italy and the United Kingdom), and whose national experts consequently completed both the questionnaires.

INVESTIGATING, CONFISCATING AND DISPOSING OF THE PROCEEDS FROM CRIME WITHIN CRIMINAL PROCEEDINGS

Part 1: Financial Investigations aimed at Locating the Proceeds from Crime within Criminal Proceedings (Investigative Phase)

1. Does a legal provision exist in your country that makes it possible to use special means of investigation (such as electronic surveillance, undercover operations, etc.) to search for the proceeds from crime?

☐	YES
☐	NO

1.1. If such a legal provision exists, how frequently are the above-mentioned special means of investigation used in practice on a scale from 1 to 5 (where 1 = never used, 5 = always used)?

1	2	3	4	5
☐	☐	☐	☐	☐

Give brief reasons for your choice.

2. Does a legal provision exist in your country that requires financial investigations to be conducted not only on the suspected criminal but also on third parties (i.e. people who are not the suspected criminal) believed to act as his/her straw men (i.e. people who have apparent, but no real power over the criminal's assets)?

☐	YES
☐	NO

2.1. If such a legal provision exists, how frequently is it applied in practice on a scale from 1 to 5 (where 1 = never applied, 5 = always applied)?

1	2	3	4	5
☐	☐	☐	☐	☐

Give brief reasons for your choice.

3. Is there a legal provision requiring (a) *banks,* (b) *other financial institutions* and (c) *non-financial institutions* to cooperate with investigative agencies in the identification of the proceeds from crime?

	YES	NO
a) *Banks*	☐	☐
b) *Other financial institutions* (which offer services such as money changing, money transmission services, financial guarantees and commitments, individual and collective portfolio management)	☐	☐
c) *Non financial institutions* (such as dealers in precious stones and metals and the real estate sector)	☐	☐

3.1. Whether this legal provision exists or not, please quantify on a scale from 1 to 5 the degree of cooperation of (a) *banks,* (b) *other financial institutions* and (c) *non financial institutions* in financial investigations (where 1 = not at all cooperative, 5 = highly cooperative):

	1	2	3	4	5
a) *Banks*	☐	☐	☐	☐	☐
b) *Other financial institutions*	☐	☐	☐	☐	☐
c) *Non financial institutions*	☐	☐	☐	☐	☐

Give brief reasons for your choices.

4. Is there a legal provision requiring a *multidisciplinary composition of the office/s conducting financial investigations in your country,* that is, the employment within these units of officers with different skills and abilities (e.g. law enforcement officers, accountants, lawyers, financial analysts, etc.)?

☐	YES
☐	NO

4.1. Whether this legal provision exists or not, please quantify on a scale from 1 to 5 the actual level of *multidisciplinary composition of the office/s conducting financial investigations in your country* (where 1 = no multidisciplinary composition, 5 = marked multidisciplinary composition):

1	2	3	4	5
☐	☐	☐	☐	☐

Give brief reasons for your choice.

5. Is there a legal provision requiring *inter-agency cooperation*, that is, cooperation between different national law enforcement agencies (police forces, revenue agencies, prosecution services, etc.) in the development of financial investigations?

☐	YES
☐	NO

5.1. Whether this legal provision exists or not, please quantify on a scale from 1 to 5 the level of *inter-agency cooperation* (where 1 = no cooperation, 5 = high level of cooperation):

1	2	3	4	5
☐	☐	☐	☐	☐

Give brief reasons for your choice.

6. Is there a legal provision requiring supergrasses (*pentiti*)/witnesses to cooperate with investigative agencies in the discovery of the proceeds from crime?

☐	YES
☐	NO

6.1. Whether this legal provision exists or not, please quantify on a scale from 1 to 5 the degree of cooperation provided by supergrasses (*pentiti*)/witnesses to financial investigations (where 1 = not cooperative, 5 = highly cooperative):

1	2	3	4	5
☐	☐	☐	☐	☐

Give brief reasons for your choice.

7. How frequently are financial investigations employed in organised crime cases, also taking into account the stage at which they are used?

☐	*Never OR rarely made, and generally at an early stage (i.e. before charges are brought)*
☐	*Never OR rarely made, and generally late (i.e. after charges)*
☐	*Sometimes made, and generally at an early stage (i.e. before charges)*
☐	*Sometimes made, and generally late (i.e. after charges)*
☐	*Often OR always made, and generally at an early stage (i.e. before charges)*
☐	*Often OR always made, and generally late (i.e. after charges)*

Give brief reasons for your choice.

8. On a scale from 1 to 5 (where 1 = inadequate, 5 = fully adequate), how would you evaluate the adequacy of (a) *the human resources* and (b) *the material resources* devoted to the identification of the proceeds from crime, with reference to their overall number (for human resources)/consistency (for material resources)?

a) *Human resources* (such as investigators, administrative personnel, etc.)	1 ☐	2 ☐	3 ☐	4 ☐	5 ☐
b) *Material resources* (such as computer facilities, etc.)	1 ☐	2 ☐	3 ☐	4 ☐	5 ☐

Give brief reasons for your choices.

9. On a scale from 1 to 5 (where 1 = no training, 5 = high level of training), please give a number to the general level of financial investigation training:

1	2	3	4	5
☐	☐	☐	☐	☐

Give brief reasons for your choice.

10. On a scale from 1 to 5 (where 1 = long, 5 = short), how would you define the period of time usually necessary to conclude financial investigations aimed at locating the proceeds from crime?

1	2	3	4	5
☐	☐	☐	☐	☐

Give brief reasons for your choice.

Part 2: Seizing and Confiscating the Proceeds from Crime within Criminal Proceedings (Judicial Phase)

11. *[Please reply to this question only if a conviction is (always or sometimes) a prerequisite for confiscation]* According to your experience, if a conviction is required for confiscation, how does this prerequisite affect, in practice, the issue of a confiscation order (e.g. due to the difficulty of obtaining a conviction) on a scale from 1 to 5 (where 1 = this prerequisite does not hamper the issue of a confiscation order, 5 = this prerequisite significantly hampers the issue of a confiscation order)?

1	2	3	4	5
☐	☐	☐	☐	☐

Give brief reasons for your choice.

12. *[Please reply to this question only if a conviction is (always or sometimes) a prerequisite for confiscation]* If a conviction is required for confiscation, is there a legal provision that makes it possible to confiscate not only the proceeds of crime from the criminal offence of which the defendant has been convicted, but also the proceeds of previous crimes of which s/he has not been convicted?

☐	YES
☐	NO

12.1. If such a legal provision exists, how is it implemented in practice on a scale from 1 to 5 (where 1 = not applied to a satisfactory extent, 5 = applied to a satisfactory extent)?

1	2	3	4	5
☐	☐	☐	☐	☐

Give brief reasons for your choice.

13. Under your legal system, once the necessary legal prerequisites (e.g. conviction) have been met, confiscating the proceeds from crime in criminal proceedings is:

☐	Always compulsory (go to question 14)
☐	Sometimes or always discretionary (go to question 13.1)

13.1. If confiscation is *sometimes or always discretionary*, how frequently is the measure applied in practice on a scale from 1 to 5 (where 1 = never applied, 5 = always applied)?

1	2	3	4	5
☐	☐	☐	☐	☐

Give brief reasons for your choice.

14. Is there a legal provision allowing for the reversal of the burden of proof, thereby placing the onus on the defendant to show the legitimate origins of his/her assets?

☐	YES
☐	NO

14.1. If such a legal provision exists, how is it implemented in practice on a scale from 1 to 5 (where 1 = not applied to a satisfactory extent, 5 = applied to a satisfactory extent)?

1	2	3	4	5
☐	☐	☐	☐	☐

Give brief reasons for your choice.

15. Does the legal system provide for (a) the confiscation of property found to be the proceeds of a crime (property confiscation), or (b) the confiscation of a sum of money equal to the value of the proceeds from crime (value confiscation), or (c) both?

☐	a) Only property confiscation is allowed
☐	b) Only value confiscation is allowed
☐	c) Both property confiscation and value confiscation are allowed

15.1. *If property confiscation is allowed in your legal system*, how is it implemented in practice on a scale from 1 to 5 (where 1 = not applied to a satisfactory extent, 5 = applied to a satisfactory extent)?

1	2	3	4	5
☐	☐	☐	☐	☐

Give brief reasons for your choice.

15.2. *If value confiscation is allowed in your legal system*, how is it implemented in practice on a scale from 1 to 5 (where 1 = not applied to a satisfactory extent, 5 = applied to a satisfactory extent)?

1	2	3	4	5
☐	☐	☐	☐	☐

Give brief reasons for your choice.

16. Does a legal provision exist which requires the seizure and confiscation of proceeds presumed to have derived from crime *if owned or held by a third person, that is, a person different from the defendant*?

☐	YES
☐	NO

16.1. If such a legal provision exists, how is it implemented in practice on a scale from 1 to 5 (where 1 = not applied to a satisfactory extent, 5 = applied to a satisfactory extent)?

1	2	3	4	5
☐	☐	☐	☐	☐

Give brief reasons for your choice.

17. Does a legal provision exist on the management of seized assets that aims at maximising their value/minimising their deterioration before they are confiscated (e.g. through the sale of the assets)?

☐	YES
☐	NO

17.1. Whether this legal provision exists or not, how would you define the current management of seized assets on a scale from 1 to 5 (where 1 = not satisfactory, i.e. not able to maximise the value/minimise the deterioration of seized assets, 5 = satisfactory, i.e. able to maximise the value/minimise the deterioration of seized assets)?

1	2	3	4	5
☐	☐	☐	☐	☐

Give brief reasons for your choice.

18. On a scale from 1 to 5 (where 1 = inadequate, 5 = fully adequate), how would you evaluate the adequacy of (a) *the human resources* and (b) *the material resources* devoted to the judicial phase, with reference to their overall number (for human resources)/consistency (for material resources)?

a) *Human resources* (such as public prosecutors, administrative personnel, etc.)	1 ☐	2 ☐	3 ☐	4 ☐	5 ☐
b) *Material resources* (such as computer facilities, etc.)	1 ☐	2 ☐	3 ☐	4 ☐	5 ☐

Give brief reasons for your choices.

19. On a scale from 1 to 5 (where 1 = no training, 5 = high level of training), please give a number to the general level of training, in the field of seizure and confiscation of the proceeds from crime, of (a) *officials who take legal action against a defendant in criminal proceedings* (such as public prosecutors) and (b) *judges*:

	1	2	3	4	5
a) Officials who take legal action against the defendant in criminal proceedings (such as public prosecutors)	☐	☐	☐	☐	☐
b) Judges	1 ☐	2 ☐	3 ☐	4 ☐	5 ☐

Give brief reasons for your choices.

20. On a scale from 1 to 5 (where 1 = incompetent, 5 = highly competent), please give a number to the general level of competence of the authority/ies managing seized assets:

1	2	3	4	5
☐	☐	☐	☐	☐

Give brief reasons for your choice.

21. On a scale from 1 to 5 (where 1 = long, 5 = short), how would you define the period of time usually necessary to conclude the judicial procedure leading to the confiscation of the proceeds from crime?

1	2	3	4	5
☐	☐	☐	☐	☐

Give brief reasons for your choice.

Part 3: Disposing of the Proceeds from Crime within Criminal Proceedings (Disposal Phase)

22. Please tick below the *disposal option(s)* allowed under your legal system. For each, please specify the *typology/ies of goods* they are associated with (cash, real property, personal property, companies, stocks, etc.).
Finally, specify how legal provisions disciplining each disposal option are applied in practice on a scale from 1 to 5 (where 1 = not applied to a satisfactory extent, 5 = applied to a satisfactory extent):

Disposal option(s) available under the legal system for confiscated assets	How are legal provisions disciplining each available disposal option applied in practice (where 1 = not applied to a satisfactory extent, 5 = applied to a satisfactory extent)?				
a) DESTRUCTION (for the following typologies of goods ______________)	1☐	2☐	3☐	4☐	5☐
b) SALE (for the following typologies of goods ______________)	1☐	2☐	3☐	4☐	5☐
c) USE FOR SOCIAL PURPOSES (for the following typologies of goods ______________)	1☐	2☐	3☐	4☐	5☐
d) RENT (for the following typologies of goods______________)	1☐	2☐	3☐	4☐	5☐
e) LIQUIDATION (for the following typologies of goods______________)	1☐	2☐	3☐	4☐	5☐
f) OTHER, I.E. ______________ (for the following typologies of goods______________)	1☐	2☐	3☐	4☐	5☐

Give brief reasons for your choices.

23. Is there a legal provision requiring *inter-agency cooperation*, that is, cooperation between the different offices involved in the disposal phase?

☐	YES
☐	NO

23.1. Whether this legal provision exists or not, please quantify on a scale from 1 to 5 the level of *inter-agency cooperation* (where 1 = no cooperation, 5 = high level of cooperation):

1	2	3	4	5
☐	☐	☐	☐	☐

Give brief reasons for your choice.

24. On a scale from 1 to 5 (where 1 = inadequate, 5 = fully adequate), how would you evaluate the adequacy of (a) *the human resources* and (b) *the material resources* devoted to the enforcement of confiscation orders/disposal of confiscated assets, with reference to their overall number (for human resources)/consistency (for material resources)?

	1	2	3	4	5
a) *Human resources* (such as officers in charge of the enforcement of confiscation orders/disposal of confiscated assets, administrative personnel, etc.)	☐	☐	☐	☐	☐
b) *Material resources* (such as computer facilities, etc.)	1 ☐	2 ☐	3 ☐	4 ☐	5 ☐

Give brief reasons for your choices.

25. On a scale from 1 to 5 (where 1 = incompetent, 5 = highly competent), please give a number to the general level of competence of the authority/ies managing confiscated assets:

1	2	3	4	5
☐	☐	☐	☐	☐

Give brief reasons for your choice.

26. On a scale from 1 to 5 (where 1 = long, 5 = short), how would you define the period of time usually necessary to dispose of confiscated assets/enforce confiscation orders?

1	2	3	4	5
☐	☐	☐	☐	☐

Give brief reasons for your choice.

INVESTIGATING, CONFISCATING AND DISPOSING OF THE PROCEEDS FROM CRIME WITHIN CIVIL PROCEEDINGS

Part 1: Financial Investigations Aimed at Locating the Proceeds from Crime Within Civil Proceedings (Investigative Phase)

1. Does a legal provision exist in your country that makes it possible to use special means of investigation (such as electronic surveillance, undercover operations, etc.) to search for the proceeds from crime?

☐	YES
☐	NO

1.1. If such a legal provision exists, how frequently are the above-mentioned special means of investigation used in practice on a scale from 1 to 5 (where 1 = never used, 5 = always used)?

1	2	3	4	5
☐	☐	☐	☐	☐

Give brief reasons for your choice.

2. Does a legal provision exist in your country that requires financial investigations to be conducted not only on the suspected criminal but also on third parties (i.e. people who are not the suspected criminal) believed to act as his/her straw men (i.e. people who have apparent, but no real power over the criminal's assets)?

☐	YES
☐	NO

2.1. If such a legal provision exists, how frequently is it applied in practice on a scale from 1 to 5 (where 1 = never applied, 5 = always applied)?

1	2	3	4	5
☐	☐	☐	☐	☐

Give brief reasons for your choice.

3. Is there a legal provision requiring (a) *banks*, (b) *other financial institutions* and (c) *non financial institutions* to cooperate with investigative agencies in the identification of the proceeds from crime?

	YES	NO
a) *Banks*	☐	☐
b) *Other financial institutions* (which offer services such as money changing, money transmission services, financial guarantees and commitments, individual and collective portfolio management)	☐	☐
c) *Non financial institutions* (such as dealers in precious stones and metals and the real estate sector)	☐	☐

3.1. Whether this legal provision exists or not, please quantify on a scale from 1 to 5 the degree of cooperation of (a) *banks,* (b) *other financial institutions* and

(c) *non financial institutions* in financial investigations (where 1 = not at all cooperative, 5 = highly cooperative):

	1	2	3	4	5
a) *Banks*	☐	☐	☐	☐	☐
b) *Other financial institutions*	☐	☐	☐	☐	☐
c) *Non financial institutions*	☐	☐	☐	☐	☐

Give brief reasons for your choices.

4. Is there a legal provision requiring a *multidisciplinary composition of the office/s conducting financial investigations in your country,* that is, the employment within these units of officers with different skills and abilities (e.g. law enforcement officers, accountants, lawyers, financial analysts, etc.)?

☐	YES
☐	NO

4.1. Whether this legal provision exists or not, please quantify on a scale from 1 to 5 the actual level of *multidisciplinary composition of the office/s conducting financial investigations in your country* (where 1 = no multidisciplinary composition, 5 = marked multidisciplinary composition):

1	2	3	4	5
☐	☐	☐	☐	☐

Give brief reasons for your choice.

5. Is there a legal provision requiring *inter-agency cooperation*, that is, cooperation between different national law enforcement agencies (police forces, revenue agencies, prosecution services, etc.) in the development of financial investigations?

☐	YES
☐	NO

5.1. Whether this legal provision exists or not, please quantify on a scale from 1 to 5 the level of *inter-agency cooperation* (where 1 = no cooperation, 5 = high level of cooperation):

1	2	3	4	5
☐	☐	☐	☐	☐

Give brief reasons for your choice.

6. Is there a legal provision requiring supergrasses (*pentiti*)/witnesses to cooperate with investigative agencies in the discovery of the proceeds from crime?

☐	YES
☐	NO

6.1. Whether this legal provision exists or not, please quantify on a scale from 1 to 5 the degree of cooperation provided by supergrasses (*pentiti*)/witnesses to financial investigations (where 1 = not cooperative, 5 = highly cooperative):

1	2	3	4	5
☐	☐	☐	☐	☐

Give brief reasons for your choice.

7. How frequently are financial investigations employed in organised crime cases, also taking into account the stage at which they are used?

☐	*Never OR rarely made, and generally at an early stage*
☐	*Never OR rarely made, and generally late*
☐	*Sometimes made, and generally at an early stage*
☐	*Sometimes made, and generally late*
☐	*Often OR always made, and generally at an early stage*
☐	*Often OR always made, and generally late*

Give brief reasons for your choice.

8. On a scale from 1 to 5 (where 1 = inadequate, 5 = fully adequate), how would you evaluate the adequacy of (a) *the human resources* and (b) *the material resources* devoted to the identification of the proceeds from crime, with reference to their overall number (for human resources)/consistency (for material resources)?

a) *Human resources* (such as investigators, administrative personnel, etc.)	1 ☐	2 ☐	3 ☐	4 ☐	5 ☐
b) *Material resources* (such as computer facilities, etc.)	1 ☐	2 ☐	3 ☐	4 ☐	5 ☐

Give brief reasons for your choices.

9. On a scale from 1 to 5 (where 1 = no training, 5 = high level of training), please give a number to the general level of financial investigation training:

1	2	3	4	5
☐	☐	☐	☐	☐

Give brief reasons for your choice.

10. On a scale from 1 to 5 (where 1 = long, 5 = short), how would you define the period of time usually necessary to conclude financial investigations aimed at locating the proceeds from crime?

1	2	3	4	5
☐	☐	☐	☐	☐

Give brief reasons for your choice.

Part 2: Seizing and Confiscating the Proceeds from Crime within Civil Proceedings (Judicial Phase)

11. Under your legal system, once the necessary legal prerequisites have been met, confiscating the proceeds from crime in civil proceedings is:

☐	Always compulsory (go to question 12)
☐	Sometimes or always discretionary (go to question 11.1)

11.1. If confiscation is *sometimes or always discretionary*, how frequently is the measure applied in practice on a scale from 1 to 5 (where 1 = never applied, 5 = always applied)?

1	2	3	4	5
☐	☐	☐	☐	☐

Give brief reasons for your choice.

12. Is there a legal provision allowing for the reversal of the burden of proof, thereby placing the onus on the defendant to show the legitimate origins of his/her assets?

☐	YES
☐	NO

12.1. If such a legal provision exists, how is it implemented in practice on a scale from 1 to 5 (where 1 = not applied to a satisfactory extent, 5 = applied to a satisfactory extent)?

1	2	3	4	5
☐	☐	☐	☐	☐

Give brief reasons for your choice.

13. Does the legal system provide for (a) the confiscation of property found to be the proceeds of a crime (property confiscation), or (b) the confiscation of a sum of

money equal to the value of the proceeds from crime (value confiscation), or (c) both?

☐	a) Only property confiscation is allowed
☐	b) Only value confiscation is allowed
☐	c) Both property confiscation and value confiscation are allowed

13.1. *If property confiscation is allowed in your legal system*, how is it implemented in practice on a scale from 1 to 5 (where 1 = not applied to a satisfactory extent, 5 = applied to a satisfactory extent)?

1	2	3	4	5
☐	☐	☐	☐	☐

Give brief reasons for your choice.

13.2. *If value confiscation is allowed in your legal system*, how is it implemented in practice on a scale from 1 to 5 (where 1 = not applied to a satisfactory extent, 5 = applied to a satisfactory extent)?

1	2	3	4	5
☐	☐	☐	☐	☐

Give brief reasons for your choice.

14. Does a legal provision exist which requires the seizure and confiscation of proceeds presumed to have derived from crime *if owned or held by a third person,* that is, *a person different from the defendant*?

☐	YES
☐	NO

14.1. If such a legal provision exists, how is it implemented in practice on a scale from 1 to 5 (where 1 = not applied to a satisfactory extent, 5 = applied to a satisfactory extent)?

1	2	3	4	5
☐	☐	☐	☐	☐

Give brief reasons for your choice.

15. Does a legal provision exist on the management of seized assets that aims at maximising their value/minimising their deterioration before they are confiscated (e.g. through the sale of the assets)?

☐	YES
☐	NO

15.1. Whether this legal provision exists or not, how would you define the current management of seized assets on a scale from 1 to 5 (where 1 = not satisfactory, i.e. not able to maximise the value/minimise the deterioration of seized assets, 5 = satisfactory, i.e. able to maximise the value/minimise the deterioration of seized assets)?

1	2	3	4	5
☐	☐	☐	☐	☐

Give brief reasons for your choice.

16. On a scale from 1 to 5 (where 1 = inadequate, 5 = fully adequate), how would you evaluate the adequacy of (a) *the human resources* and (b) *the material resources* devoted to the judicial phase, with reference to their overall number (for human resources)/consistency (for material resources)?

a) *Human resources* (such as public prosecutors, administrative personnel, etc.)	1 ☐	2 ☐	3 ☐	4 ☐	5 ☐
b) *Material resources* (such as computer facilities, etc.)	1 ☐	2 ☐	3 ☐	4 ☐	5 ☐

Give brief reasons for your choices.

17. On a scale from 1 to 5 (where 1 = no training, 5 = high level of training), please give a number to the general level of training, in the field of seizure and confiscation of the proceeds from crime, of (a) *officials who take legal action against a defendant in civil proceedings* (such as public prosecutors) and (b) *judges*:

a) *Officials who take legal action against the defendant in civil proceedings* (such as public prosecutors)	1 ☐	2 ☐	3 ☐	4 ☐	5 ☐
b) *Judges*	1 ☐	2 ☐	3 ☐	4 ☐	5 ☐

Give brief reasons for your choices.

18. On a scale from 1 to 5 (where 1 = incompetent, 5 = highly competent), please give a number to the general level of competence of the authority/ies managing seized assets:

1	2	3	4	5
☐	☐	☐	☐	☐

Give brief reasons for your choice.

19. On a scale from 1 to 5 (where 1 = long, 5 = short), how would you define the period of time usually necessary to conclude the judicial procedure leading to the

confiscation of the proceeds from crime?

1	2	3	4	5
☐	☐	☐	☐	☐

Give brief reasons for your choice.

Part 3: Disposing of the Proceeds from Crime within Civil Proceedings (Disposal Phase)

20. Please tick below the *disposal option(s)* allowed under your legal system. For each, please specify the *typology/ies of goods* they are associated with (cash, real property, personal property, companies, stocks, etc.).
Finally, specify how legal provisions disciplining each disposal option are applied in practice on a scale from 1 to 5 (where 1 = not applied to a satisfactory extent, 5 = applied to a satisfactory extent):

Disposal option(s) available under the legal system for confiscated assets	How are legal provisions disciplining each available disposal option applied in practice (where 1 = not applied to a satisfactory extent, 5 = applied to a satisfactory extent)?				
a) DESTRUCTION (for the following typologies of goods __________)	1☐	2☐	3☐	4☐	5☐
b) SALE (for the following typologies of goods __________)	1☐	2☐	3☐	4☐	5☐
c) USE FOR SOCIAL PURPOSES (for the following typologies of goods __________)	1☐	2☐	3☐	4☐	5☐
d) RENT (for the following typologies of goods __________)	1☐	2☐	3☐	4☐	5☐
e) LIQUIDATION (for the following typologies of goods __________)	1☐	2☐	3☐	4☐	5☐
f) OTHER, I.E. __________ (for the following typologies of goods __________)	1☐	2☐	3☐	4☐	5☐

Give brief reasons for your choices.

21. Is there a legal provision requiring *inter-agency cooperation*, that is, cooperation between the different offices involved in the disposal phase?

□	YES
□	NO

21.1. Whether this legal provision exists or not, please quantify on a scale from 1 to 5 the level of *inter-agency cooperation* (where 1 = no cooperation, 5 = high level of cooperation):

1	2	3	4	5
□	□	□	□	□

Give brief reasons for your choice.

22. On a scale from 1 to 5 (where 1 = inadequate, 5 = fully adequate), how would you evaluate the adequacy of (a) *the human resources* and (b) *the material resources* devoted to the enforcement of confiscation orders/disposal of confiscated assets, with reference to their overall number (for human resources)/consistency (for material resources)?

	1	2	3	4	5
a) *Human resources* (such as officers in charge of the enforcement of confiscation orders/disposal of confiscated assets, administrative personnel, etc.)	□	□	□	□	□
b) *Material resources* (such as computer facilities, etc.)	1 □	2 □	3 □	4 □	5 □

Give brief reasons for your choices.

23. On a scale from 1 to 5 (where 1 = incompetent, 5 = highly competent), please give a number to the general level of competence of the authority/ies managing confiscated assets:

1	2	3	4	5
□	□	□	□	□

Give brief reasons for your choice.

24. On a scale from 1 to 5 (where 1 = long, 5 = short), how would you define the period of time usually necessary to dispose of confiscated assets/enforce confiscation orders?

1	2	3	4	5
□	□	□	□	□

Give brief reasons for your choice.

ANNEX 2

METHODOLOGICAL APPENDIX

As shown in section 3.2, the research on which this book is based was carried out in the following four steps:

Step 1. Operationalisation of the concept 'law in action'.
Step 2. Preparation of a questionnaire, and its administration to one high profile expert per Member State by means of a telephone interview.
Step 3. Building a country profile that describes the law in action and juxtaposes it with the law in the books.
Step 4. Quantifying the law in action.

This Annex is devoted to detailed explanation of STEP 4, which involved quantification of the law in action, that is, the level of enforcement of the legal provisions (law in the books) of relevance in each of the three phases of confiscation proceedings.

After the variables measuring the law in action were identified (STEP 1) and translated into a questionnaire (STEP 2), for each variable, on the basis of the reply given by the national expert, a value was assigned to each modality on a scale from 0 to 100. The closer the value to 100, the better the law in action. The following values were assigned to the modalities of the selected variables for each of the three phases of confiscation proceedings.

FOR THE INVESTIGATIVE PHASE

VARIABLE 1. Frequency of the use of special investigative means, if their use is envisaged

1	0
2	25
3	50
4	75
5	100

where 1 = never used; 5 = always used.

VARIABLE 2. Frequency of financial investigations on third parties believed to be acting as the defendant's straw men, if such investigations of third parties are envisaged

1	0
2	25
3	50
4	75
5	100

where 1 = never made; 5 = always made.

VARIABLE 3. Level of cooperation by banks in the investigative phase

1	0
2	25
3	50
4	75
5	100

where 1 = no cooperation at all; 5 = high level of cooperation.

VARIABLE 4. Level of cooperation by non-banking financial institutions in the investigative phase

1	0
2	25
3	50
4	75
5	100

where 1 = no cooperation at all; 5 = high level of cooperation.

VARIABLE 5. Level of cooperation by non-financial institutions in the investigative phase

1	0
2	25
3	50
4	75
5	100

where 1 = no cooperation at all; 5 = high level of cooperation.

VARIABLE 6. Level of financial investigation training

1	0
2	25
3	50
4	75
5	100

where 1 = no training; 5 = high level of training.

VARIABLE 7. Level of multidisciplinary composition of the office/s conducting financial investigations

1	0
2	25
3	50
4	75
5	100

where 1 = no multidisciplinary composition; 5 = marked multidisciplinary composition.

VARIABLE 8. Level of inter-agency cooperation, that is, cooperation among different national law enforcement agencies (police forces, revenue agencies, prosecution services, etc.) in the development of financial investigations

1	0
2	25
3	50
4	75
5	100

where 1 = no cooperation; 5 = high level of cooperation.

VARIABLE 9. Degree of cooperation by informants/witnesses with financial investigations

1	0
2	25
3	50
4	75
5	100

where 1 = no cooperation at all; 5 = high level of cooperation.

VARIABLE 10. Frequency of financial investigations in organised crime cases, also taking account of the stage at which they are conducted

1. Never or rarely made, and generally late (i.e. after charges are brought)	0
2. Never or rarely made, and generally at an early stage (i.e. before charges)	20
3. Sometimes made, and generally late (i.e. after charges)	40
4. Sometimes made, and generally at an early stage (i.e. before charges)	60
5. Often or always made, and generally late (i.e. after charges)	80
6. Often or always made, and generally at an early stage (i.e. before charges)	100

VARIABLE 11. Adequacy of the human resources devoted to the identification of the proceeds from crime, with reference to their overall number

1	0
2	25
3	50
4	75
5	100

where 1 = inadequate; 5 = fully adequate.

VARIABLE 12. Adequacy of the material resources devoted to the identification of the proceeds from crime, with reference to their overall consistency

1	0
2	25
3	50
4	75
5	100

where 1 = inadequate; 5 = fully adequate.

FOR THE JUDICIAL PHASE

VARIABLE 13. Level of impediment against the issue of a confiscation order raised by the need for a conviction, if a conviction is (always or sometimes) a prerequisite for confiscation

1	100
2	75
3	50
4	25
5	0

where 1 = no impediment; 5 = significant impediment.

VARIABLE 14. Level of implementation of extended confiscation, if such a legal provision exists

1	0
2	25
3	50
4	75
5	100

where 1 = not applied to a satisfactory extent; 5 = applied to a satisfactory extent.

VARIABLE 15. Frequency of confiscation, if application of the measure is sometimes or always discretionary

1	0
2	25
3	50
4	75
5	100

where 1 = never applied; 5 = always applied.

VARIABLE 16. Level of implementation of the legal provision allowing for the reversal of the burden of proof, if such a legal provision exists

1	0
2	25
3	50
4	75
5	100

where 1 = not applied to a satisfactory extent; 5 = applied to a satisfactory extent.

VARIABLE 17. Level of implementation of property confiscation, if provided for by the legal system

1	0
2	25
3	50
4	75
5	100

where 1 = not applied to a satisfactory extent; 5 = applied to a satisfactory extent.

VARIABLE 18. Level of implementation of value confiscation, if provided for by the legal system

1	0
2	25
3	50
4	75
5	100

where 1 = not applied to a satisfactory extent; 5 = applied to a satisfactory extent.

VARIABLE 19. Level of implementation of a legal provision which requires the seizure and confiscation of proceeds presumed to have derived from crime if owned or held by a third person, if such a legal provision exists

1	0
2	25
3	50
4	75
5	100

where 1 = not applied to a satisfactory extent; 5 = applied to a satisfactory extent.

VARIABLE 20. Adequacy of the human resources devoted to the judicial phase, with reference to their overall number

1	0
2	25
3	50
4	75
5	100

where 1 = inadequate; 5 = fully adequate.

VARIABLE 21. Adequacy of the material resources devoted to the judicial phase, with reference to their overall consistency

1	0
2	25
3	50
4	75
5	100

where 1 = inadequate; 5 = fully adequate.

VARIABLE 22. Level of training of the officials (such as public prosecutors) who take legal action against defendants in criminal/civil proceedings in the field of seizure and confiscation of the proceeds from crime

1	0
2	25
3	50
4	75
5	100

where 1 = no training; 5 = high level of training.

VARIABLE 23. Level of training of judges in the field of seizure and confiscation of the proceeds from crime

1	0
2	25
3	50
4	75
5	100

where 1 = no training; 5 = high level of training.

VARIABLE 24. Level of competence of the authority/ies managing seized assets

1	0
2	25
3	50
4	75
5	100

where 1 = incompetent; 5 = highly competent.

VARIABLE 25. Level of the current management of seized assets

1	0
2	25
3	50
4	75
5	100

where 1 = not satisfactory, that is, not able to maximise the value/minimise the deterioration of seized assets; 5 = satisfactory, that is, able to maximise the value/minimise the deterioration of seized assets.

VARIABLE 26. Period of time usually necessary to conclude the judicial procedure leading to the confiscation of the proceeds from crime

1	0
2	25
3	50
4	75
5	100

where 1 = long; 5 = short.

FOR THE DISPOSAL PHASE

VARIABLE 27. Level of implementation of legal provisions disciplining each disposal option (i.e. sale, destruction, use for social purposes, rent, liquidation, other)

1	0
2	25
3	50
4	75
5	100

where 1 = not applied to a satisfactory extent; 5 = applied to a satisfactory extent.

VARIABLE 28. Level of inter-agency cooperation, that is, cooperation among the various offices involved in the disposal phase

1	0
2	25
3	50
4	75
5	100

where 1 = no cooperation; 5 = high level of cooperation.

VARIABLE 29. Adequacy of the human resources devoted to the enforcement of confiscation orders/disposal of confiscated assets, with reference to their overall number

1	0
2	25
3	50
4	75
5	100

where 1 = inadequate; 5 = fully adequate.

VARIABLE 30. Adequacy of the material resources devoted to the enforcement of confiscation orders/disposal of confiscated assets, with reference to their overall consistency

1	0
2	25
3	50
4	75
5	100

where 1 = inadequate; 5 = fully adequate.

VARIABLE 31. Level of competence of the authority/ies managing confiscated assets

1	0
2	25
3	50
4	75
5	100

where 1 = incompetent; 5 = highly competent.

VARIABLE 32. Period of time usually necessary to dispose of confiscated assets/enforce confiscation orders

1	0
2	25
3	50
4	75
5	100

where 1 = long; 5 = short.

In the case of non-reply, the variable was not taken into account in the calculation.

These values were subsequently aggregated, for each phase, into a Law in Action Index, in order to calculate an Investigative Phase Law in Action Index, a Judicial Phase Law in Action Index, and a Disposal Phase Law in Action Index. These Indexes express, on a scale from 0 to 100, the level of enforcement of the law in the books in each phase. They were obtained by calculating the average of the values assigned to the modalities of each variable for the phase. *The higher the index, the better the law in action of the phase in the country.*

The two extreme situations depicted by this quantification are the following. When one of these Indexes scores 100, it denotes the ideal situation in which the enforcement of the law in the books is the best possible. When, on the contrary, one of these Indexes scores 0, it denotes the worst possible situation in which the enforcement of the law in the books is nil.

INDEX

GPSR Compliance

The European Union's (EU) General Product Safety Regulation (GPSR) is a set of rules that requires consumer products to be safe and our obligations to ensure this.

If you have any concerns about our products, you can contact us on ProductSafety@springernature.com

In case Publisher is established outside the EU, the EU authorized representative is:

Springer Nature Customer Service Center GmbH
Europaplatz 3
69115 Heidelberg, Germany

Batch number: 10823959

Printed by Printforce, the Netherlands